D0983773

Imperialism

IMPERIALISM

A STUDY

IMPERIALISM

A STUDY

BY

J. A. HOBSON

AUTHOR OF "JOHN RUSKIN: SOCIAL REFORMER"
"THE SOCIAL PROBLEM," ETC.

NEW YORK
JAMES POTT & COMPANY
1902

Printed by
BALLANTYNE, HANSON & Co.
Edinburgh

PREFACE

THIS study of modern Imperialism is designed to give more precision to a term which is on everybody's lips and which is used to denote the most powerful movement in the current politics of the Western world. Though Imperialism has been adopted as a more or less conscious policy by several European States and threatens to break down the political isolation of the United States, Great . Britain has travelled so much faster and farther along this road as to furnish in her recent career the most profitable guidance or warning.

While an attempt is made to discover and discuss the general principles which underlie imperialist policy, the illustration of that policy is mainly derived from the progress of British Imperialism during the last generation, and proceeds rather by diagnosis than by historical description.

In Part I. the economic origins of Imperialism are traced, with such statistical measurements of its methods and results as are available.

Part II. investigates the theory and the practice of Imperialism regarded as a "mission of civilisation," in its effects upon "lower" or alien peoples, and its political and moral reactions upon the conduct and character of the Western nations engaging in it.

The book is addressed to the intelligence of the minority who are content neither to float along the tide of political opportunism nor to submit to the shove of some blind "destiny," but who desire to understand political forces in order that they may direct them.

Those readers who hold that a well-balanced judgment consists in always finding as much in favour of any political course as against it will be discontented with the treatment given here. For the study is distinctively one of social pathology, and no endeavour is made to disguise the malignity of the disease.

The statistics given in Part I. are derived, when the source is not stated, from the "Statistical Abstracts" published by the Government, reinforced, in some instances, by figures derived from the "Statesman's Year-book."

I am indebted to the editor of the "Financial Reform Almanac" for permission to reproduce the valuable diagram illustrative of British expenditure from 1870, and to the editors of the *Speaker*, the *Contemporary Review*, the *Political Science Quarterly*, and the *British Friend* for permission to embody in chapters of this volume articles printed in these magazines.

I desire also to express my gratitude to my friends Mr. Gilbert Murray and Mr. Herbert Rix for their assistance in reading most of the proof-sheets and for many valuable suggestions and corrections.

JOHN A. HOBSON.

August 1902.

CONTENTS

INTRODUCTORY

PART I

THE ECONOMICS OF IMPERIALISM

PART II

THE POLITICS OF IMPERIALISM

IMPERIALISM : A STUDY

INTRODUCTORY

NATIONALISM AND IMPERIALISM

AMID the welter of vague political abstractions to lay one's finger accurately upon any "ism" so as to pin it down and mark it out by definition seems impossible. Where meanings shift so quickly and so subtly, not only following changes of thought, but often manipulated artificially by political practitioners so as to obscure, expand, or distort, it is idle to demand the same rigour as is expected in the exact sciences. A certain broad consistency in its relations to other kindred terms is the nearest approach to definition which such a term as Imperialism admits. Nationalism, internationalism, colonialism, its three closest congeners, are equally elusive, equally shifty, and the changeful overlapping of all four demands the closest vigilance of students of modern politics.

During the nineteenth century the struggle towards nationalism, or establishment of political union on a basis of nationality, has been a dominant factor alike in dynastic movements and as an inner motive in the life of masses of population. That struggle, in external politics, has sometimes taken a disruptive form, as in the case of Greece, Servia, Roumania, and Bulgaria breaking from Ottoman rule, and the detachment of North Italy from

A

her unnatural alliance with the Austrian Empire. In other cases it has been a unifying or a centralising force, enlarging the area of nationality, as in the case of Italy and the Pan-Slavist movement in Russia. Sometimes nationality has been taken as a basis of federation of States, as in United Germany and in North America.

It is true that the forces making for political union have sometimes gone further, making for federal union of diverse nationalities, as in the cases of Austria-Hungary, Norway and Sweden, and the Swiss Federation. But the general tendency has been towards welding into large strong national unities the loosely related States and provinces with shifting attachments and alliances which covered large areas of Europe since the break-up of the Empire. This has been the most definite achievement of the nineteenth century. The force of nationality, operating in this work, is quite as visible in the failures to achieve political freedom as in the successes; and the struggles of Irish, Poles, Finns, Hungarians, and Czechs to resist the forcible subjection to or alliance with stronger neighbours brings out in its full vigour the powerful sentiment of nationality.

The middle of the century was especially distinguished by a series of definitely "nationalist" revivals, some of which found important interpretation in dynastic changes, while others were crushed or collapsed. Holland, Poland, Belgium, Norway, the Balkans, formed a vast arena for these struggles of national forces.

The close of the third quarter of the century saw Europe fairly settled into large national States or federations of States, though in the nature of the case there can be no finality, and Italy still looks to Trieste, as Germany to Austria, for the fulfilment of her manifest destiny.

This passion and the dynastic forms it helped to mould and animate are largely attributable to the fierce prolonged resistance which peoples, both great and small, were called on to maintain against the imperial designs of Napoleon. The national spirit of England was roused by the tenseness of the struggle to a self-consciousness it had never experienced since "the spacious days of great Elizabeth." Jena made Prussia into a great nation; the Moscow campaign brought Russia into the field of European nationalities as a constant factor in politics, opening her for the first time to the full tide of Western ideas and influences.

Turning from this territorial and dynastic nationalism to the spirit of racial, linguistic, and economic solidarity which has been the underlying motive, we find a still more remarkable movement. Local particularism on the one hand, vague cosmopolitanism upon the other, yielded to a ferment of nationalist sentiment, manifesting itself among the weaker peoples not merely in a sturdy and heroic resistance against political absorption or territorial nationalism, but in a passionate revival of decaying customs, language, literature, and art; while it bred in more dominant peoples strange ambitions of national "destiny" and an attendant spirit of Chauvinism.

The true nature and limits of nationality have never been better stated than by J. S. Mill.

"A portion of mankind may be said to constitute a nation if they are united among themselves by common sympathies which do not exist between them and others. This feeling of nationality may have been generated by various causes. Sometimes it is the effect of identity of race and descent. Community of language and community of religion greatly contribute to it. Geographical limits are one of the causes. But the strongest of all is identity of political antecedents, the possession of a national history and consequent community of recollections, collective pride and humiliation, pleasure and regret, connected with the same incidents in the past." [1]

It is a debasement of this genuine nationalism, by attempts to overflow its natural banks and absorb the near or distant territory of reluctant and unassimilable peoples, that marks the passage from nationalism to a spurious colonialism on the one hand, Imperialism on the other.

Colonialism, where it consists in the migration of part of a nation to vacant or sparsely peopled foreign lands, the emigrants carrying with them full rights of citizenship in the mother country, or else establishing local self-government in close conformity with her institutions and under her final control, may be considered a genuine expansion of nationality, a territorial enlargement of the stock, language and institutions of the nation. Few colonies in history have, however, long remained in this condition when they have been remote from the mother country. Either they have severed the connection and set up for themselves as separate nationalities, or they have been kept in complete political bondage so far as all major processes of government are concerned, a condition to which the term Imperialism is at least as appropriate as colonialism. The only form of distant colony which can be regarded as a clear expansion of nationalism is the self-governing British colony in Australasia and Canada, and even in these cases local conditions may generate a separate nationalism based on a strong consolidation of colonial interests and sentiments alien from and conflicting with those of the mother nation. In other " self-governing " colonies, as in Cape Colony and Natal,

[1] " Representative Government," chap. xvi.

where the majority of whites are not descended from British settlers, and where the presence of subject or "inferior" races in vastly preponderating numbers, and alien climatic and other natural conditions, mark out a civilisation distinct from that of the "mother country," the conflict between the colonial and the imperial ideas has long been present in the forefront of the consciousness of politicians. When Lord Rosmead spoke of the permanent presence of the imperial factor as "simply an absurdity," and Mr. Rhodes spoke of its "elimination," they were championing a "colonialism" which is more certain in the course of time to develop by inner growth into a separate "nationalism" than in the case of the Australasian and Canadian colonies, because of the wider divergence, alike of interests and radical conditions of life, from the mother nation. Our other colonies are plainly representative of the spirit of Imperialism rather than of colonialism. No considerable proportion of the population consists of British settlers living with their families in conformity with the social and political customs and laws of their native land: in most instances they form a small minority wielding political or economic sway over a majority of alien and subject people, themselves under the despotic political control of the Imperial Government or its local nominees. This, the normal condition of a British colony, is well-nigh universal in the colonies of other European countries. The "colonies" which France and Germany establish in Africa and Asia are in no real sense plantations of French and German national life beyond the seas; nowhere, not even in Algeria, do they represent true European civilisation; their political and economic structure of society is wholly alien from that of the mother country.

Colonialism, in its best sense, is a natural overflow of nationality; its test is the power of colonists to transplant the civilisation they represent to the new natural and social environment in which they find themselves. We must not be misled by names; the "colonial" party in Germany and France is identical in general aim and method with the "imperialist" party in England, and the latter is the truer title. Professor Seeley well marked the nature of Imperialism. "When a State advances beyond the limits of nationality its power becomes precarious and artificial. This is the condition of most empires, and it is the condition of our own. When a nation extends itself into other territories the chances are that it cannot destroy or completely drive out, even if it succeeds in conquering, them. When this happens it has a great and permanent difficulty to contend with, for the subject or rival nationalities cannot be properly assimilated, and remain as a permanent cause of weakness and danger."[1]

The novelty of the recent Imperialism regarded as a policy consists chiefly in its adoption by several nations. The notion of a number of competing empires is essentially modern. The root idea of empire in the ancient and mediæval world was that of a federation of States, under a hegemony, covering in general terms the entire known or recognised world, such as was held by Rome under the so-called *pax Romana*. When Roman citizens, with full civic rights, were found all over the explored world, in Africa and Asia, as well as in Gaul and Britain, Imperialism contained a genuine element of internationalism. With the fall of Rome this conception of a single empire wielding political authority over the civilised world did not disappear. On the contrary, it

[1] "Expansion of England," lect. iii.

survived all the fluctuations of the Holy Roman Empire. Even after the definite split between the Eastern and Western sections had taken place at the close of the fourth century, the theory of a single State, divided for administrative purposes, survived. Beneath every cleavage or antagonism, and notwithstanding the severance of many independent kingdoms and provinces, this ideal unity of the empire lived. It formed the conscious avowed ideal of Charlemagne, though as a practical ambition confined to Western Europe. Rudolph of Habsburg not merely revived the idea, but laboured to realise it through Central Europe, while his descendant Charles V. gave a very real meaning to the term by gathering under the unity of his imperial rule the territories of Austria, Germany, Spain, the Netherlands, Sicily, and Naples. In later ages this dream of a European Empire animated the policy of Peter the Great, Catherine, and Napoleon. Nor is it impossible that Kaiser Wilhelm III. holds a vision of such a world-power.

Political philosophers in many ages, Vico, Macchiavelli, Dante, Kant, have speculated on an empire as the only feasible security for peace, a hierarchy of States conforming on the larger scale to the feudal order within the single State.

Thus empire was identified with internationalism, though not always based on a conception of equality of nations. The break-up of the Central European Empire, with the weakening of nationalities that followed, evoked a new modern sentiment of internationalism which, through the eighteenth century, was a flickering inspiration in the intellectual circles of European States. "The eve of the French Revolution found every wise man in Europe—Lessing, Kant, Goethe, Rousseau, Lavater, Condorcet, Priestley, Gibbon, Franklin—more of a citizen

of the world than of any particular country. Goethe
confessed that he did not know what patriotism was, and
was glad to be without it. Cultured men of all countries were at home in polite society everywhere. Kant
was immensely more interested in the events of Paris
than in the life of Prussia. Italy and Germany were
geographical expressions ; those countries were filled
with small States in which there was no political life, but
in which there was much interest in the general progress
of culture. The Revolution itself was at bottom also
human and cosmopolitan. It is, as Lamartine said, ' a
date in the human mind,' and it is because of that fact
that all the carping of critics like Taine cannot prevent
us from seeing that the character of the men who led the
great movements of the Revolution can never obliterate
the momentous nature of the Titanic strife. The soldiers
of the Revolution who, barefooted and ragged, drove the
insolent reactionaries from the soil of France were fighting not merely for some national cause, but for a cause
dimly perceived to be the cause of general mankind.
With all its crudities and imperfections, the idea of the
Revolution was that of a conceived body of Right in
which all men should share." [1]

This early flower of humane cosmopolitanism was
destined to wither before the powerful revival of nationalism which marked the next century. Even in the
narrow circles of the cultured classes it easily passed
from a noble and a passionate ideal to become a vapid
sentimentalism, and after the brief flare of 1848 among
the continental populace had been extinguished, little
remained but a dim smouldering of the embers. Even
the Socialism which upon the continent retains a measure of the spirit of internationalism is so tightly con-

[1] W. Clarke, *Progressive Review*, February 1897.

fined within the national limits, in its struggle with bureaucracy and capitalism, that "the international" expresses little more than a holy aspiration, and has little opportunity of putting into practice the genuine sentiments of brotherhood which its prophets have always preached.

Thus the triumph of nationalism seems to have crushed the rising hope of internationalism. Yet it would appear that there is no essential antagonism between them. A true strong internationalism in form or spirit would rather imply the existence of powerful self-respecting nationalities which seek union on the basis of common national needs and interests. Such a historical development would be far more conformable to laws of social growth than the rise of anarchic cosmopolitanism from individual units amid the decadence of national life.

Nationalism is a plain highway to internationalism, and if it manifests divergence we may well suspect a perversion of its nature and its purpose. Such a perversion is Imperialism, in which nations trespassing beyond the limits of facile assimilation transform the wholesome stimulative rivalry of varied national types into the cut-throat struggle of competing empires.

. Not only does aggressive Imperialism defeat the movement towards internationalism by fostering animosities among competing empires: its attack upon the liberties and the existence of weaker or lower races stimulates in them a corresponding excess of national self-consciousness. A nationalism that bristles with resentment and is all astrain with the passion of self-defence is only less perverted from its natural genius than the nationalism which glows with the animus of greed and self-aggrandisement at the expense of others. From

this aspect aggressive Imperialism is an artificial stimulation of nationalism in peoples too foreign to be
absorbed and too compact to be permanently crushed.
We have welded Africanderdom into just such a strong
dangerous nationalism, and we have joined with other
nations in creating a resentful nationalism hitherto unknown in China. The injury to nationalism in both
cases consists in converting a cohesive, pacific, internal
force into an exclusive, hostile force, a perversion of
the true power and use of nationality. The worst and
most certain result is the retardation of internationalism. The older nationalism was primarily an
inclusive sentiment; its natural relation to the same
sentiment in another people was lack of sympathy, not
open hostility; there was no inherent antagonism
to prevent nationalities from growing and thriving side
by side. Such in the main was the nationalism of
the earlier nineteenth century, and the politicians of
Free Trade had some foundation for their dream of
a quick growth of effective, informal internationalism
by peaceful, profitable intercommunication of goods and
ideas among nations recognising a just harmony of
interests in free peoples.

The overflow of nationalism into imperial channels
quenched all such hopes. While co-existent nationalities are capable of mutual aid involving no direct antagonism of interests, co-existent empires following each
its own imperial career of territorial and industrial
aggrandisement are natural necessary enemies. The
full nature of this antagonism on its economic side is
not intelligible without a close analysis of those conditions of modern capitalist production which compel
an ever keener "fight for markets," but the political
antagonism is obvious.

The scramble for Africa and Asia has virtually re-cast the policy of all European nations, has evoked alliances which cross all natural lines of sympathy and historical association, has driven every continental nation to consume an ever-growing share of its material and human resources upon military and naval equipment. has drawn the great new power of the United States from its isolation into the full tide of competition; and, by the multitude, the magnitude, and the suddenness of the issues it throws on to the stage of politics, has be-come a constant agent of menace and of perturbation to the peace and progress of mankind. The new policy has exercised the most notable and formidable influence upon the conscious statecraft of the nations which indulge in it. While producing for popular consumption doctrines of national destiny and imperial missions of civilisation, contradictory in their true import, but sub-sidiary to one another as supports of popular Imperialism, it has evolved a calculating, greedy type of Macchiavellian-ism, entitled "real-politik" in Germany, where it was made, which has remodelled the whole art of diplomacy and has erected national aggrandisement without pity or scruple as the conscious motive force of foreign policy. Earth hunger and the scramble for markets are respon-sible for the openly avowed repudiation of treaty obliga-tions which Germany, Russia, and England have not scrupled to defend. The sliding scale of diplomatic language, hinterland, sphere of interest, sphere of in-fluence, paramountcy, suzerainty, protectorate, veiled or open, leading up to acts of forcible seizure or annexation which sometimes continue to be hidden under "lease," "rectification of frontier," "concession," and the like, is the invention and expression of this cynical spirit of Imperialism. While Germany and Russia have per-

haps been more open in their professed adoption of the
material gain of their country as the sole criterion of
public conduct, other nations have not been slow to
accept the standard. Though the conduct of nations
in dealing with one another has commonly been determined at all times by selfish and short-sighted considerations, the conscious, deliberate adoption of this standard
at an age when the intercourse of nations and their
interdependence for all essentials of human life grow
ever closer is a retrograde step fraught with grave perils
to the cause of civilisation.

PART I

THE ECONOMICS OF IMPERIALISM

CHAPTER I

THE MEASURE OF IMPERIALISM

QUIBBLES about the modern meaning of the term Imperialism are best resolved by reference to concrete facts in the history of the last thirty years. During that period a number of European nations, Great Britain being first and foremost, have annexed or otherwise asserted political sway over vast portions of Africa and Asia, and over numerous islands in the Pacific and elsewhere. The extent to which this policy of expansion has been carried on, and in particular the enormous size and the peculiar character of the British acquisitions, are not adequately realised even by those who pay some attention to Imperial politics.

The following lists, giving the area and, where possible, the population of the new acquisitions, are designed to give definiteness to the term Imperialism. Though derived from official sources, they do not, however, profess strict accuracy. The sliding scale of political terminology along which no-man's land, or hinterland, passes into some kind of definite protectorate is often applied so as to conceal the process; "rectification" of a fluid frontier is continually taking place; paper "partitions" of spheres of influence or protection in Africa and Asia are often obscure, and in some cases the area and the population are highly speculative.

In a few instances it is possible that portions of territory put down as acquired since 1870 may have been ear-marked by a European Power at some earlier date. But care is taken to include only such territories as have come within this period under the definite political control of the Power to which they are assigned. The figures in the case of Great Britain are so startling as to call for a little further interpretation. I have thought it right to add to the recognised list of colonies and protectorates the " veiled Protectorate " of Egypt, with its vast Soudanese claim, the entire territories assigned to Chartered Companies, and the native or feudatory States in India which acknowledge our paramountcy by the admission of a British Agent or other official endowed with real political control.

All these lands are rightly accredited to the British Empire, and if our past policy is still pursued, the intensive as distinct from the extensive Imperialism will draw them under an ever-tightening grasp.

In a few other instances, as, for example, in West Africa, countries are included in this list where some small dominion had obtained before 1870, but where the vast majority of the present area of the colony is of recent acquisition. Any older colonial possession thus included in Lagos or Gambia is, however, far more than counterbalanced by the increased area of the Gold Coast Colony, which is not included in this list, and which grew from 29,000 square miles in 1873 to 39,000 square miles in 1893.

	Date of Acquisition.	Area. Square Miles	Population.
EUROPE—			
Cyprus	1878	3,584	227,900
AFRICA—			
Zanzibar and Pemba . .	1888		200,000
East Africa Protectorate .	1895	1,000,000	2,500,000
Uganda Protectorate . .	1894–1896	140,000	3,800,000
Somali Coast Protectorate	1884–1885	68,000	(?)
British Central Africa Protectorate . . .	1889	42,217	688,049
Lagos	to 1899	21,000	3,000,000
Gambia	to 1888	3,550	215,000
Ashantee	1896–1901	70,000	2,000,000
Niger Coast Protectorate .	1885–1898	400,000 to 500,000	25,000,000 to 40,000,000
Egypt	1882	400,000	9,734,405
Egyptian Soudan . .	1882	950,000	10,000,000
Griqualand West . .	1871–1880	15,197	83,373
Zululand	1879–1897	10,521	240,000
British Bechuanaland . .	1885	51,424	72,736
Bechuanaland Protectorate.	1891	213,000	200,000
Transkei	1879–1885	2,535	153,582
Tembuland	1885	4,155	180,130
Pondoland	1894	4,040	188,000
Griqualand East . . .	1879–1885	7,511	152,609
British South Africa Charter	1889	750,000	321,000
Transvaal	1900	119,139	870,000
Orange River Colony . .	1900	48,826	207,503
ASIA—			
Hong Kong (littoral) . .	1898	376	100,000
Wei-hai-wei	...	270	118,000
Socotra	1886	1,382	10,000
Upper Burma . . .	1887	83,473	2,046,933
Baluchistan	1876–1889	130,000	500,000
Sikkim	1890	2,818	30,000
Rajputana (States) . .		128,022	12,186,352
Burma (States) . .	since 1881	62,661	785,800
Jammu and Kashmir .		80,000	2,543,952
Malay Protected States .	1883–1895	24,849	620,000
North Borneo Company .	1881	31,106	175,000
North Borneo Protectorate	1888	...	...
Sarawak	1888	50,000	500,000
British New Guinea . .	1888	90,540	350,000
Fiji Islands	1874	7,740	122,676

The list is by no means complete. It takes no account of several large regions which have passed under the control of our Indian Government as native or feudatory States, but of which no statistics of area or popula-

B

tion, even approximate, are available. Such are the Shan States, the Burma Frontier, and the Upper Burma Frontier, the districts of Chitral, Bajam, Swat, Waziristan, which came under our "sphere of influence" in 1893, and have been since taken under a closer protectorate. The increase of British India itself between 1871 and 1891 amounted to an area of 104,993 square miles, with a population of 25,330,000, while no reliable measurement of the formation of new native States within that period and since is available. Many of the measurements here given are in round numbers, indicative of their uncertainty, but they are taken, wherever available, from official publications of the Colonial Office, corroborated or supplemented from the "Statesman's Year-book." They will by no means comprise the full tale of our expansion during the thirty years, for many enlargements made by the several colonies themselves are omitted. But taken as they stand they make a formidable addition to the growth of an Empire whose nucleus is only 120,000 square miles, with 40,000,000 population.

For so small a nation to add to its domains in the course of a single generation an area of 4,754,000 square miles,[1] with an estimated population of 88,000,000, is a historical fact of great significance.

Accepting Sir Robert Giffen's estimate[2] of the size of our Empire (including Egypt and the Soudan) at about 13,000,000 square miles, with a population of some 400 to 420 millions (of whom about 50,000,000 are of British race and speech), we find that one-third of this

[1] Sir R. Giffen gives the figures as 4,204,690 square miles for the period 1870-1898.
[2] "The Relative Growth of the Component Parts of the Empire," a paper read before the Colonial Institute, January 1898.

Empire, containing quite one-fourth of the total population of the Empire, has been acquired within the last generation. This is in tolerably close agreement with other independent estimates.[1]

The character of this Imperial expansion is clearly exhibited in the list of new territories.

Though, for convenience, the year 1870 has been taken as indicative of the beginning of a conscious policy of Imperialism, it will be evident that the movement did not attain its full impetus until the middle of the eighties. The vast increase of territory, and the method of wholesale partition which assigned to us great tracts of African land, may be dated from about 1884. Within fifteen years some three and three-quarter

[1] BRITISH COLONIES AND DEPENDENCIES, 1900.

	Area. Square Miles.	Estimated Population.
EUROPEAN DEPENDENCIES . . .	119	204,421
ASIATIC DEPENDENCIES—		
India (1,800,258 square miles, 287,223,431 inhabitants) . Others (27,321 square miles, 4,363,257 inhabitants) . .	1,827,579	291,586,688
AFRICAN COLONIES	535,398	6,773,360
AMERICAN COLONIES	3,952,572	7,260,169
AUSTRALASIAN COLONIES . . .	3,175,840	5,009,281
Total	9,491,508	310,833,919
PROTECTORATES—		
Asia	120,400	1,200,000
Africa (including Egypt, Egyptian Soudan)	3,530,000	54,730,000
Oceania	800	30,000
Total Protectorates . . .	3,651,200	55,960,000
Grand total	13,142,708	366,793,919

(Compiled from Morris' "History of Colonisation," vol. ii. p. 87, and "Statesman's Year-book," 1900.)

millions of square miles have been added to the British
Empire.[1]

Nor does Great Britain stand alone in this
enterprise. The leading characteristic of modern Imperialism, the competition of rival Empires, is the product of this same period. The close of the Franco-
German war marks the beginning of a new colonial policy
in France and Germany, destined to take effect in the
next decade. It was not unnatural that the newly-
founded German Empire, surrounded by powerful
enemies and doubtful allies, and perceiving its more
adventurous youth drawn into the United States and
other foreign lands, should form the idea of a colonial
empire. During the seventies a vigorous literature

[1] "Liberalism and the Empire," p. 341.

	1884–1900.	Area. Square Miles.	Population.
British New Guinea . .	1884	90,540	350,000
Nigeria	1884	(?) 450,000	(?) 30,000,000
Pondoland . . .	1884	4,040	188,000
Somaliland . . .	1884	68,000	(?)
Bechuanaland . .	1884–1885	264,000	272,000
Upper Burma . . .	1886	83,470	2,947,000
British East Africa . .	1886	860,000	2,500,000
Zululand (with Tongaland) .	1887	15,000	240,000
Sarawak and Brunei . .	1888	65,000	545,000
Pahang (Straits Settlements) .	1888	10,000	57,000
Rhodesia	1889	470,000	718,000
Zanzibar	1890	1,020	200,000
British Central Africa . .	1891	42,217	900,000
Uganda	1894	150,000	4,000,000
Ashantee. . . .	1896	21,000	(?) 3,000,000
Wei-hai-wei . . .	1898	270	118,000
Kow-lung	1898	400	100,000
Soudan	1898	950,000	(?) 10,000,000
Transvaal and Orange River Colony . . .	1900	167,000	1,301,000
Total . .		3,711,957	57,436,000

Total area, British Empire, January 1884—square miles, 8,059,179.
Population, 248,000,000.

sprang up in advocacy of the policy[1] which took shape a little later in the powerful hands of Bismarck. The earliest instance of official aid for the promotion of German commerce abroad occurred in 1880 in the Government aid granted to the "German Commercial and Plantation Association of the Southern Seas." German connection with Samoa dates from the same year, but the definite advance of Germany upon its Imperialist career began in 1884, with a policy of African protectorates and annexations of Oceanic islands. During the next fifteen years she brought under her colonial sway about 1,000,000 square miles, with an estimated population of 14,000,000. Almost the whole of this territory is tropical, and the white population forms a total of a few thousands.

Similarly in France a great revival of the old colonial spirit took place in the early eighties, the most influential of the revivalists being the eminent economist, M. Paul Leroy-Beaulieu. The extension of empire in Senegal and Sahara in 1880 was followed next year by the annexation of Tunis, and France was soon actively engaged in the scramble for Africa in 1884, while at the same time she was fastening her rule on Tonking and Laos in Asia. Her acquisitions since 1880 (exclusive of the extension of New Caledonia and its dependencies) amount to an area of over three and a half million square miles, with a native population of some 37,000,000, almost the whole tropical or sub-tropical, inhabited by lower races and incapable of genuine French colonisation.

Italian aspirations took similar shape from 1880 onwards, though the disastrous experience of the Abyssinian expeditions has given a check to Italian Imperialism. Her

[1] Fabri's *Bedarf Deutschland der Colonien* was the most vigorous and popular treatise.

possessions in East Africa are confined to the northern colony of Eritrea and the protectorate of Somaliland.

Of the other European States, two only, Portugal[1] and Belgium, enter directly into the competition of the new Imperialism. The African arrangements of 1884–6 assigned to Portugal the large district of Angola on the Congo Coast, while a large strip of East Africa passed definitely under her political control in 1891. The anomalous position of the great Congo Free State, ceded to the King of Belgium in 1883, and growing since then by vast accretions, must be regarded as involving Belgium in the competition for African empire.

Spain may be said to have definitely retired from imperial competition. The large and important possessions of Holland in the East and West Indies, though involving her in imperial politics to some degree, belong to older colonialism: she takes no part in the new imperial expansion.

Russia, the only active expansionist country of the North, stands alone in the character of her imperial growth, which differs from other Imperialism in that it has been principally Asiatic in its achievements and has proceeded by direct extension of imperial boundaries, partaking to a larger extent than in the other cases of a regular colonial policy of settlement for purposes of agriculture and industry. It is, however, evident that Russian expansion, though of a more normal and natural order than that which characterises the new Imperialism, comes definitely into contact and into competition with the claims and aspirations of the latter in Asia, and has been advancing rapidly during the period which is the object of our study.

[1] Portugal's true era of Imperialism in Africa, however, dates back two centuries. See Theal's fascinating story of the foundation of a Portuguese Empire in "Beginnings of South African History" (Fisher Unwin).

The recent entrance of the powerful and progressive
nation of the United States of America upon Imperialism
by the annexation of Hawaii and the taking over of the
relics of ancient Spanish empire not only adds a new formidable competitor for trade and territory, but changes and
complicates the issues.   As the focus of political attention
and activity shifts more to the Pacific States, and the commercial aspirations of America are more and more set
upon trade with the Pacific islands and the Asiatic coast,
the same forces which are driving European States along
the path of territorial expansion seem likely to act upon
the United States, leading her to a virtual abandonment
of the principle of American isolation which has hitherto
dominated her policy.

The following comparative table of colonisation, compiled from the "Statesman's Year-book" for 1900 by
Mr. H. C. Morris,[1] marks the present expansion of the
political control of Western nations :—

	Number of Colonies.	Area. Square Miles.		Population.	
		Mother Country.	Colonies, &c.	Mother Country.	Colonies, &c.
United Kingdom	50	120,979	11,605,238	40,559,954	345,222,239
France .	33	204,092	3,740,756	38,517,975	56,401,860
Germany . .	13	208,830	1,027,120	52,279,901	14,687,000
Netherlands .	3	12,648	782,862	5,074,632	35,115,711
Portugal .	9	36,038	801,100	5,049,729	9,148,707
Spain . .	3	197,670	243,877	17,565,632	136,000
Italy . . .	2	110,646	188,500	31,856,675	850,000
Austria-Hungary	2	241,032	23,570	41,244,811	1,568,092
Denmark . .	3	15,289	86,634	2,185,335	114,229
Russia . .	3	8,660,395	255,550	128,932,173	15,684,000
Turkey . .	4	1,111,741	465,000	23,834,500	14,956,236
China . .	5	1,336,841	2,881,560	386,000,000	16,680,000
U.S.A. . .	6	3,557,000	172,091	77,000,000	10,544,617
Total . .	136	15,813,201	22,273,858	850,103,317	521,108,791

The political nature of the new British Imperialism
may be authoritatively ascertained by considering the

[1] *Cf.* his "History of Colonisation," vol. ii. p. 318 (Macmillan & Co.).

governmental relations which the newly annexed territories hold with the Crown.

Officially,[1] British "colonial possessions" fall into
three classes—(1) "Crown colonies, in which the Crown
has the entire control of legislation, while the administration is carried on by public officers under the control
of the Home Government; (2) colonies possessing representative institutions, but not responsible government,
in which the Crown has no more than a veto on legislation, but the Home Government retains the control of
public affairs; (3) colonies possessing representative institutions and responsible government, in which the Crown
has only a veto on legislation, and the Home Government
has no control over any officer except the Governor."

Now, of the thirty-nine separate areas which have
been annexed by Great Britain since 1870 as colonies
or protectorates, not a single one ranks in class 2 or
3. The new Imperialism has established no single
British colony endowed with responsible government or
representative institutions. Nor, with the exception of
the three new States in South Africa, where white settlers
live in some numbers, is it seriously pretended that any
of these annexed territories is being prepared and educated
for representative, responsible self-government; and even
in these South African States there is no serious intention,
either on the part of the Home Government or of the
colonists, that the majority of the inhabitants shall have
any real voice in the government.

It is true that some of these areas enjoy a measure
of self-government, as protectorates or as feudatory States,
under their own native princes. But all these in major
matters of policy are subject to the absolute rule of the
British Government, or of some British official, while the

[1] See the "Colonial Office List."

general tendency is towards drawing the reins of arbitrary control more tightly over protectorates, converting them into States which are in substance, though not always in name, Crown colonies.   With the exception of a couple of experiments in India, the tendency everywhere has been towards a closer and more drastic imperial control over the territories that have been annexed, transforming protectorates, company rule, and spheres of influence into definite British States of the Crown colony order.

This is attributable, not to any greed of tyranny on the part of the Imperial Government, but to the conditions imposed upon our rule by considerations of climate and native population.   Almost the whole of this new territory is tropical, or so near to the tropics as to preclude genuine colonisation of British settlers, while in those few districts where Europeans can work and breed, as in parts of South Africa and Egypt, the preoccupation of the country by large native populations of "lower races" precludes any considerable settlement of British workers and the safe bestowal of the full self-government which prevails in Australasia and Canada.

The same is true to an even more complete extent of the Imperialism of other continental countries.   The new Imperialism has nowhere extended the political and civil liberties of the mother country to any part of the vast territories which, since 1870, have fallen under the government of Western civilised Powers.   Politically, the new Imperialism is an expansion of autocracy.

Taking the growth of Imperialism as illustrated in the recent expansion of Great Britain and of the chief continental Powers, we find the distinction between Imperialism and colonisation, set forth in the opening chapter, closely borne out by facts and figures, and warranting the following general judgments:—

First—Almost the whole of recent imperial expansion is occupied with the political absorption of tropical or sub-tropical lands in which white men will not settle with their families.

Second—Nearly all the lands are thickly peopled by " lower races."

Thus this recent imperial expansion stands entirely distinct from the colonisation of sparsely peopled lands in temperate zones, where white colonists carry with them the modes of government, the industrial and other arts of the civilisation of the mother country. The " occupation " of these new territories is comprised in the presence of a small minority of white men, officials, traders, and industrial organisers, exercising political and economic sway over great hordes of population regarded as inferior and as incapable of exercising any considerable rights of self-government, in politics or industry.

APPENDIX.

Expansion of Chief European Powers since 1884.

	Date of Acquisition.	Area. Square Miles.	Population.
FRANCE.			
Asia—			
Tonking and Laos	1884–1893	210,370	13,500,000
Africa—			
Tunis	1881	50,840	1,500,000
Sahara Region	...	1,684,000	2,500,000
Senegal (extension)	1880	200,000	3,500,000
Military Territories	1893	700,000	4,000,000
Dahomey	1893	60,000	1,000,000
Congo	1884	450,000	8,000,000
Comoro Islands	1886	620	53,000
Madagascar	1896	227,750	2,500,000
Oceania—			
(Extensions of New Caledonia and dependencies	...	...	...
Total		3,583,580	36,553,000

	Date of Acquisition.	Area. Square Miles.	Population.
GERMANY.			
AFRICA—			
Togoland	1884	33,000	2,500,000
Kamerun	1884	191,130	3,500,000
German South-West Africa .	1884–1890	322,450	200,000
German East Africa . .	1885–1890	384,180	8,000,000
ASIA—			
Kiauchau (with sphere of influence in Shantung) }	1897	200	60,000
Kaiser Wilhelm's Land .	1885–1886	70,000	110,000
Bismarck Archipelago . .	1885	20,000	188,000
Solomon Islands . . .	1886	4,200	45,000
Marshall Islands . . .	1886	150	13,000
Caroline Islands . . } Pelew Islands . . }	1899	560	40,000
Marianne Islands . . .	1899	250	2,000
Samoan Island, Savaii Upolu	...	100	29,100
Total . . .		1,026,220	16,687,100
RUSSIA.			
ASIA—			
Bokhara (dependency). .	1873	92,000	2,500,000
Khiva (dependency) . .	1872	22,320	800,000
Kwang-Tung . . .	1898	...	...
Manchuria (military occupation) . . . }	1900	...	...
BELGIUM.			
Congo Free State . .	1883–1894	900,000	30,000,000
PORTUGAL.			
AFRICA—			
Cape Verde Islands . .	1896	1,480	114,130
Guinea	1886	4,440	820,000
Angola	1886	484,800	4,119,000
East Africa . . .	1891	301,000	3,120,000
ASIA—			
Goa, Damoa, Tunis, &c. .	1887	9,036	860,000
Macao	1886	4	78,627
Total . . .		800,760	9,111,757

BRITISH AFRICA IN 1902.

BRITISH AFRICA IN 1873.

CHAPTER II

THE COMMERCIAL VALUE OF IMPERIALISM

THE absorption of so large a proportion of public interest, energy, blood and money in seeking to procure colonial possessions and foreign markets would seem to indicate that Great Britain obtains her chief livelihood by external trade. Now this is not the case. Large as is our foreign and colonial trade in volume and in value, essential as is much of it to our national well-being, nevertheless it furnishes a small proportion of the real income of the nation.

, Although the volume and value of home industries are not directly calculable, the total income of the nation, comprising profits, wages, rents, and other gains from all sources, is approximately estimated at £1,700,000,000 per annum. This sum, of course, covers all payments, not only for productive services of land, capital and labour in the making and distributing of material wealth, but for professional and personal services as well. Real income in the shape of goods or services to this amount is consumed or saved within the year.

Now the total value of the import and export trade of Great Britain in 1898 (we take this year as the latest normal one for the purpose, later years being disturbed by the war factor) amounted to £765,000,000. If we were to take the very liberal allowance of 5 per cent. as profit upon this turnover of trade, the annual income directly derived from our external trade would amount to a little over £38,000,000, or about one forty-fifth part of our total income.

If one is estimating the total income directly derived from taking part in processes of external trade, it would be necessary to add the salaries of commercial clerks, rents of offices, &c., paid by British mercantile firms engaged in this trade. Even then the total income derived from external trade would only play a small part in the total income of Great Britain.

"But surely," it will be said, "you do not restrict the worth of our foreign trade to gains derived from the trading processes. The whole of the value of the exports of home produce, amounting in 1898 to £233,000,000, should be reckoned as income derived from or dependent on external trade for the purpose of this comparison, for it represents payments in the shape of profits, wages, rents, &c., made to persons in Great Britain who have produced the goods that are exported: destroy this export trade and you annihilate all this income." This plausible presentation of the matter rests, however, upon shallow economic analysis. It is an excellent thing to have a wide and various foreign market, but we cannot admit that the capital and labour which made the export goods must have remained without employment if this foreign outlet for the goods they made had not existed. It is an advantage to our manufacturers that foreigners are willing to compete with home consumers for the purchase of their manufactures, and particular industries have grown and thriven by this enlargement of their market. The particular direction in which large quantities of capital and labour have been employed has been determined by these external markets. But

we are not entitled to conclude that if this export trade
had not grown up this capital and labour would have
been without productive employment, though some of
it must have been differently employed. The assumption that home demand is a fixed amount, and that
any commodities produced in excess of this amount
must find a foreign market or remain unsold, is quite
unwarranted. On the contrary, there is no necessary
limit to the quantity of capital and labour which can
be employed in producing goods for the home market,
if the productive power is disposed in industries which
meet the rising demands of the consumer. Whatever
quantity of wealth is produced in this country can
be bought and consumed in this country, because with
everything that is produced a corresponding power to
purchase and consume is created. The pressure to
find external markets, though urgent enough in many
trades, is not based on any natural economic necessity.
There is no natural limit to the quantity of wealth
which can be produced, exchanged, and consumed
within Great Britain except the limits imposed by
restricted natural resources and the actual condition
of the arts of industry.[1] Without, then, disputing the
great utility of foreign trade to us, I would insist that
the money income regarded as derived from foreign
trade ought to be confined to the sum of the superior
prices obtained for the goods sold abroad over those
which could have been obtained for them (or for the
goods which could have been produced in their place
by the same factors of production) in the home market.

Whatever value such considerations justify us in
setting upon the external trade of Great Britain, they

[1] For the necessity, other than natural, which gives such great importance to foreign trade, see chap. vi.

do not justify the weight this trade exercises as a determinant of our commercial policy.

Moreover, it should be borne in mind that whereas during the first seven decades of the century, before any strong, definite, or continuous imperialistic policy was maintained, England's foreign trade was advancing faster than her home trade, the three decades during which our public policy has been consciously dominated by a struggle for external markets show no increase in the value of our external trade comparable with the increase of our home trade. Between 1870 and 1898 the total income of the nation from all sources has grown from about £1,200,000,000 to £1,700,000,000. The following table gives the yearly figures of our import and export trade during that same period, the quinquennial average, and the value per head of the population :—

Year.	Trade (in Millions).	Value per Head of Population.	Year.	Trade (in Millions).	Value per Head of Population.
		£ s. d.			£ s. d.
1870 . . .	547		1885 . . .	642	
1871 . . .	615		1886 . . .	619	
1872 . . .	669		1887 . . .	643	
1873 . . .	682		1888 . . .	686	
1874 . . .	668		1889 . . .	743	
Average	636	19 19 3	Average	666	18 4 5
1875 . . .	655		1890 . . .	749	
1876 . . .	632		1891 . . .	744	
1877 . . .	647		1892 . . .	715	
1878 . . .	616		1893 . . .	682	
1879 . . .	612		1894 . . .	682	
Average	632	18 16 6	Average	715	18 14 10
1880 . . .	697		1895 . . .	703	
1881 . . .	694		1896 . . .	738	
1882 . . .	720		1897 . . .	745	
1883 . . .	732		1898 . . .	765	
1884 . . .	686				
Average	706	20 1 3	Average	737	19 7 10

C

Although the real increase in volume of external trade is considerable when the fall of general prices since 1870 is taken into account, it is quite evident that neither the volume nor the value of external trade has kept pace during this period with the volume and the value of internal trade. While the total income per head of the population has certainly increased by as much as 20 per cent., the value of external trade per head has actually shrunk.

Next, let us inquire whether the vast outlay of energy and money upon imperial expansion is attended by a growing trade within the Empire as compared with foreign trade. In other words, does the policy tend to make us more and more an economically self-sufficing Empire? Does trade follow the flag?

The following figures represent the proportion which our trade with our colonies and possessions bears to our foreign trade during the latter half of the nineteenth century :—

PERCENTAGES OF TOTAL VALUES.[1]

Annual Averages.	Imports into Great Britain from		Exports from Great Britain to	
	Foreign Countries.	British Possessions.	Foreign Countries.	British Possessions.
1855–1859	76.5	23.5	68.5	31.5
1860–1864	71.2	28.8	66.6	33.4
1865–1869	76.0	24.0	72.4	27.6
1870–1874	78.0	22.0	74.4	25.6
1875–1879	77.9	22.0	66.9	33.1
1880–1884	76.5	23.5	65.5	34.5
1885–1889	77.1	22.9	65.0	35.0
1890–1894	77.1	22.9	67.6	34.4
1895–1898	78.6	21.4	66.0	34.0

[1] This table, as distinguished from those following, is based on figures which include in the export trade only British and Irish produce, and do not include export of "foreign and colonial produce."

A longer period has here been taken as a basis of comparison in order to bring out clearly the central truth, viz. that our modern imperialist policy has had no appreciable influence whatever upon the determination of our external trade. The proportion of our exports and our imports, as between foreign countries and our own possessions, is virtually the same in the first period, 1855-59, and the last period, 1895-98, nor, with one exception, has it varied widely during the entire half-century. That exception consists in a notable drop in the proportion of exports to our possessions in the period 1865–74 ; after the recovery from that depression, in 1875–79, there is no considerable change. Although since 1870 such vast additions have been made to British possessions, involving a corresponding reduction in the number or size of " foreign countries," this imperial expansion is attended by no increase in the proportion of intra-imperial trade as represented in the imports and exports of Great Britain.

A somewhat closer study of the trade statistics of the last decade of the nineteenth century emphasises the recent tendency.

TRADE WITH FOREIGN COUNTRIES AND BRITISH POSSESSIONS
(IN MILLION £).

Imports.

Year.	From Foreign Countries.	From British Possessions.	Percentage from British Possessions.
1891	336	99	23
1892	326	98	23
1893	313	92	23
1894	314	94	23
1895	321	96	23
1896	349	93	21
1897	357	94	21
1898	371	100	22
1899	378	107	22
1900	414	109	21

TRADE WITH FOREIGN COUNTRIES AND BRITISH POSSESSIONS
(IN MILLION £).

Exports.

Year.	To Foreign Countries.	To British Possessions.	Percentage to British Possessions.
1891	216	93	30
1892	211	81	28
1893	198	79	29
1894	195	79	29
1895	210	76	26
1896	206	90	30
1897	207	87	30
1898	204	90	30
1899	235	94	29
1900	252	102	29

Value of new ships sold to foreigners first entered in export returns
in 1899—1899, £9,196,000 ; 1900, £8,588,000.

The elaborate statistical investigation of Professor
Alleyne Ireland into the trade of our colonial possessions
strikes a still heavier blow at the notion that trade
follows the flag. Taking the same period, he establishes
the following two facts :—

"The total import trade of all the British colonies
and possessions has increased at a much greater rate than
the imports from the United Kingdom." "The total
exports of all the British colonies and possessions have
increased at a much greater rate than the exports to the
United Kingdom." [1]

The following table [2] shows the gradual decline in
the importance to the colonies of the commercial connection with Great Britain since 1872-75, as illustrated
in the proportion borne in the value of their exports
from and their imports to Great Britain as compared

[1] Page 125.
[2] Founded on the tables of Professor Ireland ("Tropical Civilisation,"
pp. 98-101), and revised up to date from figures in the Statistical Abstract
of Colonial Possessions, Cd. 307.

with the value of the total imports and exports of the British colonies and possessions :—

Four-Yearly Averages.	Percentages of Imports into Colonies, &c., from Great Britain.	Percentages of Exports from Colonies, &c., into Great Britain.
1856–1859	46.5	57.1
1860–1863	41.0	65.4
1864–1867	38.9	57.6
1868–1871	39.8	53.5
1872–1875	43.6	54.0
1876–1879	41.7	50.3
1880–1883	42.8	48.1
1884–1887	38.5	43.0
1888–1891	36.3	39.7
1892–1895	32.4	36.6
1896–1899	32.5	34.9

In other words, while Great Britain's dependence on her Empire for trade is stationary, the dependence of her Empire upon her for trade is rapidly diminishing.

Closer attention to the special period when imperial expansion has been in full activity—1884 to the end of the century—enforces the lesson still more powerfully.

Year.	Exports and Imports of Great Britain (in Million £).	Imports and Export Trade of Great Britain with Possessions (in Million £).
1884	686	184
1885	642	170
1886	619	164
1887	643	166
1888	686	179
1889	743	188
1890	749	191
1891	744	193
1892	715	179
1893	682	170
1894	682	172
1895	703	172
1896	738	184
1897	745	183
1898	765	190

The actual condition of British trade with foreign countries and with the chief groups of the colonies respectively may be indicated by the following statement [1] for the year ending December 1901 :—

	Imports from.		Exports to.	
	Value.	Per-centage.	Value.	Per-centage.
	£		£	
Foreign Countries . .	417,615,000	80	178,450,000	63½
British India . .	38,001,000	7	39,753,000	14
Australasia . .	34,682,000	7	26,932,000	9½
Canada	19,775,000	4	7,797,000	3
British South Africa	5,155,000	1	17,006,000	6
Other British Possessions	7,082,000	1	10,561,000	4
Total . .	522,310,000	100	280,499,000	100

It is thus clearly seen that while imperial expansion is attended by no increase in the value of our trade with our colonies and dependencies, a considerable increase in the value of our trade with foreign nations has taken place. Did space permit, it could be shown that the greatest increase of our foreign trade is with that group of industrial nations whom we regard as our industrial enemies, and whose political enmity we are in danger of arousing by our policy of expansion—France, Germany, Russia, and the United States.

Our import trade with the United States alone is greater than with the whole of our colonies. In 1898, the last normal year, the aggregate trade with foreign countries in British produce was £520,877,107, with our possessions £182,660,716. In 1898 the imports from the United States were £126,062,155, and from our possessions £99,433,995. The total imports were £470,544,702, so that the imports from our possessions constituted about one-fifth of the whole.

One more point of supreme significance in its bearing

[1] "Cobden Club Leaflet," 123, by Harold Cox.

on the new Imperialism remains. We have already drawn attention to the radical distinction between genuine colonialism and Imperialism. This distinction is strongly marked in the statistics of the progress of our commerce with our foreign possessions.

The following table indicates the movement of our commerce during the last three decades of the nineteenth century with India, the technically self-governing colonies, and the other colonies respectively :—

TRADE OF THE EMPIRE WITH GREAT BRITAIN.

(ooo omitted in amount columns.)

Annual Average of 1867–71.						
	Total Imports.	Imports from Britain.	Percentage of British Imports.	Total Exports.	Exports to Britain.	Percentage of Exports to Britain.
	£	£		£	£	
India	45,818	31,707	69.2	56,532	29,738	52.6
Self-governing Colonies	42,612	24,502	57.5	42,386	23,476	55.4
Other Colonies . .	23,161	7,955	34.3	23,051	10,698	46.4
Annual Average of 1892–96.						
India	52,577	37,811	71.9	68,250	22,656	33.2
Self-governing Colonies	74,572	44,133	59.2	83,528	58,714	70.3
Other Colonies . .	39,835	10,443	26.2	36,626	10,987	29.3

(Professor Flux, "The Flag and Trade," *Journal of Statistical Society*, Sept. 1899, vol. lxii. pp. 496–98.)

Professor Flux thus summarises the chief result of this comparison : "The great source of growth of Britain's colonial trade is very clearly shown to be the growth of trade with the colonies to which self-government ·has been granted. Their foreign trade has nearly doubled, and the proportion of it which is carried on with the mother country has increased from about 56½ per cent. to 65 per cent." This testimony of trade to the virtues of self-government cannot, however, be pressed very far, as is proved by classifying the same set of facts upon another *fundamentum divisionis.*

The distinction of self-governing and other colonies is almost identical with that between tropical and non-tropical colonies. The latter distinction, however, does not admit so much exactitude, though it is even more important in the instructive light it throws upon the economic character of Imperialism.

Regarded in a specifically political manner, Imperialism would seem confined to those colonies and possessions to which responsible self-government is denied, and which are governed by the will of Great Britain. But if due weight is assigned to economic as well as to formally political conditions, all possessions where the mass of the inhabitants enjoy no real share in such self-government as is accorded must be included. This extends the imperialist area so as to make it cover the important cases of Cape Colony and Natal, where the conditions are essentially lacking in popular self-government,

VALUE OF EXPORTS OF PRODUCE AND MANUFACTURES OF THE UNITED KINGDOM TO BRITISH COLONIES AND POSSESSIONS.

(Cape Colony and Natal included under Tropics.)

	1884	1885	1886	1887
Tropics	46,006,946	43,420,915	43,565,649	45,649,905
Other Colonies	34,869,842	34,574,005	32,105,752	29,720,351
	1888	1889	1890	1891
Tropics	49,044,638	49,956,824	54,542,324	50,853,312
Other Colonies	35,196,875	33,322,166	32,828,059	35,102,776
	1890	1893	1894	1895
Tropics	45,943,912	47,736,754	48,242,074	45,236,549
Other Colonies	28,804,605	24,413,409	24,546,471	24,960,745
	1896	1897	1898	
Tropics	54,539,233	51,437,539	53,579,233	...
Other Colonies	29,597,704	29,237,524	29,847,538	...

In this table the "other colonies" consist of Australasia, Canada, Newfoundland, the Channel Islands, Gibraltar, and Malta.

While the export trade to the whole number of colonies and possessions shows a slight absolute growth of value, having risen from £80,875,946 in 1884 to £83,426,761 in 1898, that between the mother country and the non-tropical possessions shows a considerable decline, more than compensated by the growth of trade with the tropical colonies. But further investigation makes it quite evident that this result and various others depend entirely upon the classification of Cape Colony and Natal, which rank for statistical purposes as pivotal colonies, carrying with them the balance of advantage to tropical and non-tropical, self-governing and imperialist States, according as we place them.

For during this period the exports to these South African colonies show an increase from £4,102,281 to £12,199,810. Hence, if these colonies, with their quite abnormal conditions, are excluded, the small rise of colonial exports as a whole becomes a considerable decline. If, having regard to the semi-tropical character of Natal, destined in all probability to be exploited chiefly by Coolie and Kaffir labour, and the great tropical hinterland fed by the trade of Cape Colony, we reckon these colonies in the tropical class, that entire class presents a favourable appearance as compared with the non-tropical colonies.

A strict interpretation of self-government will, by including Cape Colony and Natal (though the latter only obtained full self-government in 1893), throw the advantage on the side of the self-governing colonies, as against the imperially governed colonies. If, however, having regard to the virtual exclusion from all political power of the great majority of the population of these South African colonies, we refuse to rank them with Canada and Australasia, this argument for self-government on economic grounds disappears.

The real distinction which the facts and figures serve to emphasise is that between the tropical and the non-tropical colonies; and their political bearing rests upon the fact that the new Imperialism is perforce driven more and more into the annexation and administration of tropical countries. Taking under survey our whole Empire, we reach the conclusion that, excluding our commerce with India, the smallest, least valuable, and most uncertain trade is that done with our tropical possessions, and in particular with those which have come under imperial control since 1870. The only considerable increase of our import trade since 1884 is from our genuine colonies in Australasia, North America, and Cape Colony; the trade with India has been stagnant, while that with our tropical colonies in Africa and the West Indies has been in most cases irregular and dwindling. Our export trade exhibits the same general character, save that Australia and Canada show a growing resolution to release themselves from dependence upon British manufactures; the trade with the tropical colonies, though exhibiting some increase, is very small and very fluctuating.

As for the territories acquired under the new Imperialism, except in one instance, no serious attempt to regard them as satisfactory business assets is possible.[1] Egypt alone yields a trade of some magnitude; of the

[1] The following are the official figures, as far as accessible, of import and export trade with our recently acquired tropical or sub-tropical possessions for 1900 and for (1898):—

	Imports from.	Exports to (including British, Colonial, and Foreign Merchandise).
	£	£
Cyprus	110,286 (137,934)	59,055 (77,883)
Zanzibar and Pemba . . .	195,480 (154,437)	78,876 (122,072)
Other East African Territories (Somaliland, Uganda, East Africa Protectorate)	3,874 (2,068)	145,229 (149,646)
Niger Coast Protectorate . .	987,717 (377,545)	808,567 (706,206)
Egypt	12,585,578 (8,855,689)	6,159,468 (4,626,881)
Lagos	367,631 (1,133,646)	595,928 (578,196)
Gambia	22,372 (54,229)	91,124 (91,376)
British Central Africa Protectorate (1899)	[159,435]	[79,349]
North Borneo Company . . .	3,885 (1,601)	12,119 (15,859)
Malay Protectorate States (1899) . .	[11,200,000]	[6,800,000]
British New Guinea . . .	250 (190)	1,626 (1,049)
Fiji Islands	17,720 (135)	32,571 (18,135)
Leeward Islands (1899) . . .	60,210	148,020
Windward Islands (1899) . . .	230,290	280,540

The present public value of some of our latest acquisitions in Africa is concisely indicated by the following official return of revenue and expenditure:—

UGANDA.

					Revenue.	Expenditure.
1894–5	.	.	.	.	£7,577	£63,937
1896–7	.	.	.	.	39,191	147,641
1901–2	.	.	.	.	52,050	224,731

BRITISH EAST AFRICA.

					Revenue.	Expenditure.
1891–2	.	.	.	.	£16,919	£12,951
1901–2	.	.	.	.	83,619	180,118

BRITISH CENTRAL AFRICA.

					Revenue.	Expenditure.
1901–2	.	.	.	.	£52,785	£104,612

The figures are taken from the annual accounts laid before Parliament by the Comptroller and Auditor-General, and from the Estimates of the Protectorates for the year 1901–2, the completed accounts not having yet been received.

other possessions, three only—Lagos, Niger Coast Protectorate, and North Borneo—are proved to do a trade with Great Britain exceeding one million pounds in value.   In fact, excluding Egypt, the whole volume of this trade, so far as it is officially recorded, does not amount to ten million pounds; and though the actual trade is doubtless in excess of this sum, it forms an infinitesimal addition to the commercial resources of our nation.   Apart from its quantity, the quality of the new tropical export trade is of the lowest, consisting for the most part, as the analysis of the Colonial Office shows, of the cheapest textile goods of Lancashire, the cheapest metal goods of Birmingham and Sheffield, and large quantities of gunpowder, spirits, and tobacco.

Such evidence leads to the following conclusions bearing upon the economics of the new Imperialism. First, the external trade of Great Britain bears a small and diminishing proportion to its internal industry and trade.   Secondly, of the external trade, that with British possessions bears a diminishing proportion to that with foreign countries.   Thirdly, of the trade with British possessions, the tropical trade, and in particular the trade with the new tropical possessions, is the smallest, least progressive, and most fluctuating in quantity, while it is lowest in the character of the goods which it embraces.

APPENDIX.

COMPARISON OF 18 CHIEF EXPORTS (COVERING 59.4 PER CENT. OF OUR EXPORTS, 1870–79) DURING PERIODS 1870–79 AND 1890–99. + denotes increase, – decrease.

	Value.	Quantity.	Price.
	Per Cent.	Per Cent.	Per Cent.
Beer and Ale	– 20	– 7½	– 13
Coal	+ 100	+ 140	– 18
Cotton Yarn	– 32	+ 9	– 36
Cotton Goods	– 9	+ 36	– 33
Cotton Goods (printed and dyed)	+ 1	+ 59	– 70
Cotton Thread	+ 90	+ 130	– 11
Fresh Herrings	+ 57	+ 98	– 14
Jute Goods	+ 58	+ 145	– 53
Linen Goods	– 42	– 17	– 30
Linen Yarn	– 43	– 38	– 13
Iron (pig and puddled)	– 29	same.	– 27
Iron (bar, angle, bolt, rod)	– 56	– 39	– 29
Rails	– 51	– 8	– 48
Tin-plates	+ 36	+ 150	– 48
Total Iron and Steel	– 8	+ 20	...
Copper	+ 55	+ 130	– 38
Spirits	+ 480	+ 183	+ 94
Woollen and Worsted Yarn	– 5½	+ 56	– 37
Woollen and Worsted Tissues	– 29	– 36	+ 14

AVERAGE EXPORTS PER HEAD OF POPULATION.

	£	s.	d.			£	s.	d.
1870–74	7	7	5	Average 1870–79		6	9	0
1875–79	6	0	7					
1880–84	6	12	11	,, 1880–89		6	8	3
1885–89	6	3	7					
1890–94	6	3	2	,, 1890–99		6	1	8
1895–99	6	0	3					

(*Economic Review*, January 1902; "Thirty Years' Export Trade," Barnard Ellinson.)

CHAPTER III

IMPERIALISM AS AN OUTLET FOR POPULATION

THERE is a widely prevalent belief that imperial expansion is desirable, or even necessary, in order to absorb and utilise the surplus of our ever-growing population. "The reproductive powers of nature," runs the argument, "brook no restraint: the most dominant force in history is the tendency of population to overflow its ancient banks, seeking fuller and easier subsistence. Great Britain is one of the most congested areas in the world; her growing population cannot find enough remunerative occupation within these islands; professional and working-classes alike find it more and more difficult to earn a decent and secure living, every labour market is overstocked, emigration is a prime economic necessity. Now, those who under such pressure leave our shores consist largely of the strongest and most energetic stuff the nation contains. Many of these people, whose permanent alienation would be a heavy loss, have been saved to the Empire by the policy of imperial expansion: they have settled either in vacant places of the earth which they have seized and kept under British rule, or in places where they have set up a definitely British supremacy over lower races of existing inhabitants. It is our most urgent national interest that this surplus emigrant population shall settle in lands which are under the British flag, and we must therefore maintain a constant policy of extending the political control of Great Britain so as to cover the new homes to which these people betake themselves in pursuit of employment." This motive is closely linked with other economic motives relating to trade and investments. The establishment of British trade, and especially of British capital, in foreign lands naturally attracts a certain British population; traders, engineers, overseers, and mechanics are needed as entrepreneurs and managers. So wherever a new area is opened up to our trade and capital the nucleus of an outlander population is formed. Hence, of necessity, springs up a crop of political issues, an outlander problem: the British outlanders not satisfied with the foreign rule demand the intervention of their home Government. Thus the duty of protecting British subjects in a foreign country is identified with the duty of protecting British property, not merely the personal property of the outlanders, often a trivial matter, but the far larger stakes of the home investors. But apart from these cases of special interest, wherever any considerable number of British subjects settles in a savage or semi-civilised country they have a "right" to British protection, and since that protection can seldom be made effective without the exercise of direct British authority, the imperial ægis of Great Britain must be spread over all such areas, when a convenient occasion for such expansion presents itself.

Such is the accepted theory and practice. What validity does it possess as an argument for recent imperial expansion? Let me first ask: Is England over-populated now, and is the prospect of further increase such as to compel us to "peg out claims for posterity" in other parts of the world? The facts are these. Great Britain is not so thickly populated as certain prosperous industrial areas in Germany, the Netherlands, and China: along with every recent growth of population has come a far greater growth of wealth and of the power to purchase food and other subsistence. The modern specialisation of industry has caused a congestion of population upon certain spots which may be injurious in some ways to the well-being of the nation, but it cannot be regarded as over-population in the sense of a people outgrowing the means of subsistence. Nor have we reason to fear such over-population in the future. It is true that our manufactures and commerce may not continue to grow as rapidly as in the past, though we have no clear warrant from industrial statistics for this judgment: but if this be so, neither is our population likely to increase so fast. Of this we have clear statistical evidence: the diminution of the rate of growth of our population, as disclosed by the two latest censuses, is such as to justify the conclusion that, if the same forces continue to operate, the population of Great Britain will be stationary by the middle of the century.

There exists, then, no general necessity for a policy of expansion in order to provide for over-population, present or prospective. But supposing it were necessary for an increasing surplus of our population to emigrate, is it necessary for us to spend so large a part of our national resources, and to incur such heavy risks, in seizing new territory for them to settle upon?

The total emigration of Britons represents no large proportion of the population; that proportion during the recent years of imperial expansion has perceptibly diminished: of the emigrants a small proportion settles in British possessions, and an infinitesimally small fraction settles in the countries acquired under the new Imperialism. These most instructive facts are established by the following official table, giving the statistics of emigration from 1884, the year from which the full tide of imperial expansion is to be dated:—

NUMBER OF OUTWARD-BOUND PASSENGERS OF BRITISH AND IRISH ORIGIN, FROM THE UNITED KINGDOM TO COUNTRIES OUT OF EUROPE.

Year.	Passengers to					Total.
	United States.	British North America.	Australia and New Zealand.	Cape of Good Hope and Natal.	Other Places.	
1884	155,280	31,134	44,255	...	11,510	242,179
1885	137,687	19,828	39,395	...	10,724	207,644
1886	152,710	24,745	43,076	3,897	8,472	232,900
1887	201,526	32,025	34,183	4,909	8,844	281,487
1888	195,986	34,853	31,127	6,466	11,496	279,928
1889	168,771	28,269	28,294	13,884	14,577	253,795
1890	152,413	22,520	21,179	10,321	11,683	218,116
1891	156,395	21,578	19,547	9,090	11,897	218,507
1892	150,039	23,254	15,950	9,891	10,908	210,042
1893	148,949	24,732	11,203	13,097	10,833	208,814
1894	104,001	17,459	10,917	13,177	10,476	156,030
1895	126,502	16,622	10,567	20,234	11,256	185,181
1896	98,921	15,267	10,354	24,594	12,789	161,925
1897	85,324	15,571	12,061	21,109	12,395	146,460
1898	80,494	17,640	10,693	19,756	12,061	140,644
1899	92,482	16,410	11,467	14,432	11,571	146,362
1900	102,797	18,443	14,922	20,815	11,848	168,825

Regarded as a measure of the outflow of "surplus" population, even these figures are excessive in two ways. In the first place, they include considerable numbers of travellers and casual visitors who are not real emigrants. Secondly, to measure aright the net emigration, we must set against these figures the immigration figures. The net reduction of our population by emigration is thus reduced to an average, during the last five years, of 87,224 per annum.

Considering that the term "other places" includes the entire non-European world, outside Canada, Aus-

D

tralasia, and South Africa, it is clear that the rest of our
Empire absorbs at most a very few thousands, while the
number of industrial settlers in our new tropical dominions must be a mere handful. A certain quantity of
military and official employment is afforded by the new
Imperialism to the influential upper classes, a few
engineers, missionaries, prospectors, and overseers of
trading and industrial undertakings get temporary posts,
but as a contribution towards the general field of
employment the new Imperialism is an utterly insignificant factor.

No substantial settlement of Britons is taking place
upon any of the areas of the Empire acquired since 1870,
excepting the Transvaal and the Orange River Colony,
nor is it likely that any such settlement will take place.
The tropical character of most lands acquired under the new
Imperialism renders genuine colonisation impossible: there
is no true British settlement in these places; a small
number of men spend a short broken period in precarious
occupations as traders, engineers, missionaries, overseers.
The new Empire is even more barren for settlement than
for profitable trade.

CHAPTER IV

ECONOMIC PARASITES OF IMPERIALISM

I

SEEING that the Imperialism of the last three decades is clearly condemned as a business policy, in that at enormous expense it has procured a small, bad, unsafe increase of markets, and has jeopardised the entire wealth of the nation in rousing the strong resentment of other nations, we may ask, "How is the British nation induced to embark upon such unsound business?" The only possible answer is that the business interests of the nation as a whole are subordinated to those of certain sectional interests that usurp control of the national resources and use them for their private gain. This is no strange or monstrous charge to bring; it is the commonest disease of all forms of government. The famous words of Sir Thomas More are as true now as when he wrote them: "Everywhere do I perceive a certain conspiracy of rich men seeking their own advantage under the name and pretext of the commonwealth."

Although the new Imperialism has been bad business for the nation, it has been good business for certain classes and certain trades within the nation. The vast expenditure on armaments, the costly wars, the grave risks and embarrassments of foreign policy, the stoppage of political and social reforms within Great Britain, though fraught with great injury to the nation, have served well the present business interests of certain industries and professions.

It is idle to meddle with politics unless we clearly recognise this central fact and understand what these sectional interests are which are the enemies of national safety and the commonwealth. We must put aside the merely sentimental diagnosis which explains wars or other national blunders by outbursts of patriotic animosity or errors of statecraft. Doubtless at every outbreak of war not only the man in the street but the man at the helm is often duped by the cunning with which aggressive motives and greedy purposes dress themselves in defensive clothing. There is, it may be safely asserted, no war within memory, however nakedly aggressive it may seem to the dispassionate historian, which has not been presented to the people who were called upon to fight as a necessary defensive policy, in which the honour, perhaps the very existence, of the State was involved.

The disastrous folly of these wars, the material and moral damage inflicted even on the victor, appear so plain to the disinterested spectator that he is apt to despair of any State attaining years of discretion, and inclines to regard these natural cataclysms as implying some ultimate irrationalism in politics. But careful analysis of the existing relations between business and politics shows that the aggressive Imperialism which we seek to understand is not in the main the product of blind passions of races or of the mixed folly and ambition of politicians. It is far more rational than at first sight appears. Irrational from the standpoint of the whole nation, it is rational enough from the standpoint of certain classes in the nation. A completely socialist State which kept good books and presented regular balance-sheets of expenditure and assets would soon discard Imperialism; an intelligent *laissez-faire* democracy which gave duly proportionate weight in its policy to all economic interests alike would do the same. But a State in which certain well-organised business interests are able to outweigh the weak, diffused interest of the community is bound to pursue a policy which accords with the pressure of the former interests.

In order to explain Imperialism on this hypothesis we have to answer two questions. Do we find in Great Britain to-day any well-organised group of special commercial and social interests which stand to gain by aggressive Imperialism and the militarism it involves? If such a combination of interests exists, has it the power to work its will in the arena of politics?

What is the direct economic outcome of Imperialism? A great expenditure of public money upon ships, guns, military and naval equipment and stores, growing and productive of enormous profits when a war, or an alarm of war, occurs; new public loans and important fluctuations in the home and foreign Bourses; more posts for soldiers and sailors and in the diplomatic and consular services; improvement of foreign investments by the substitution of the British flag for a foreign flag; acquisition of markets for certain classes of exports, and some protection and assistance for trades representing British houses in these manufactures; employment for engineers, missionaries, speculative miners, ranchers and other emigrants.

Certain definite business and professional interests feeding upon imperialistic expenditure, or upon the results of that expenditure, are thus set up in opposition to the common good, and, instinctively feeling their way to one another, are found united in strong sympathy to support every new imperialist exploit.

If the £60,000,000 which may now be taken as a minimum expenditure on armaments in time of peace were subjected to a close analysis, most of it would be traced directly to the tills of certain big firms engaged in building warships and transports, equipping and coaling them, manufacturing guns, rifles, and ammunition, supplying horses, waggons, saddlery, food, clothing for the services, contracting for barracks, and for other large irregular needs. Through these main channels the millions flow to feed many subsidiary trades, most of which are quite aware that they are engaged in executing contracts for the services. Here we have an important nucleus of commercial Imperialism. Some of these trades, especially the shipbuilding, boiler-making, and gun and ammunition making trades, are conducted by large firms with immense capital, whose heads are well aware of the uses of political influence for trade purposes.

These men are Imperialists by conviction; a pushful policy is good for them.

With them stand the great manufacturers for export trade, who gain a living by supplying the real or artificial wants of the new countries we annex or open up. Manchester, Sheffield, Birmingham, to name three representative cases, are full of firms which compete in pushing textiles and hardware, engines, tools, machinery, spirits, guns, upon new markets. The public debts which ripen in our colonies, and in foreign countries that come under our protectorate or influence, are largely loaned in the shape of rails, engines, guns, and other materials of civilisation made and sent out by British firms. The making of railways, canals, and other public works, the establishment of factories, the development of mines, the improvement of agriculture in new countries, stimulate a definite interest in important manufacturing industries which feeds a very firm imperialist faith in their owners.

The proportion which such trade bears to the total industry of Great Britain is very small, but some of it is extremely influential and able to make a definite impression upon politics, through chambers of commerce, Parliamentary representatives, and semi-political, semi-commercial bodies like the Imperial South African Association or the China League.

The shipping trade has a very definite interest which makes for Imperialism. This is well illustrated by the policy of State subsidies now claimed by shipping firms as a retainer, and in order to encourage British shipping for purposes of imperial safety and defence.

The services are, of course, imperialist by conviction and by professional interest, and every increase of the army and navy enhances their numerical strength and the political power they exert. The abolition of purchase in the army, by opening the profession to the upper middle classes, greatly enlarged this most direct feeder of imperial sentiment. The potency of this factor is, of course, largely due to the itch for glory and adventure among military officers upon disturbed or uncertain frontiers of the Empire. This has been a most prolific source of expansion in India. The direct professional influence of the services carries with it a less organised but powerful sympathetic support on the part of the aristocracy and the wealthy classes, who seek in the services careers for their sons.

To the military services we may add the Indian Civil Service and the numerous official and semi-official posts in our colonies and protectorates. Every expansion of the Empire is also regarded by these same classes as affording new openings for their sons as ranchers, planters, engineers, or missionaries. This point of view is aptly summarised by a high Indian official, Sir Charles Crossthwaite, in discussing British relations with Siam. "The real question was who was to get the trade with them, and how we could make the most of them, so as to find fresh markets for our goods and also employment for those superfluous articles of the present day, our boys."

From this standpoint our colonies still remain what James Mill cynically described them as being, "a vast system of outdoor relief for the upper classes."

In all the professions, military and civil, the army, diplomacy, the church, the bar, teaching and engineering, Greater Britain serves for an overflow, relieving the congestion of the home market and offering chances to more reckless or adventurous members, while it furnishes a convenient limbo for damaged characters and careers. The actual amount of profitable employment thus furnished by our recent acquisitions is inconsiderable, but it arouses that disproportionate interest which always attaches to the margin of employment. To extend this margin is a powerful motive in Imperialism.

These influences, primarily economic, though not unmixed with other sentimental motives, are particularly operative in military, clerical, academic, and Civil Service circles, and furnish an interested bias towards Imperialism throughout the educated classes.

II

By far the most important economic factor in Imperialism is the influence relating to investments. The growing cosmopolitanism of capital is the greatest economic change of this generation. Every advanced industrial nation is tending to place a larger share of its capital outside the limits of its own political area, in foreign countries, or in colonies, and to draw a growing income from this source.

No exact or even approximate estimate of the total amount of the income of the British nation derived from foreign investments is possible. We possess, however, in the income-tax assessments an indirect measurement of certain large sections of investments, from which we can form some judgment as to the total size of the income from foreign and colonial sources, and the rate of its growth.

INCOME FROM FOREIGN INVESTMENTS ASSURED TO INCOME-TAX.

	1884.	1888.	1892.	1896.	1900.
	£	£	£	£	£
From Indian public revenue	2,607,942	3,130,959	3,203,573	3,475,751	3,587,919
Indian rails	4,544,466	4,841,647	4,580,797	4,543,969	4,693,795
Colonial and foreign public securities, &c.	13,233,271	16,757,736	14,949,017	16,419,933	18,394,380
Railways out of United Kingdom	3,777,592	4,178,456	8,013,838	13,032,556	14,043,107
Foreign and colonial investments	9,665,853	18,069,573	23,981,545	17,428,870	19,547,685
	33,829,124	46,978,371	54,728,770	54,901,079	60,266,886

From this table it appears that the period of energetic Imperialism has been coincident with a remarkable growth in the income from external investments. The income from these sources has nearly doubled in the period 1884–1900, while the portion derived from foreign railways and foreign and colonial investments has increased at a still more rapid rate.

These figures only give the foreign income which can be identified as such. To them must be added a

large amount of income which escapes these income-tax
returns, including considerable sums which would appear
as profits of businesses carried on in the United Kingdom,
such as insurance companies, investment trusts, and land
mortgage companies, many of which derive a large part
of their income from foreign investments.   How rapid is
the growth of this order of investment is seen from the
published returns of investments of life insurance companies, which show that their investments in mortgages
outside the United Kingdom had grown from about
£6,000,000 in 1890 to £13,000,000 in 1898.

Sir R. Giffen estimated the income derived from
foreign sources as profit, interest and pensions in 1882 at
£70,000,000, and in a paper read before the Statistical
Society in March 1899 he estimated the income from
these same sources for the current year at £90,000,000.
It is probable that this last figure is an underestimate,
for if the items of foreign income not included as such
under the income-tax returns bear the same proportion to those included as in 1882, the present total of
income from foreign and colonial investments should be
£120,000,000 rather than £90,000,000.   Sir R. Giffen
hazards the calculation that the new public investments
abroad in the sixteen years 1882–1898 amounted to
over £800,000,000, " and though part of the sum may
have been nominal only, the real investment must have
been enormous."

Mr. Mulhall gives the following estimate of the size and
growth of our foreign and colonial investments since 1862:

Year.	Amount.	Annual Increase.
	£	Per Cent.
1862	144,000,000	...
1872	600,000,000	45.6
1882	875,000,000	27.5
1893	1,698,000,000	74.8

This last amount is of especial interest, because it represents the most thorough investigation made by a most competent economist for the "Dictionary of Political Economy." The investments included under this figure may be classified under the following general heads :—

Loans.	Million £.	Railways.	Million £.	Sundries.	Million £.
Foreign . .	525	U.S.A. . .	120	Banks . .	50
Colonial . .	225	Colonial . .	140	Lands . .	100
Municipal .	20	Various . .	128	Mines, &c. .	390
	770		388		540

In other words, in 1893 the British capital invested abroad represented about 15 per cent. of the total wealth of the United Kingdom : nearly one-half of this capital was in the form of loans to foreign and colonial Governments; of the rest a large proportion was invested in railways, banks, telegraphs, and other public services, owned, controlled, or vitally affected by Governments, while most of the remainder was placed in lands and mines, or in industries directly dependent on land values.

Income-tax returns and other statistics descriptive of the growth of these investments indicate that the total amount of British investments abroad at the end of the nineteenth century cannot be set down at a lower figure than £2,000,000,000. Considering that Sir R. Giffen regarded as "moderate" the estimate of £1,700,000,000 in 1892, the figure here named is probably below the truth.

Now, without placing any undue reliance upon these estimates, we cannot fail to recognise that in dealing with these foreign investments we are facing by far the most important factor in the economics of Imperialism. Whatever figures we take, two facts are evident. First, that the income derived as interest upon foreign investments enormously exceeds that derived as profits upon ordinary export and import trade. Secondly, that while our foreign and colonial trade, and presumably the income from it, are growing but slowly, the share of our import values representing income from foreign investments is growing very rapidly.

In a former chapter I pointed out how small a proportion of our national income appeared to be derived as profits from external trade. It seemed unintelligible that the enormous costs and risks of the new Imperialism should be undertaken for such small results in the shape of increase to external trade, especially when the size and character of the new markets acquired were taken into consideration. The statistics of foreign investments, however, shed clear light upon the economic forces which are dominating our policy. While the manufacturing and trading classes make little out of their new markets, paying, if they knew it, much more in taxation than they get out of them in trade, it is quite otherwise with the investor.

It is not too much to say that the modern foreign policy of Great Britain is primarily a struggle for profitable markets of investment. To a larger extent every year Great Britain is becoming a nation living upon tribute from abroad, and the classes who enjoy this tribute have an ever-increasing incentive to employ the public policy, the public purse, and the public force to extend the field of their private investments, and to safeguard and improve their existing investments. This is, perhaps, the most important fact in modern politics, and the obscurity in which it is wrapped constitutes the gravest danger to our State.

What is true of Great Britain is true likewise of

France, Germany, the United States, and of all countries in which modern capitalism has placed large surplus savings in the hands of a plutocracy or of a thrifty middle class. A well-recognised distinction is drawn between creditor and debtor countries. Great Britain has been for some time by far the largest creditor country, and the policy by which the investing classes use the instrument of the State for private business purposes is most richly illustrated in the recent history of her wars and annexations. But France, Germany, and the United States are advancing fast along the same path. The nature of these imperialist operations is thus set forth by the Italian economist Loria :—

"When a country which has contracted a debt is unable, on account of the slenderness of its income, to offer sufficient guarantee for the punctual payment of interest, what happens? Sometimes an out-and-out conquest of the debtor country follows. Thus France's attempted conquest of Mexico during the second empire was undertaken solely with the view of guaranteeing the interest of French citizens holding Mexican securities. But more frequently the insufficient guarantee of an international loan gives rise to the appointment of a financial commission by the creditor countries in order to protect their rights and guard the fate of their invested capital. The appointment of such a commission literally amounts in the end, however, to a veritable conquest. We have examples of this in Egypt, which has to all practical purposes become a British province, and in Tunis, which has in like manner become a dependency of France, who supplied the greater part of the loan. The Egyptian revolt against the foreign domination issuing from the debt came to nothing, as it met with invariable opposition from capitalistic combinations, and Tel-el-Kebir's success, bought with money, was the most brilliant victory wealth has ever obtained on the field of battle."[1]

But, though useful to explain certain economic facts, the terms "creditor" and "debtor," as applied to countries, obscure the most significant feature of this Imperialism.   For though, as appears from the analysis given above, much, if not most, of the debts are "public," the credit is nearly always private, though sometimes, as in the case of Egypt, its owners succeed in getting their Government to enter a most unprofitable partnership, guaranteeing the payment of the interest, but not sharing in it.

Aggressive Imperialism, which costs the tax-payer so dear, which is of so little value to the manufacturer and trader, which is fraught with such grave incalculable peril to the citizen, is a source of great gain to the investor who cannot find at home the profitable use he seeks for his capital, and insists that his Government should help him to profitable and secure investments abroad.

If, contemplating the enormous expenditure on armaments, the ruinous wars, the diplomatic audacity of knavery by which modern Governments seek to extend their territorial power, we put the plain, practical question, *Cui bono?* the first and most obvious answer is, The investor.

The annual income Great Britain derives from commissions on her whole foreign and colonial trade, import and export, is estimated by Sir R. Giffen[2] at £18,000,000 for 1899, taken at 2½ per cent., upon a turnover of

---

[1] Loria, "The Economic Foundations of Politics," p. 273 (Sonnenschein).
[2] *Journal of the Statistical Society*, vol. xlii. p. 9.

£800,000,000. This is the whole that we are entitled
to regard as profits on external trade. Considerable as
this sum is, it cannot serve to yield an economic motive-
power adequate to explain the dominance which business
considerations exercise over our imperial policy. Only
when we set beside it some £90,000,000 or £100,000,000,
representing pure profit upon investments, do we understand whence the economic impulse to Imperialism is
derived.

Investors who have put their money in foreign lands,
upon terms which take full account of risks connected
with the political conditions of the country, desire to use
the resources of their Government to minimise these risks,
and so to enhance the capital value and the interest of
their private investments. The investing and speculative
classes in general also desire that Great Britain should
take other foreign areas under her flag in order to secure
new areas for profitable investment and speculation.

III

If the special interest of the investor is liable to
clash with the public interest and to induce a wrecking
policy, still more dangerous is the special interest of the
financier, the general dealer in investments. In large
measure the rank and file of the investors are, both for
business and for politics, the cat's-paws of the great financial
houses, who use stocks and shares not so much as investments to yield them interest, but as material for
speculation in the money market. In handling large
masses of stocks and shares, in floating companies, in
manipulating fluctuations of values, the magnates of the
Bourse find their gain. These great businesses—banking,

broking, bill discounting, loan floating, company promoting—form the central ganglion of international capitalism. United by the strongest bonds of organisation, always in closest and quickest touch with one another, situated in the very heart of the business capital of every State, controlled, so far as Europe is concerned, chiefly by men of a single and peculiar race, who have behind them many centuries of financial experience, they are in a unique position to control the policy of nations. No great quick direction of capital is possible save by their consent and through their agency. Does any one seriously suppose that a great war could be undertaken by any European State, or a great State loan subscribed, if the house of Rothschild and its connections set their face against it?

Every great political act involving a new flow of capital, or a large fluctuation in the values of existing investments, must receive the sanction and the practical aid of this little group of financial kings. These men, holding their realised wealth and their business capital, as they must, chiefly in stocks and bonds, have a double stake, first as investors, but secondly and chiefly as financial dealers. As investors, their political influence does not differ essentially from that of the smaller investors, except that they usually possess a practical control of the businesses in which they invest. As speculators or financial dealers they constitute, however, the gravest single factor in the economics of Imperialism.

To create new public debts, to float new companies, and to cause constant considerable fluctuations of values are three conditions of their profitable business. Each condition carries them into politics, and throws them on the side of Imperialism.

The public financial arrangements for the Philippine

war put several millions of dollars into the pockets of Mr. Pierpont Morgan and his friends; the China-Japan war, which saddled the Celestial Empire for the first time with a public debt, and the indemnity which she will pay to her European invaders in connection with the recent conflict, bring grist to the financial mills in Europe; every railway or mining concession wrung from some reluctant foreign potentate means profitable business in raising capital and floating companies. A policy which rouses fears of aggression in Asiatic states, and which fans the rivalry of commercial nations in Europe, evokes vast expenditure on armaments, and ever-accumulating public debts, while the doubts and risks accruing from this policy promote that constant oscillation of values of securities which is so profitable to the skilled financier. There is not a war, a revolution, an anarchist assassination, or any other public shock, which is not gainful to these men; they are harpies who suck their gains from every new forced expenditure and every sudden disturbance of public credit. To the financiers "in the know" the Jameson raid was a most advantageous coup, as may be ascertained by a comparison of the "holdings" of these men before and after that event; the terrible sufferings of England and South Africa in the war, which is a sequel of the raid, is a source of immense profit to the big financiers who have best held out against the uncalculated waste, and have recouped themselves by profitable war contracts and by "freezing out" the smaller interests in the Transvaal. These men are the only certain gainers from the war, and most of their gains are made out of the public losses of their adopted country or the private losses of their fellow-countrymen.

The policy of these men, it is true, does not necessarily make for war; where war would bring about too

E

great and too permanent a damage to the substantial fabric of industry, which is the ultimate and essential basis of speculation, their influence is cast for peace, as in the dangerous quarrel between Great Britain and the United States regarding Venezuela. But every increase of public expenditure, every oscillation of public credit short of this collapse, every risky enterprise in which public resources can be made the pledge of private speculations, is profitable to the big money-lender and speculator.

The wealth of these houses, the scale of their operations, and their cosmopolitan organisation make them the prime determinants of imperial policy. They have the largest definite stake in the business of Imperialism, and the amplest means of forcing their will upon the policy of nations.

In view of the part which the non-economic factors of patriotism, adventure, military enterprise, political ambition, and philanthropy play in imperial expansion, it may appear that to impute to financiers so much power is to take a too narrowly economic view of history. And it is true that the motor-power of Imperialism is not chiefly financial: finance is rather the governor of the imperial engine, directing the energy and determining its work: it does not constitute the fuel of the engine, nor does it directly generate the power. Finance manipulates the patriotic forces which politicians, soldiers, philanthropists, and traders generate; the enthusiasm for expansion which issues from these sources, though strong and genuine, is irregular and blind; the financial interest has those qualities of concentration and clear-sighted calculation which are needed to set Imperialism to work. An ambitious statesman, a frontier soldier, an over-zealous missionary, a pushing trader, may suggest or even initiate a step of imperial expansion, may assist in educating patriotic public opinion to the urgent need of some fresh advance, but the final determination rests with the financial power.   The direct influence exercised by great financial houses in " high politics " is supported by the control which they exercise over the body of public opinion through the Press, which, in every "civilised" country, is becoming more and more their obedient instrument.   While the specifically financial newspaper imposes " facts " and " opinions " on the business classes, the general body of the Press comes more and more under the conscious or unconscious domination of financiers.   The case of the South African Press, whose agents and correspondents fanned the martial flames in this country, was one of open ownership on the part of South African financiers, and this policy of owning newspapers for the sake of manufacturing public opinion is common in the great European cities.   In Berlin, Vienna, and Paris many of the influential newspapers are held by financial houses, which use them, not primarily to make direct profits out of them, but in order to put into the public mind beliefs and sentiments which will influence public policy and thus affect the money market. In Great Britain this policy has not gone so far, but the alliance with finance grows closer every year, either by financiers purchasing a controlling share of newspapers, or by newspaper proprietors being tempted into finance. Apart from the financial Press, and financial ownership of the general Press, the City notoriously exercises a subtle and abiding influence upon leading London newspapers, and through them upon the body of the provincial Press, while the entire dependence of the Press for its business profits upon its advertising columns involves a peculiar reluctance to oppose the organised financial classes with whom rests the control of so much advertising business.   Add to this the natural sympathy with a sensational policy which a cheap Press always manifests, and it becomes evident that the Press is strongly biassed towards Imperialism, and lends itself with great facility to the suggestion of financial or political Imperialists who desire to work up patriotism for some new piece of expansion.

Such is the array of distinctively economic forces making for Imperialism, a large loose group of trades and professions seeking profitable business and lucrative employment from the expansion of military and civil services, from the expenditure on military operations, the opening up of new tracts of territory and trade with the same, and the provision of new capital which these operations require, all these finding their central guiding and directing force in the power of the general financier.

The play of these forces does not openly appear. They are essentially parasites upon patriotism, and they adapt themselves to its protecting colours. In the mouths of their representatives are noble phrases, expressive of their desire to extend the area of civilisation, to establish good government, promote Christianity, extirpate slavery, and elevate the lower races. Some of the business men who hold such language may entertain a genuine, though usually a vague, desire to accomplish these ends, but they are primarily engaged in business, and they are not unaware of the utility of the more unselfish forces in furthering their ends.   Their true attitude of mind is expressed by Mr. Rhodes in his famous description of " Her Majesty's Flag " as " the greatest commercial asset in the world."[1]

[1] It will be observed that this, like not a few other words of revelation, has been doctored in the volume, " Cecil Rhodes: his Political Life and Speeches," by " Vindex ".(p. 823).

CHAPTER V

IMPERIALISM BASED ON PROTECTION

A BUSINESS man estimating the value of an extension of his business will set the increased costs against the increased takings. Is it unreasonable that a business nation should adopt the same course ? From this standpoint our increased military and naval expenditure during recent years may be regarded primarily as insurance premiums for protection of existing colonial markets and current outlay on new markets.

In order to test the finance of the new Imperialism, let us compare the growth of expenditure on armaments and wars since 1884 with the increased value of colonial trade :—

Year.	Armaments and War.	Colonial Trade. Import and Export Trade with Possessions.
	£	£
1884	27,864,000	184,000,000
1885	30,577,000	170,000,000
1886	39,538,000	164,000,000
1887	31,768,000	166,000,000
1888	30,609,000	179,000,000
1889	30,536,000	188,000,000
1890	32,772,000	191,000,000
1891	33,488,000	193,000,000
1892	33,312,000	179,000,000
1893	33,423,000	170,000,000
1894	33,566,000	172,000,000
1895	35,593,000	172,000,000
1896	38,334,000	184,000,000
1897	41,453,000	183,000,000
1898	40,395,000	190,000,000

Now, though there are no means of ear-marking the expenditure which might rank as insurance upon old markets or that which is spent upon acquiring new markets, it is not unreasonable to saddle the new Imperialism with the whole of the increase and to set against it the value of the trade of the new acquisitions. For though it might be claimed that the aggressive commercialism of rival European States has raised the insurance rate upon the old markets, it cannot be contended that Great Britain's expenditure on armaments need have increased had she adopted firmly and consistently the full practice of Cobdenism, a purely defensive attitude regarding her existing Empire and a total abstinence from acquisition of new territory. The increased hostility of foreign nations towards us may be regarded as entirely due to the aggressive Imperialism of the last thirty years, and the increased expenditure on armaments may, therefore, reasonably rank in a business balance-sheet as a cost of that policy.

So taken, this new expenditure is nothing else than a huge business blunder. An individual doing business in this fashion could not avoid bankruptcy, and a nation, however rich, pursuing such a policy is loaded with a millstone which must eventually drag her down.

In total contravention of our theory that trade rests upon a basis of mutual gain to the nations that engage in it, we have undertaken enormous expenses with the object of " forcing " new markets, and the markets we have forced are small, precarious, and unprofitable. The only certain and palpable result of the expenditure has been to keep us continually embroiled with the very nations that are our best customers, and with whom, in spite of everything, our trade makes the most satisfactory advance.

Not only are these markets not worth what they cost us, but the assumption that our trade would have been proportionately less had they fallen into the hands of rival and Protectionist nations is quite groundless.   If, instead of squandering money upon these recent territorial acquisitions, we had let any or all of them pass into the possession of France, Germany, or Russia, in order that these . countries might spend their money, instead of us spending our money, in acquiring and developing them, is it certain that our foreign trade would not have grown by at least as much as our colonial trade might have shrunk ?   The assumption that there is only a given quantity of trade, and that if one nation gets any portion of it another nation loses just so much, shows a blind ignorance of the elements of international trade.   It arises from a curiously perverse form of separatism which insists upon a nation keeping a separate account with every other nation, and ignoring altogether the roundabout trade which is by far the most important business of an advanced industrial nation.

France seizing Madagascar practically extirpates direct British trade with the Malagasy ; Germany, by her occupation of Shan-tung, deprives us of all possibility of trade with this Chinese province.   But it by no means follows that France and Germany can or will keep to themselves the whole advantage of these new markets. To make any such supposition implies a complete abandonment of the principles of Free Trade.   Even were the whole of China portioned out among the other industrial nations, each imposing tariffs which virtually prohibited direct trade between Great Britain and China —the most extreme assumption of a hostile attitude—it by no means follows that England would not reap enormous benefits from the expansion of her foreign trade, attributable in the last resort to the opening up of China. Even the feeblest recognition of the intricacies of foreign trade should make us aware that an increased trade with France, Germany, or Russia, either directly or through other nations trading with them, might give us our full share of the wealth of Chinese trade, and prove as beneficial as any direct share of trade with China which at great expense and peril we might secure. The assignment of spheres of influence in China or in Africa to France, Germany, or Russia, which they may seek to monopolise for purposes of trade, does not imply, as seems to be believed, a corresponding loss of markets to England. The intricate and ever-growing industrial co-operation of the civilised nations through trade does not permit any nation to keep to herself the gain of any market she may hold. It is not difficult to conceive cases where another nation might enjoy a larger share of the results of a trade than the nation which owned the private markets of this trade.

These are or were the commonplaces of the economics of Free Trade, the plainest lessons of enlightened common sense. Why are they forgotten?

The answer is that Imperialism repudiates Free Trade, and rests upon an economic basis of Protection. Just in so far as an Imperialist is logical does he become an open and avowed Protectionist.

If the fact of France or Germany seizing for its exclusive use a market which we might have seized necessarily reduces our aggregate external trade by the amount of this market, it is only reasonable that when we seize a territory we should take the same means to keep its market for ourselves. Imperialism, when it has shaken off the " old gang " of politicians who had swallowed Free Trade doctrine when they were young, will openly adopt the Protectionism required to round off this policy.

Imperialism naturally strives to fasten to the mother country the markets of each new territorial acquisition, convinced that only by such separate increments can the aggregate of our trade grow ; and by the success of this policy it must justify the enormous national outlay which Imperialism involves. Free Trade trusts for the increase of our foreign trade to the operation of the self-interest of other trading nations. Her doctrine is that, though it were better for us and for them that they should give us free admission to their colonial and home markets, their protective tariff, even though it prohibits us from trading directly with their colonies, does not shut us out from all the benefits of their colonial development. Through the ordinary operation of competition in European markets the rubber trade which France does in East Africa helps to increase the supply and to keep down the price of " rubber " for English consumers, just as the bounties which continental countries pay to sugar producers enable British boys and girls to enjoy cheap sweets.

There is, then, nothing vaguely hypothetical about these indirect gains. Every business man can trace certain concrete advantages of goods and prices which come to us from the development of colonies by Protectionist countries. The " open door " is an advantage to our trade, but not a necessity. If we have to spend vast sums and incur vast risks in keeping " doors open " against the wishes of our best customers, it is more profitable to let them close these doors and take our gain by the more indirect but equally certain processes of roundabout trade. At present Great Britain is in a stronger position than any other nation to practise this policy of abstinence, because she possesses in her carrying trade by sea a most effective guarantee that she will obtain an adequate share of the net gains from new markets opened up by foreign nations. Though no complete statistics are available, it is known that a very large proportion of the trade, not only between England and foreign countries, but between foreign countries trading among themselves and with their possessions, is carried by British ships. So long as this continues, England, apart from her share obtained in roundabout trade, must participate directly and in a most important manner in the trade advantages of foreign markets belonging to our European trade competitors.

These considerations ought to make us willing that other nations should do their share of expansion and development, well contented to await the profit which must accrue to us from every increase of world-wealth through ordinary processes of exchange. We have done our share, and more, of the costly, laborious, and dangerous work of opening up new countries to the general trade of Western industrial nations; our recent ventures have been more expensive and less profitable to us than the earlier ones, and any further labours of expansion seem to conform to a law of diminishing returns, yielding smaller and more precarious increments of trade to a larger outlay of material and intellectual capital. Have we not reached, or even passed, the limit of the most profitable outlay of our national energy and resources? Will not enlightened self-interest impel us to leave to other active and ambitious nations—France, Russia, Germany, America—the work of developing new tropical or sub-tropical countries? If it is necessary that Western industrial civilisation shall undertake the political and commercial management of the whole world, let these nations take their share. Why should we do all the work and get so little from it? On the assumption that backward countries must be developed by foreign countries for the general good, a reasonable economy of power will apportion the work which remains to the "Imperialism" of other nations. Even if these other nations were disposed to shirk their share, it would pay us better to persuade them to undertake it rather than further to load our overladen shoulders. Since these other nations are not only eager to do their share, but by their jealousy at our undertaking their work continually threaten to wreck the peace of Europe, it seems sheer madness for Great Britain to weaken herself politically and financially by any further process of expansion.

APPENDIX.

NATIONAL EXPENDITURE AND ARMAMENTS.

For the Year ending 31st March.	Expenditure on Armaments, Exclusive of War Charges.			Extra-ordinary War Expenditure.[1]	Total Expenditure on War and Armaments.	Total National Expenditure.
	Army.	Navy.	Total.			
	£	£	£	£	£	£
1895 . . .	17,900,000	17,545,000	35,445,000	...	35,445,000	93,918,421
1896 . . .	18,460,000	19,724,000	38,184,000	...	38,184,000	97,764,357
1897 . . .	18,270,000	22,170,000	40,440,000	...	40,440,000	101,476,669
1898 . . .	19,330,000	20,850,000	40,180,000	...	40,180,000	102,935,994
1899 . . .	20,000,000	24,068,000	44,068,000	...	44,068,000	108,150,236
1900 . . .	20,600,000	26,000,000	46,600,000	23,000,000	69,600,000	133,722,407
1901 . . .	24,473,000	29,520,000	53,993,000	67,237,000	121,230,000	183,592,264
1902 . . .	29,312,000	31,030,000	60,342,000	69,830,000	130,172,000	195,522,000
1903 . . . "Estimates."	29,665,000	31,255,000	60,920,000	59,050,000	119,970,000	188,469,000

[1] As given in the various "Statements of Revenue and Expenditure as laid before the House by the Chancellor of the Exchequer when opening the Budget," but omitting the "Interest on the War Debt." In his Budget Speech on 14th April 1902, Sir Michael Hicks-Beach estimated the total cost of the wars in South Africa and China during the three years ending 31st March 1902 as £165,034,000. Of this sum £45,420,000 had been defrayed out of revenue and by the suspension of the Sinking Fund (£4,640,000 a year), while £119,614,000 had been added to the Debt.

CHAPTER VI

THE ECONOMIC TAPROOT OF IMPERIALISM

No mere array of facts and figures adduced to illustrate the economic nature of the new Imperialism will suffice to dispel the popular delusion that the use of national force to secure new markets by annexing fresh tracts of territory is a sound and a necessary policy for an advanced industrial country like Great Britain. It has indeed been proved that recent annexations of tropical countries, procured at great expense, have furnished poor and precarious markets, that our aggregate trade with our colonial possessions is virtually stationary, and that our most profitable and progressive trade is with rival industrial nations, whose territories we have no desire to annex, whose markets we cannot force, and whose active antagonism we are provoking by our expansive policy.

But these arguments are not conclusive. It is open to Imperialists to argue thus: "We must have markets for our growing manufactures, we must have new outlets for the investment of our surplus capital and for the energies of the adventurous surplus of our population : such expansion is a necessity of life to a nation with our great and growing powers of production. An ever larger share of our population is devoted to the manufactures and commerce of towns, and is thus dependent for life and work upon food and raw materials from foreign lands. In order to buy and pay for these things we must sell our goods abroad. During the first three-quarters of the cen-

tury we could do so without difficulty by a natural expansion of commerce with continental nations and our
colonies, all of which were far behind us in the main arts
of manufacture and the carrying trades. So long as
England held a virtual monopoly of the world markets
for certain important classes of manufactured goods, Imperialism was unnecessary. During the last thirty years
this manufacturing and trading supremacy has been
greatly impaired: other nations, especially Germany, the
United States, and Belgium, have advanced with great
rapidity, and while they have not crushed or even stayed
the increase of our external trade, their competition is
making it more and more difficult to dispose of the full
surplus of our manufactures at a profit. The encroachments made by these nations upon our old markets, even
in our own possessions, make it most urgent that we
should take energetic means to secure new markets.
These new markets must lie in hitherto undeveloped
countries, chiefly in the tropics, where vast populations
live capable of growing economic needs which our manufacturers and merchants can supply. Our rivals are
seizing and annexing territories for similar purposes, and
when they have annexed them close them to our trade.
The diplomacy and the arms of Great Britain must be
used in order to compel the owners of the new markets
to deal with us : and experience shows that the safest
means of securing and developing such markets is by
establishing ' protectorates ' or by annexation. The present value of these markets must not be taken as a final
test of the economy of such a policy ; the process of educating civilised needs which we can supply is of necessity
a gradual one, and the cost of such Imperialism must be
regarded as a capital outlay, the fruits of which posterity
will reap. The new markets may not be large, but they

form serviceable outlets for the overflow of our great textile and metal industries, and, when the vast Asiatic and African populations of the interior are reached, a rapid expansion of trade may be expected to result.

"Far larger and more important is the pressure of capital for external fields of investment. Moreover, while the manufacturer and trader are well content to trade with foreign nations, the tendency for investors to work towards the political annexation of countries which contain their more speculative investments is very powerful. Of the fact of this pressure of capital there can be no question. Large savings are made which cannot find any profitable investment in this country; they must find employment elsewhere, and it is to the advantage of the nation that they should be employed as largely as possible in lands where they can be utilised in opening up markets for British trade and employment for British enterprise.

"However costly, however perilous, this process of imperial expansion may be, it is necessary to the continued existence and progress of our nation;[1] if we abandoned it we must be content to leave the development of the world to other nations, who will everywhere cut into our trade, and even impair our means of securing the food and raw materials we require to support our population. Imperialism is thus seen to be, not a choice, but a necessity."

The practical force of this economic argument in politics is strikingly illustrated by the recent history of the United States. Here is a country which suddenly breaks through a conservative policy, strongly held by

---

[1] "And why, indeed, are wars undertaken, if not to conquer colonies which permit the employment of fresh capital, to acquire commercial monopolies, or to obtain the exclusive use of certain highways of commerce?" (Loria, "Economic Foundations of Society," p. 267).

both political parties, bound up with every popular instinct and tradition, and flings itself into a rapid imperial career for which it possesses neither the material nor the moral equipment, risking the principles and practices of liberty and equality by the establishment of militarism and the forcible subjugation of peoples which it cannot safely admit to the condition of American citizenship.

Is this a mere wild freak of spread-eaglism, a burst of political ambition on the part of a nation coming to a sudden realisation of its destiny ? Not at all. The spirit of adventure, the American " mission of civilisation," are, as forces making for Imperialism, clearly subordinate to the driving force of the economic factor. The dramatic character of the change is due to the unprecedented rapidity of the industrial revolution in the United States during the last two decades. During that period the United States, with her unrivalled natural resources, her immense resources of skilled and unskilled labour, and her genius for invention and organisation, has developed the best equipped and most productive manufacturing economy the world has yet seen. Fostered by rigid protective tariffs, her metal, textile, tool, clothing, furniture, and other manufactures have shot up in a single generation from infancy to full maturity, and, having passed through a period of intense competition, are attaining, under the able control of great trust-makers, a power of production greater than has been attained in the most advanced industrial countries of Europe.

An era of cut-throat competition, followed by a rapid process of amalgamation, has thrown an enormous quantity of wealth into the hands of a small number of captains of industry. No luxury of living to which this class could attain kept pace with its rise of income,

and a process of automatic saving set in upon an unprecedented scale. The investment of these savings in
other industries helped to bring these under the same
concentrative forces. Thus a great increase of savings
seeking profitable investment is synchronous with a
stricter economy of the use of existing capital. No
doubt the rapid growth of a population, accustomed to a
high and an always ascending standard of comfort, absorbs in the satisfaction of its wants a large quantity of
new capital. But the actual rate of saving, conjoined
with a more economical application of forms of existing
capital, has exceeded considerably the rise of the national
consumption of manufactures. The power of production
has far outstripped the actual rate of consumption, and,
contrary to the older economic theory, has been unable to
force a corresponding increase of consumption by lowering prices.

This is no mere theory. The history of any of the
numerous trusts or combinations in the United States
sets out the facts with complete distinctness. In the
free competition of manufactures preceding combination
the chronic condition is one of " over-production," in the
sense that all the mills or factories can only be kept at
work by cutting prices down towards a point where the
weaker competitors are forced to close down, because
they cannot sell their goods at a price which covers the
true cost of production. The first result of the successful
formation of a trust or combine is to close down the
worse equipped or worse placed mills, and supply the
entire market from the better equipped and better placed
ones. This course may or may not be attended by a rise
of price and some restriction of consumption : in some
cases trusts take most of their profits by raising prices,
in other cases by reducing the costs of production

through employing only the best mills and stopping the waste of competition.

For the present argument it matters not which course is taken; the point is that this concentration of industry in "trusts," "combines," &c., at once limits the quantity of capital which can be effectively employed and increases the share of profits out of which fresh savings and fresh capital will spring. It is quite evident that a trust which is motived by cut-throat competition, due to an excess of capital, cannot normally find inside the "trusted" industry employment for that portion of the profits which the trust-makers desire to save and to invest. New inventions and other economies of production or distribution within the trade may absorb some of the new capital, but there are rigid limits to this absorption. The trust-maker in oil or sugar must find other investments for his savings: if he is early in the application of the combination principles to his trade, he will naturally apply his surplus capital to establish similar combinations in other industries, economising capital still further, and rendering it ever harder for ordinary saving men to find investments for their savings.

Indeed, the conditions alike of cut-throat competition and of combination attest the congestion of capital in the manufacturing industries which have entered the machine economy. We are not here concerned with any theoretic question as to the possibility of producing by modern machine methods more goods than can find a market. It is sufficient to point out that the manufacturing power of a country like the United States may grow so fast as to exceed the demands of the home market. No one acquainted with trade will deny a fact which all American economists assert, that this is the condition which the United States has reached within the last few years,

F

so far as the more developed industries are concerned. Her manufactures are saturated with capital and can absorb no more. One after another they are seeking refuge from the waste of competition in "combines" which secure a measure of profitable peace by restricting the quantity of operative capital. Industrial and financial princes in oil, steel, sugar, railroads, banking, &c., are faced with the dilemma of either spending more than they know how to spend, or forcing markets outside the home area. Two economic courses are open to them, both leading towards an abandonment of the political isolation of the past and the adoption of imperialist methods in the future. Instead of shutting down inferior mills and rigidly restricting output to correspond with profitable sales in the home markets, they may employ their full productive power, applying their savings to increase their business capital, and, while still regulating output and prices for the home market, may "hustle" for foreign markets, dumping down their surplus goods at prices which would not be possible save for the .profitable nature of their home market. So likewise they may employ their savings in seeking investments outside their country, first repaying the capital borrowed from Great Britain and other countries for the early development of their railroads, mines and manufactures, and afterwards becoming themselves a creditor class to foreign countries.

It is this sudden demand for foreign markets for manufactures and for investments which is avowedly responsible for the adoption of Imperialism as a political policy and practice by the Republican party to which the great industrial and financial chiefs belong, and which belongs to them. The adventurous enthusiasm of President Roosevelt and his "manifest destiny" and

" mission of civilisation " party must not deceive us.
It is Messrs. Rockefeller, Pierpont Morgan, Hanna,
Schwab, and their associates who need Imperialism
and who are fastening it upon the shoulders of the
great Republic of the West.   They need Imperialism because they desire to use the public resources of
their country to find profitable employment for the
capital which otherwise would be superfluous.

It is not indeed necessary to own a country in order
to do trade with it or to invest capital in it, and doubtless the United States can find some vent for their surplus goods and capital in European countries.   But
these countries are for the most part able to make
provision for themselves; most of them have erected
tariffs against manufacturing imports, and even Great
Britain is being urged to defend herself by reverting to
Protection.   The big American manufacturers and financiers will be compelled to look to China and the Pacific
and to South America for their most profitable chances;
Protectionists by principle and practice, they will insist
upon getting as close a monopoly of these markets as
they can secure, and the competition of Germany, England, and other trading nations will drive them to the
establishment of special political relations with the
markets they most prize.   Cuba, the Philippines, and
Hawaii are but the *hors d'œuvre* to whet an appetite for
an ampler banquet.   Moreover, the powerful hold upon
politics which these industrial and financial magnates
possess forms a separate stimulus, which, as we have
shown, is operative in Great Britain and elsewhere; the
public expenditure in pursuit of an imperial career will
be a separate immense source of profit to these men,
as financiers negotiating loans, shipbuilders and owners

handling subsidies, contractors and manufacturers of armaments and other imperialist appliances.

The suddenness of this political revolution is due to the rapid manifestation of the need. During a period of ten years the United States has nearly trebled the value of its manufacturing export trade, and, if the rate of progress of the last few years continues, within this decade it will overtake our more slowly advancing export trade, and stand first in the list of manufacture-exporting nations.[1]

This is the avowed ambition, and no idle one, of the keenest business men of America; and with the natural resources, the labour and the administrative talents at their disposal, it is quite likely they will achieve their object.[2] The stronger and more direct control over politics exercised in America by business men enables

[1] EXPORT TRADE OF UNITED STATES, 1890–1900.

Year.	Agriculture.	Manufactures.	Miscellaneous.
	£	£	£
1890	125,756,000	31,435,000	13,019,000
1891	146,617,000	33,720,000	11,731,000
1892	142,508,000	30,479,000	11,660,000
1893	123,810,000	35,484,000	11,653,000
1894	114,737,000	35,557,000	11,168,000
1895	104,143,000	40,230,000	12,174,000
1896	132,992,000	50,738,000	13,639,000
1897	146,059,000	55,923,000	13,984,000
1898	170,383,000	61,585,000	14,743,000
1899	156,427,000	76,157,000	18,002,000
1900	180,931,000	88,281,000	21,389,000

The statistics for 1901, however, show a distinct check in manufacturing exports, marking a drop of some £9,200,000 as compared with the figures for 1900.

[2] "We hold now three of the winning cards in the game for commercial greatness, to wit—iron, steel and coal. We have long been the granary of the world, we now aspire to be its workshop, then we want to be its clearing-house" (The President of the American Bankers' Association at Denver, 1898).

them to drive more quickly and more straightly along the line of their economic interests than in Great Britain. American Imperialism is the natural product of the economic pressure of a sudden advance of capitalism which cannot find occupation at home and needs foreign markets for goods and for investments.

The same needs exist in European countries, and, as is admitted, drive Governments along the same path. Over-production in the sense of an excessive manufacturing plant, and surplus capital which cannot find sound investments within the country, force Great Britain, Germany, Holland, France to place larger and larger portions of their economic resources outside the area of their present political domain, and then stimulate a policy of political expansion so as to take in the new areas. The economic sources of this movement are laid bare by periodic trade-depressions due to an inability of producers to find adequate and profitable markets for what they can produce. The Majority Report of the Commission upon the Depression of Trade in 1885 put the matter in a nut-shell. "That, owing to the nature of the times, the demand for our commodities does not increase at the same rate as formerly; that our capacity for production is consequently in excess of our requirements, and could be considerably increased at short notice; that this is due partly to the competition of the capital which is being steadily accumulated in the country." The Minority Report straightly imputes the condition of affairs to "over-production." Germany is at the present time suffering severely from what is called a glut of capital and of manufacturing power: she must have new markets; her Consuls all over the world are "hustling" for trade; trading settlements are forced upon Asia Minor; in East and West Africa, in China and else-

where the German Empire is impelled to a policy of
colonisation and protectorates as outlets for German
commercial energy.

Every improvement of methods of production, every
concentration of ownership and control, seems to ac-
centuate the tendency. As one nation after another
enters the machine economy and adopts advanced industrial methods, it becomes more difficult for its
manufacturers, merchants, and financiers to dispose
profitably of their economic resources, and they are
tempted more and more to use their Governments in
order to secure for their particular use some distant
undeveloped country by annexation and protection.

The process we may be told is inevitable, and so
it seems upon a superficial inspection. Everywhere
appear excessive powers of production, excessive capital
in search of investment. It is admitted by all business
men that the growth of the powers of production in
their country exceeds the growth in consumption, that
more goods can be produced than can be sold at a
profit, and that more capital exists than can find remunerative investment.

It is this economic condition of affairs that forms
the taproot of Imperialism. If the consuming public
in this country raised its standard of consumption to
keep pace with every rise of productive powers, there
could be no excess of goods or capital clamorous to
use Imperialism in order to find markets: foreign
trade would indeed exist, but there would be no difficulty in exchanging a small surplus of our manufactures
for the food and raw material we annually absorbed,
and all the savings that we made could find employment,
if we chose, in home industries.

There is nothing inherently irrational in such a

supposition. Whatever is, or can be, produced, can be consumed, for a claim upon it, as rent, profit, or wages, forms part of the real income of some member of the community, and he can consume it, or else exchange it for some other consumable with some one else who will consume it. With everything that is produced a consuming power is born. If then there are goods which cannot get consumed, or which cannot even get produced because it is evident they cannot get consumed, and if there is a quantity of capital and labour which cannot get full employment because its products cannot get consumed, the only possible explanation of this paradox is the refusal of owners of consuming power to apply that power in effective demand for commodities.

It is, of course, possible that an excess of producing power might exist in particular industries by misdirection, being engaged in certain manufactures, whereas it ought to have been engaged in agriculture or some other use. But no one can seriously contend that such misdirection explains the recurrent gluts and consequent depressions of modern industry, or that, when over-production is manifest in the leading manufactures, ample avenues are open for the surplus capital and labour in other industries. The general character of the excess of producing power is proved by the existence at such times of large bank stocks of idle money seeking any sort of profitable investment and finding none.

The root questions underlying the phenomena are clearly these: "Why is it that consumption fails to keep pace automatically in a community with power of production?" "Why does under-consumption or over-saving occur?" For it is evident that the consuming power, which, if exercised, would keep tense the reins of production, is in part withheld, or in other words is "saved" and stored up for investment. All saving for investment does not imply slackness of production; quite the contrary. Saving is economically justified, from the social standpoint, when the capital in which it takes material shape finds full employment in helping to produce commodities which, when produced, will be consumed. It is saving in excess of this amount that causes mischief, taking shape in surplus capital which is not needed to assist current consumption, and which either lies idle, or tries to oust existing capital from its employment, or else seeks speculative use abroad under the protection of the Government.

But it may be asked, "Why should there be any tendency to over-saving? why should the owners of consuming power withhold a larger quantity for savings than can be serviceably employed?" Another way of putting the same question is this, "Why should not the pressure of present wants keep pace with every possibility of satisfying them?" The answer to these pertinent questions carries us to the broadest issue of the distribution of wealth. If a tendency to distribute income or consuming power according to needs were operative, it is evident that consumption would rise with every rise of producing power, for human needs are illimitable, and there could be no excess of saving. But it is quite otherwise in a state of economic society where distribution has no fixed relation to needs, but is determined by other conditions which assign to some people a consuming power vastly in excess of needs or possible uses, while others are destitute of consuming power enough to satisfy even the full demands of physical efficiency. The following illustration may serve to make the issue clear. "The volume of production has been constantly rising owing to the development of modern machinery. There are two main channels to carry off these products—one channel carrying off the product destined to be consumed by the workers, and the other channel carrying off the remainder to the rich. The workers' channel is in rockbound banks that cannot enlarge, owing to the competitive wage system preventing wages rising *pro rata* with increased efficiency. Wages are based upon cost of living, and not upon efficiency of labour. The miner in the poor mine gets the same wages per day as the miner in the adjoining rich mine. The owner of the rich mine gets the advantage—not his labourer. The channel which conveys the goods destined to supply the rich is itself divided into two streams. One stream carries off what the rich 'spend' on themselves for the necessities and luxuries of life. The other is simply an 'overflow' stream carrying off their 'savings.' The channel for spending, *i.e.* the amount wasted by the rich in luxuries, may broaden somewhat, but owing to the small number of those rich enough to indulge in whims it can never be greatly enlarged, and at any rate it bears such a small proportion to the other channel that in no event can much hope of avoiding a flood of capital be hoped for from this division. The rich will never be so ingenious as to spend enough to prevent overproduction. The great safety overflow channel which has been continuously more and more widened and deepened to carry off the ever-increasing flood of new capital is that division of the stream which carried the savings of the rich, and this is not only suddenly found to be incapable of further enlargement, but actually seems to be in the process of being dammed up." [1]

[1] "The Significance of the Trust," by H. G. Wilshire.

Though this presentation over-accentuates the cleavage between rich and poor and over-states the weakness of the workers, it gives forcible and sound expression to a most important and ill-recognised economic truth. The "overflow" stream of savings is of course fed not exclusively from the surplus income of "the rich"; the professional and industrial middle classes, and to some slight extent the workers, contribute. But the "flooding" is distinctly due to the automatic saving of the surplus income of rich men. This is of course particularly true of America, where multi-millionaires rise quickly and find themselves in possession of incomes far exceeding the demands of any craving that is known to them. To make the metaphor complete, the overflow stream must be represented as re-entering the stream of production and seeking to empty there all the "savings" that it carries. Where competition remains free, the result is a chronic congestion of productive power and of production, forcing down home prices, wasting large sums in advertising and in pushing for orders, and periodically causing a crisis followed by a collapse, during which quantities of capital and labour lie unemployed and unremunerated. The prime object of the trust or other combine is to remedy this waste and loss by substituting regulation of output for reckless overproduction. In achieving this it actually narrows or even dams up the old channels of investment, limiting the overflow stream to the exact amount required to maintain the normal current of output. But this rigid limitation of trade, though required for the separate economy of each trust, does not suit the trust-maker, who is driven to compensate for strictly regulated industry at home by cutting new foreign channels as outlets for his productive power and his excessive savings.

Thus we reach the conclusion that Imperialism is the endeavour of the great controllers of industry to broaden the channel for the flow of their surplus wealth by seeking foreign markets and foreign investments to take off the goods and capital they cannot sell or use at home.

The fallacy of the supposed inevitability of imperial expansion as a necessary outlet for progressive industry is now manifest. It is not industrial progress that demands the opening up of new markets and areas of investment, but mal-distribution of consuming power which prevents the absorption of commodities and capital within the country. The over-saving which is the economic root of Imperialism is found by analysis to consist of rents, monopoly profits, and other unearned or excessive elements of income, which, not being earned by labour of head or hand, have no legitimate *raison d'être*. Having no natural relation to effort of production, they impel their recipients to no corresponding satisfaction of consumption: they form a surplus wealth, which, having no proper place in the normal economy of production and consumption, tends to accumulate as excessive savings. Let any turn in the tide of politico-economic forces divert from these owners their excess of income and make it flow, either to the workers in higher wages, or to the community in taxes, so that it will be spent instead of being saved, serving in either of these ways to swell the tide of consumption—there will be no need to fight for foreign markets or foreign areas of investment.

Many have carried their analysis so far as to realise the absurdity of spending half our financial resources in fighting to secure foreign markets at times when hungry mouths, ill-clad backs, ill-furnished houses indicate countless unsatisfied material wants among our own population. If we may take the careful statistics of Mr. Rowntree[1] for our guide, we shall be aware that more than one-fourth of the population of our towns is living at a standard which is below bare physical efficiency. If, by some economic readjustment, the products which flow from the surplus saving of the rich to swell the overflow streams could be diverted so as to raise the incomes and the standard of consumption of this inefficient fourth, there would be no need for pushful Imperialism, and the cause of social reform would have won its greatest victory.

It is not inherent in the nature of things that we should spend our natural resources on militarism, war, and risky, unscrupulous diplomacy, in order to find markets for our goods and surplus capital. An intelligent progressive community, based upon substantial equality of economic and educational opportunities, will raise its standard of consumption to correspond with every increased power of production, and can find full employment for an unlimited quantity of capital and labour within the limits of the country which it occupies. Where the distribution of incomes is such as to enable all classes of the nation to convert their felt wants into an effective demand for commodities, there can be no over-production, no under-employment of capital and labour, and no necessity to fight for foreign markets.

The most convincing condemnation of the current economy is conveyed in the difficulty which producers everywhere experience in finding consumers for their products : a fact attested by the prodigious growth of classes of agents and middlemen, the multiplication of every sort of advertising, and the general increase of the distributive classes. Under a sound economy the

[1] "Poverty: A Study of Town Life."

pressure would be reversed : the growing wants of progressive societies would be a constant stimulus to the inventive and operative energies of producers, and would form a constant strain upon the powers of production. The simultaneous excess of all the factors of production, attested by frequently recurring periods of trade depression, is a most dramatic exhibition of the false economy of distribution. It does not imply a mere miscalculation in the application of productive power, or a brief temporary excess of that power; it manifests in an acute form an economic waste which is chronic and general throughout the advanced industrial nations, a waste contained in the divorcement of the desire to consume and the power to consume.

If the apportionment of income were such as to evoke no excessive saving, full constant employment for capital and labour would be furnished at home. This, of course, does not imply that there would be no foreign trade. Goods that could not be produced at home, or produced as well or as cheaply, would still be purchased by ordinary process of international exchange, but here again the pressure would be the wholesome pressure of the consumer anxious to buy abroad what he could not buy at home, not the blind eagerness of the producer to use every force or trick of trade or politics to find markets for his " surplus " goods.

The struggle for markets, the greater eagerness of producers to sell than of consumers to buy, is the crowning proof of a false economy of distribution. Imperialism is the fruit of this false economy; " social reform " is its remedy. The primary purpose of " social reform," using the term in its economic signification, is to raise the wholesome standard of private and public consumption for a nation, so as to enable the nation to live up to its highest standard of production. Even those social reformers who aim directly at abolishing or reducing some bad form of consumption, as in the Temperance movement, generally recognise the necessity of substituting some better form of current consumption which is more educative and stimulative of other tastes, and will assist to raise the general standard of consumption.

There is no necessity to open up new foreign markets; the home markets are capable of indefinite expansion. Whatever is produced in England can be consumed in England, provided that the " income," or power to demand commodities, is properly distributed. This only appears untrue because of the unnatural and unwholesome specialisation to which this country has been subjected, based upon a bad distribution of economic resources, which has induced an overgrowth of certain manufacturing trades for the express purpose of effecting foreign sales. If the industrial revolution had taken place in an England founded upon equal access by all classes to land, education and legislation, specialisation in manufactures would not have gone so far (though more intelligent progress would have been made, by reason of a widening of the area of selection of inventive and organising talents); foreign trade would have been less important, though more steady; the standard of life for all portions of the population would have been high, and the present rate of national consumption would probably have given full, constant, remunerative employment to a far larger quantity of private and public capital than is now employed.[1] For the over-saving or wider

---

[1] The classical economists of England, forbidden by their theories of parsimony and of the growth of capital to entertain the notion of an indefinite expansion of home markets by reason of a constantly rising standard of national comfort, were early driven to countenance a doctrine of the necessity of finding external markets for the investment of capital.

consumption that is traced to excessive incomes of the rich is a suicidal economy, even from the exclusive standpoint of capital; for consumption alone vitalises capital and makes it capable of yielding profits. An economy that assigns to the "possessing" classes an excess of consuming power which they cannot use, and cannot convert into really serviceable capital, is a dog-in-the-manger policy. The social reforms which deprive the possessing classes of their surplus will not, therefore, inflict upon them the real injury they dread; they can only use this surplus by forcing on their country a wrecking policy of Imperialism. The only safety of nations lies in removing the unearned increments of income from the possessing classes, and adding them to the wage-income of the working classes or to the public income, in order that they may be spent in raising the standard of consumption.

Social reform bifurcates, according as reformers seek to achieve this end by raising wages or by increasing public taxation and expenditure. These courses are not essentially contradictory, but are rather complementary. Working-class movements aim, either by private co-operation or by political pressure on legislative and administrative government, at increasing the proportion of the national income which accrues to labour in the form of wages, pensions, compensation for injuries, &c. State Socialism aims at getting for the direct use of the whole society an increased share of the "social values" which arise from the closely and essentially co-operative work of an industrial society, taxing property and in-

So J. S. Mill: "The expansion of capital would soon reach its ultimate boundary if the boundary itself did not continually open and leave more space" ("Political Economy"). And before him Ricardo (in a letter to Malthus): "If with every accumulation of capital we could take a piece of fresh fertile land to our island, profits would never fall."

comes so as to draw into the public exchequer for public expenditure the "unearned elements" of income, leaving to individual producers those incomes which are necessary to induce them to apply in the best way their economic energies, and to private enterprises those businesses which do not breed monopoly, and which the public need not or cannot undertake. These are not, indeed, the sole or perhaps the best avowed objects of social reform movements. But for the purposes of this analysis they form the kernel.

Trade Unionism and Socialism are thus the natural enemies of Imperialism, for they take away from the "imperialist" classes the surplus incomes which form the economic stimulus of Imperialism.

This does not pretend to be a final statement of the full relations of these forces. When we come to political analysis we shall perceive that the tendency of Imperialism is to crush Trade Unionism and to "nibble" at or parasitically exploit State Socialism. But, confining ourselves for the present to the narrowly economic setting, Trade Unionism and State Socialism may be regarded as complementary forces arrayed against Imperialism, in as far as, by diverting to working-class or public expenditure elements of income which would otherwise be surplus savings, they raise the general standard of home consumption and abate the pressure for foreign markets. Of course, if the increase of working-class income were wholly or chiefly "saved," not spent, or if the taxation of unearned incomes were utilised for the relief of other taxes borne by the possessing classes, no such result as we have described would follow. There is, however, no reason to anticipate this result from trade-union or socialistic measures. Though no sufficient natural stimulus exists to force the well-to-do classes to spend in further luxuries the surplus incomes which they save, every working-class family is subject to powerful stimuli of economic needs, and a reasonably governed State would regard as its prime duty the relief of the present poverty of public life by new forms of socially useful expenditure.

But we are not here concerned with what belongs to the practical issues of political and economic policy. It is the economic theory for which we claim acceptance— a theory which, if accurate, dispels the delusion that expansion of foreign trade, and therefore of empire, is a necessity of national life.

Regarded from the standpoint of economy of energy, the same "choice of life" confronts the nation as the individual. An individual may expend all his energy in acquiring external possessions, adding field to field, barn to barn, factory to factory—may "spread himself" over the widest area of property, amassing material wealth which is in some sense "himself" as containing the impress of his power and interest. He does this by specialising upon the lower acquisitive plane of interest at the cost of neglecting the cultivation of the higher qualities and interests of his nature. The antagonism is not indeed absolute. Aristotle has said, "We must first secure a livelihood and then practise virtue." Hence the pursuit of material property as a reasonable basis of physical comfort would be held true economy by the wisest men; but the absorption of time, energy, and interest upon such quantitative expansion at the necessary cost of starving the higher tastes and faculties is condemned as false economy. The same issue comes up in the business life of the individual: it is the question of intensive *versus* extensive cultivation. A rude or ignorant farmer, where land is plentiful, is apt to spread

G

his capital and labour over a large area, taking in new tracts and cultivating them poorly. A skilled, scientific farmer will study a smaller patch of land, cultivate it thoroughly, and utilise its diverse properties, adapting it to the special needs of his most remunerative markets. The same is true of other businesses; even where the economy of large-scale production is greatest there exists some limit beyond which the wise business man will not go, aware that in doing so he will risk by enfeebled management what he seems to gain by mechanical economies of production and market.

Everywhere the issue of quantitative *versus* qualitative growth comes up. This is the entire issue of empire. A people limited in number and energy and in the land they occupy have the choice of improving to the utmost the political and economic management of their own land, confining themselves to such accessions of territory as are justified by the most economical disposition of a growing population; or they may proceed, like the slovenly farmer, to spread their power and energy over the whole earth, tempted by the speculative value or the quick profits of some new market, or else by mere greed of territorial acquisition, and ignoring the political and economic wastes and risks involved by this imperial career. It must be clearly understood that this is essentially a choice of alternatives; a full simultaneous application of intensive and extensive cultivation is impossible. A nation may either, following the example of Denmark or Switzerland, put brains into agriculture, develop a finely varied system of public education, general and technical, apply the ripest science to its special manufacturing industries, and so support in progressive comfort and character a considerable population upon a strictly limited area; or it may, like

Great Britain, neglect its agriculture, allowing its lands to go out of cultivation and its population to grow up in towns, fall behind other nations in its methods of education and in the capacity of adapting to its uses the latest scientific knowledge, in order that it may squander its pecuniary and military resources in forcing bad markets and finding speculative fields of investment in distant corners of the earth, adding millions of square miles and of unassimilable population to the area of the Empire.

The driving forces of class interest which stimulate and support this false economy we have explained. No remedy will serve which permits the future operation of these forces. It is idle to attack Imperialism or Militarism as political expedients or policies unless the axe is laid at the economic root of the tree, and the classes for whose interest Imperialism works are shorn of the surplus revenues which seek this outlet.

CHAPTER VII

IMPERIALIST FINANCE

THE analysis of economic forces in the foregoing chapter explains the character which public finance assumes in States committed to an imperialist policy. Imperialism, as we see, implies the use of the machinery of government by private interests, mainly capitalist, to secure for them economic gains outside their country. The dominance of this factor in public policy imposes a special character alike upon expenditure and taxation.

The accompanying diagram brings into clear light the main features of the national expenditure of Great Britain during the last three decades of the nineteenth century.

The first feature is the rate of growth of national expenditure taken as a whole. This growth has been far faster than the growth of foreign trade. For whereas the average yearly value of our foreign trade for 1870–75, amounting to £636,000,000, increased in the period 1895–98 to £737,000,000, the average public expenditure advanced over the same period from £63,160,000 to £94,450,000. It is faster than the growth of the aggregate national income, which, according to the rough estimates of statisticians, advanced during the same period from about £1,200,000,000 to £1,700,000,000. The rate of growth has greatly quickened during the later half of the period in question, for, leaving out of consideration war expenditure,

GRANTS IN AID OF
LOCAL TAXATION

EDUCATION

CIVIL SERVICES

NAVAL & MILITARY
EXPENDITURE.

NATIONAL DEBT
(Payment of Interest and
Repayment of Capital).

COST OF COLLECTION

Years ending March 31st

Denotes Exception

Population
32,205,444

Population
32,749,167

1870
£
61,000,000

1871
£
61,800,000

1872
£
62,900,000

1873
£
61,900,000

1874
£
67,570,000

1875
£
65,000,000

| 1870 | 1871 | 1872 | 1873 | 1874 | 1875 |

LIBERAL GOVERNMENT.

GLADSTONE MINISTRY.

From Dec. 9, 1868, to Feb. 21, 1874.   From Fe

T(

the rise of ordinary imperial expenditure has been from
£87,423,000 in 1888 to £128,600,000 in 1900.

The most salient feature of the diagram is the small
proportion of the national revenue expended for what
may be regarded as directly productive purposes of
government. Roughly speaking, three-quarters of the
money goes for naval and military expenditure, and for
the payment of military debts, about five shillings in the
pound being available for education, civil government,
and the dubious policy of grants in aid of local taxation.[1]

The only satisfactory incident disclosed by the table
is the growing amount and proportion of public money
spent on education. A substantial part of the sum
expended as aid to local taxation has simply gone as a
dole to landowners.

The direct military and naval expenditure during the
period has increased faster than the total expenditure, the
growth of trade, of national income, or any other general
indication of national resources. In 1875 the army and
navy cost less than 24½ millions out of a total expenditure of 65 millions; in 1898 they cost nearly 43 millions
out of a total of 99 millions.

The enormous expenditure upon the South African
war will admittedly be followed by a demand for a large
permanent increase in these branches of expenditure,
amounting to an addition of not less than £15,000,000
per annum.

This growth of naval and military expenditure from
about 25 to 60 millions in a little over a quarter of a
century is the most significant fact of imperialist finance.
The financial, industrial, and professional classes, who, we

[1] A portion of the money expended under the head National Debt
should, however, be regarded as productively expended, since it has gone
towards reduction of the debt. Between 1875 and 1900 a reduction of
£140,000,000, equal to about £5,800,000 per annum, has been effected.

have shown, form the economic core of Imperialism, have used their political power to extract these sums from the nation in order to improve their investments and open up new fields for capital, and to find profitable markets for their surplus goods, while out of the public sums expended on these objects they reap other great private gains in the shape of profitable contracts, and lucrative or honourable employment.

The financial and industrial capitalists who have mainly engineered this policy, employing their own genuine convictions to conceal their ill-recognised business ends, have also made important bribes or concessions to other less directly benefited interests in order to keep their sympathy and ensure their support.

This explains the large and growing grants in aid of local taxation, almost the whole of which, interpreted by a scientific regard to incidence of taxation, must be considered as a subsidy to landowners. The support of the Church and of the liquor trade has been more cheaply purchased; the former by relief of rates on tithes and increased grants for Church schools, the latter by a policy of masterly inaction in the matter of temperance reforms and special consideration in regard to taxation.

In making the capitalist-imperialist forces the pivot of financial policy, I do not mean that other forces, industrial and political, have no independent aims and influences, but simply that the former group must be regarded as the true determinant in the interpretation of actual policy.

We have identified almost all the organised interests, commonly summed under the head of .Capitalism, including land capital, with Imperialism. Most of them participate directly in one or other of the two sorts of gain which attend this policy: the interest, trade profits, or employment furnished by the imperialist policy, or the interest, profit, or employment connected with military and civil expenditure itself.

It cannot be too clearly recognised that increasing public expenditure, apart from all political justification, is a direct source of gain to certain well-organised and influential interests, and to all such Imperialism is the chief instrument of such increasing expenditure. .

While the directors of this definitely parasitic policy are capitalists, the same motives appeal to special classes of the workers. In many towns most important trades are dependent upon Government employment or contracts; the Imperialism of the metal and shipbuilding centres is attributable in no small degree to this fact. Members of Parliament freely employ their influence to secure contracts and direct trade to their constituents, and every growth of public expenditure enhances this dangerous bias.

The clearest significance of imperialist finance, however, appears on the side, not of expenditure, but of taxation. The object of those economic interests which use the public purse for purposes of private gain is in large measure defeated if they have first to find the money to fill that purse. To avert the direct incidence of taxation from their own shoulders on to those of other classes or of posterity is a natural policy of self-defence.

A sane policy of taxation would derive the whole or the main part of the national revenue from unearned increments of land values and from profits in trades which, by virtue of some legal or economic protection screening them from close competition, are able to earn high rates of interest or profit. Such taxation would be borne most easily, falling upon unearned elements of incomes, and would cause no disturbance of industry.

This, however, would imply the taxation of precisely those elements which constitute the economic taproot of Imperialism. For it is precisely the unearned elements of income which tend towards an automatic process of accumulation, and which, by swelling the stream of surplus capital seeking markets of investment or markets for the surplus goods it helps to make, direct political forces into Imperialism. A sound system of taxation would, therefore, strike at the very root of the malady.

On the other hand, were the capitalist-imperialist forces openly to shift the burden of taxation on to the shoulders of the people, it would be difficult under popular forms of government to operate such an expensive policy. The people must pay, but they must not know they are paying, or how much they are paying, and the payment must be spread over as long a period as possible.

To take a concrete example from recent history. The medley of financial and political interests which inveigled Great Britain into spending some two hundred millions of public money, in order to obtain for them control of the land and mineral resources of the South African Republics, could not possibly have achieved their object if they had been compelled to raise the money by sending round a tax-gatherer to take from every citizen in hard cash the several pounds which constituted his share of the taxes—the share which by more crooked ways was to be got out of him.

To support Imperialism by direct taxation of incomes or property would be impossible. Where any real forms of popular control existed, militarism and wars would be impossible if every citizen was made to realise their cost by payments of hard cash. Imperialism, therefore, makes everywhere for indirect taxation; not chiefly on grounds of convenience, but for purposes of concealment.

Or perhaps it would be more just to say that Imperialism takes advantage of the cowardly and foolish preference which the average man everywhere exhibits for being tricked out of his contribution to the public funds, using this common folly for its own purposes. It is seldom possible for any Government, even in the stress of some grave emergency, to impose an income-tax; even a property-tax is commonly evaded in all cases of personal property, and is always unpopular. The case of England is an exception which really proves the rule.

The repeal of import duties and the establishment of Free Trade marked the political triumph of the new manufacturing and commercial plutocracy over the land-owning aristocracy. Free Trade was so profitable to the former classes in securing cheap importation of raw materials and in cheapening the subsistence of labour at a time when England's priority in new industrial methods offered an indefinitely rapid expansion of trade that they were willing to support the reimposition of the income-tax which Peel proposed in 1842 in order to enable him to repeal or reduce the import duties. When the sudden financial stress of the Crimean war came on the country the Free Trade policy was in the prime of its popularity and success, and a Liberal ministry, in preference to a reversion to Protection which would otherwise have been inevitable, gave permanency to the tax, extending the area of its application and making its removal more difficult by further repeals of import duties. No Government could now remove it, for the new unpopularity caused by finding adequate substitutes would have outweighed the credit gained by its removal, while its productivity and calculability are advantages shared in an equal degree by no other mode of taxation.

Some allowance may also be made for the principles and personal convictions of political financiers trained in the English science of political economy, and still more for the temptation of competing parties to seek the favour of the newly enfranchised populace by a well-paraded policy of class taxation. The seething revolutionism of the mid-century throughout Europe, the rapid growth of huge industrial centres throughout England, with their masses of ill-explored poverty and their known aptitude for ignorant agitation, made the establishment of formal democracy seem a most hazardous experiment, and both parties were in a mood to conciliate the new monster by doles or bribery. When the break-up of the old Liberal party in 1885–86 had for the first time thrown the vast preponderance of personal property on to the same side as real property, a genuinely democratic budget with a progressive income-tax and a substantial death duty became possible and seemed expedient. It is not necessary to deny that Sir William Harcourt and his colleagues were sincerely convinced of the justice as well as the expediency of this policy; but it must be remembered that no alternative was open, in face of the need of increased funds for Imperialism and education, except a *volte face* upon the Free Trade principles they had most stoutly championed, and a dangerous attack upon trade interests which might recoil upon the working classes, whose cause they were anxious to espouse. The financial attack on " property," embodied in the progressive income-tax and death duties, must be regarded, then, as an exceptional policy, due mainly to a combination of two causes—the difficulty of reverting suddenly to the abandoned practice of Protection, and the desire to conciliate the favour of the new unknown democracy.

Hence the anomaly of Imperialism attended by direct taxation. In no other country have the political conditions operated so. Upon the Continent Militarism and Imperialism have thriven upon indirect taxation, and have enabled the agricultural and manufacturing interests to defeat easily any movement towards Free Trade by urging the needs of revenue through tariffs. In Great Britain it seems unlikely that the policy of direct taxation upon property and income for imperial purposes will be carried any further. The Government of the propertied classes has almost shaken itself free from the traditions of Free Trade; many of the leaders and the overwhelming majority of the rank and file are avowed Protectionists so far as agriculture and certain staple industries are concerned. They are no longer seriously frightened by the power of the people as implied by a popular franchise, nor are they prepared to conciliate it by further taxes upon property; they have experimented with the temper of "the monster," and they think that by the assistance of "the trade" and the Church he is quite manageable, and can be cajoled into paying for Imperialism through protective duties. "Panem et circenses" interpreted into English means cheap booze and Mafficking. Popular education, instead of serving as a defence, is an incitement towards Imperialism; it has opened up a panorama of vulgar pride and crude sensationalism to a great inert mass who see current history and the tangled maze of world movements with dim, bewildered eyes, and are the inevitable dupes of the able organised interests who can lure, or scare, or drive them into any convenient course.

Had the Liberal party stood by the principles of peace, retrenchment, and reform, refusing to go beyond the true "colonialism" of such men as Molesworth, and rejecting the temptations to a "spirited foreign policy" dictated by bond-holders, they might now be able to resist the attack upon Free Trade which seems inevitable. But a Liberal party committed to a militant Imperialism whose rapidly growing expense is determined chiefly by the conduct of foreign Powers and the new arts of scientific warfare is in a hopeless dilemma. Its position as a buffer party between the propertied classes organised as Conservatism and the unorganised pressure of a loose set of forces striving to become a socialist Labour party dictates moderation, and the personnel of its leaders still drawn from the propertied classes prevents it from making any bold attempt to work Imperialism upon a basis of direct taxation upon property, raising the income and property taxes to cover every increasing need of imperialist finance. It has neither the pluck nor the principle to renounce Imperialism or to insist that the classes who seek to benefit by it shall pay for it.

There is then no reason to impute to Liberalism either the desire or the power to defray the expenses of militant Imperialism by a further pursuance of progressive taxation of incomes and property. While the conveniences of finance may prevent the repeal of taxation which is so productive, it will not be carried further; when expenditure is placed again upon a normal footing the income-tax will be reduced and all increase of normal expenditure (estimated recently by a statistical authority at £20,000,000 for military services alone) will be defrayed by indirect taxation.

Now any considerable calculable increase of revenue by indirect taxation means the abandonment of Free Trade. A large steady income of such a kind can only be raised by duties upon imports of necessaries and prime conveniences of life and trade. It is of course quite immaterial to urge that taxation for revenue is not Protection. If import duties are raised on sugar and tea, if they are imposed upon wheat and flour, foreign meat and raw materials of our staple manufactures, or upon finished manufactured goods competing in our market, it matters not that the object be revenue, the economic effect is Protection.

It is probable that imperialist finance is not yet prepared to admit the name or the full economic policy of Protection. The preparatory steps can find other names. A countervailing duty upon beet-sugar poses as an instrument of Free Trade: once admitted, it introduces a whole train of countervailing duties by parity of reasoning. A tax on prison-made goods, on the ground that they are subsidised and so produced under "cost" price, is logically followed by similar protection against all products of "sweated" foreign industry. An export duty upon coal may well be followed by similar duties on the export of engines and machinery, which similarly aid the growth of our manufacturing rivals. But the most formidable mask of Protection will take the shape of military necessity. A military nation surrounded by hostile empires must have within her boundaries adequate supplies of the sinews of war, efficient recruits, and a large food supply. We cannot safely rely upon the fighting capacities of a town-bred population, or upon food supplies from foreign lands. Both needs demand that checks be set upon the excessive concentration of our population in towns, and that a serious attempt be made to revive agriculture and restore the people to the soil.

There are two methods which seem possible. The one is a large radical scheme of land reform interfering with the rights of landowners by compulsory purchase or leasing on the part of public bodies, with powers to

establish large numbers of small farmers on the soil with
loans of capital sufficient to enable them to live and work
upon the soil.   The other method is Protection, the
re-imposition of taxes on imported grain, cattle, fruit,
and dairy produce, with the object of stimulating agriculture and keeping the population on the soil.

Given the political sway of the possessing classes, it
is certain that the latter course will be preferred.   The
landowning and the industrial interests are now sufficiently blended to render it impossible for the town
industrialist to refuse assistance to the rural landowner.
The recent dole in relief of rates is a convincing testimony to this truth.   Political economists may prove that
the chief result of " Protection," in as far as it protects,
is to raise the rent of land, that a corn tax will raise the
price of bread, and by raising real wages injure profits,
and that if the tax really succeeded in stimulating intensive cultivation and self-sufficiency for food supply it
would not assist the revenue.   The Protectionist will not
be dismayed by the contradictory positions he is required
to hold, for he will be aware that the people whose votes
he craves cannot hold two arguments in their heads at
the same time for purposes of comparison.

The demand for agricultural protection in order to
keep upon the soil a peasantry with sound physique and
military aptitudes is likely to outweigh all economic
objections in the near future, and it is quite possible that
Protection may here be tempered by such carefully
devised land reforms as shall place a new " yeoman "
class upon British soil, and a substantial sum as purchase
money plus compensation for disturbance in the pockets
of British landlords.

One other secret avenue to Protection is through the
shipbuilding trade.   Here is a case not for taxation but for

bounties. If England is to be strong for contest in war and trade she must keep open for herself the highways of commerce, and must own ships and men adaptable for purposes of defence. England's great foreign trade was undoubtedly built up in the first instance by the aid of the navigation laws, and the same combination of political exigencies and commercial interests will make towards a revival of this policy. Such are the main streams of tendency towards Protection. But there is no reason to suppose that the policy will be confined to agriculture, sugar and other subsidised imports, export duties upon coal, and bounties on shipbuilding. The leading branches of the textile, metal, and other staple manufactures whose monopoly even in the home market is threatened by the progressive industries of Germany, Holland, and the United States have long lost that confident reliance on Free Trade which they entertained when England's paramountcy in the manufacturing arts was unquestioned. The local specialisation of industries places a most formidable weapon in the hands of the protectionist politician. In spite of the financial and intellectual aid given to the Free Trade movement by certain manufacturing interests, Protection stands as the producer's policy, Free Trade as the consumer's. The specialisation of localities enables a politician to appeal to the separate trade interests of a single town or neighbourhood, and to convince not only its capitalists but its workers of the gain that would accrue to them if their trade was protected against what is termed unfair competition of foreigners: nothing is said about what they will lose as consumers in the diminished purchasing power of their profits and wages, the result of Protection to the trades of other localities. This appeal made to the separate interests of producers is almost certain to be successful in a people of low education and intelligence. Any attempt to put the other side by representing the result of Protection to be a general rise of prices is commonly met by a confident denial that this result will follow, though it is commonly admitted that wages and profits will rise in the particular local trade to whose self-interest the protectionist appeal is addressed.

It is, however, probable that an attempt will be made to conceal the whole character of the protectionist policy by a misty atmosphere of Imperialism. Protection will not be Protection, but Free Trade within the Empire; a protectionist tariff will hide its exclusive side and masquerade as an Imperial Zollverein. Great economic changes, requiring the use of political machinery, invent that machinery. The Imperialism of England, essentially though not exclusively an economic thing, will strive to cover the protective system of finance it favours, by a great political achievement, entitled Federation of the Empire. This avenue to Protection would in any case have been essayed by Imperialism, as indeed the curious attempt of Mr. Chamberlain in 1897 testifies. The abnormally rapid swelling of financial needs due to the disastrous policy in South Africa merely precipitates this policy and gives it political occasion. It will be sought to exploit the enthusiastic loyalty of the colonists exhibited in their rally round the mother country in the South African war for purposes of formal federation on a basis which shall bind them to contribute money and men to the protection and expansion of the Empire. The probability of success in this attempt to secure imperial federation is a matter for separate consideration. It is here named as one of the avenues to Protection.

In many ways it thus appears that Protection is the natural ally of Imperialism.

The economic root of Imperialism is the desire of strong organised industrial and financial interests to secure and develop at the public expense and by the public force private markets for their surplus goods and their surplus capital. War, militarism, and a "spirited foreign policy" are the necessary means to this end. This policy involves large increase of public expenditure. If they had to pay the cost of this policy out of their own pockets in taxation upon incomes and property, the game would not be worth the candle, at any rate so far as markets for commodities are concerned. They must find means of putting the expense upon the general public. But in countries where a popular franchise and representative government exist this cannot be successfully done in an open manner. Taxation must be indirect and must fall upon such articles of consumption or general use as are part of the general standard of consumption and will not shrink in demand or give way to substitutes under the process of taxation. This protection not only serves the purposes of imperial finance, taxing the impotent and ignorant consumer for the imperial gains of the influential economic interests, but it seems to furnish them a second gain by securing to them as producers their home market which is threatened by outside competition, and enabling them to raise their prices to the home consumers and so reap a rise of profits. To those who regard foreign trade in its normal condition as a fair interchange of goods and services, it may seem difficult to understand how these economic interests expect to exclude foreign goods from their market, while at the same time pushing their goods in foreign markets. But we must remind such economists that the prime motive force here is not trade but investment: a surplus of exports over imports is

H

sought as the most profitable mode of investment, and when a nation, or more strictly its investing classes, is bent on becoming a creditor or parasitic nation to an indefinite extent, there is no reason why its imports and exports should balance even over a long term of years. The whole struggle of so-called Imperialism upon its economic side is towards a growing parasitism, and the classes engaged in this struggle require Protection as their most serviceable instrument.

The nature and object of Protection as a branch of imperialist finance is best illustrated in the case of Great Britain, because the necessity of subverting an accepted Free Trade policy lays bare the different methods of Protection and the forces upon which it relies. In other nations committed to or entering upon an imperialist career with the same ganglia of economic interests masquerading as patriotism, civilisation, and the like, Protection has been the traditional finance, and it has only been necessary to extend it and direct it into the necessary channels.

Protection, however, is not the only appropriate financial method of Imperialism. There is at any given time some limit to the quantity of current expenditure which can be met by taxing consumers. The policy of Imperialism to be effective requires at times the outlay of large unforeseen sums on wars and military equipment. These cannot be met by current taxation. They must be treated as capital expenditure, the payment of which may be indefinitely deferred or provided by a slow and suspensible sinking fund.

The creation of public debts is a normal and a most imposing feature of Imperialism. Like Protection, it also serves a double purpose, not only furnishing a second means of escaping taxation upon income and property otherwise inevitable, but providing a most useful form of investment for idle savings waiting for more profitable employment. The creation of large growing public debts is thus not only a necessary consequence of an imperialist expenditure too great for its current revenue, or of some sudden forced extortion of a war indemnity or other public penalty. It is a direct object of imperialist finance to create further debts, just as it is an object of the private money-lender to goad his clients into pecuniary difficulties in order that they may have recourse to him. Analysis of foreign investments shows that public or State-guaranteed debts are largely held by investors and financiers of other nations; and recent history shows, in the cases of Egypt, Turkey, China, the hand of the bond-holder, and of the potential bond-holder, in politics. This method of finance is not only profitable in the case of foreign nations, where it is a chief instrument or pretext for encroachment. It is of service to the financial classes to have a large national debt of their own. The floating of and the dealing in such public loans are a profitable business, and are means of exercising important political influences at critical junctures. Where floating capital constantly tends to excess, further debts are serviceable as a financial drainage scheme.

Imperialism with its wars and its armaments is undeniably responsible for the growing debts of the continental nations, and while the unparalleled industrial prosperity of Great Britain and the isolation of the United States have enabled these great nations to escape this ruinous competition during recent decades, the period of their immunity is over; both, committed as they seem to an Imperialism without limit, will succumb more and more to the money-lending classes dressed as Imperialists and patriots.

PART II

THE POLITICS OF IMPERIALISM

CHAPTER I

THE POLITICAL SIGNIFICANCE OF IMPERIALISM

I

THE curious ignorance which prevails regarding the political character and tendencies of Imperialism cannot be better illustrated than by the following passage from a learned work upon "The History of Colonisation":[1] "The extent of British dominion may perhaps be better imagined than described, when the fact is appreciated that, of the entire land surface of the globe, approximately one-fifth is actually or theoretically under that flag, while more than one-sixth of all the human beings living in this planet reside under one or the other type of English colonisation. The names by which authority is exerted are numerous, and processes are distinct, but the goals to which this manifold mechanism is working are very similar. According to the climate, the natural conditions and the inhabitants of the regions affected, procedure and practice differ. The means are adapted to the situation; there is not any irrevocable, immutable line of policy; from time to time, from decade to decade, English statesmen have applied different treatments to the same territory. Only one fixed rule of action seems to exist; it is to promote the interests of the colony to the utmost, to develop its scheme of government as rapidly as possible, and eventually to elevate it from the position of inferiority

[1] Morris, vol. ii. p. 80.

to that of association.   Under the charm of this beneficent spirit the chief colonial establishments of Great
Britain have already achieved substantial freedom, without dissolving nominal ties; the other subordinate
possessions are aspiring to it, while, on the other hand,
this privilege of local independence has enabled England
to assimilate with ease many feudatory States into the
body politic of her system."   Here then is the theory
that Britons are a race endowed, like the Romans, with
a genius for government, that our colonial and imperial
policy is animated by a resolve to spread throughout the
world the arts of free self-government which we enjoy at
home,[1] and that in truth we are accomplishing this work.

Now, without discussing here the excellencies or the
defects of the British theory and practice of representative self-government, to assert that our "fixed rule of
action" has been to educate our dependencies in this
theory and practice is quite the largest misstatement
of the facts of our colonial and imperial policy that is
possible.   Upon the vast majority of the populations
throughout our Empire we have bestowed no real powers
of self-government, nor have we any serious intention
of doing so, or any serious belief that it is possible
for us to do so.

Of the three hundred and sixty-seven millions of
British subjects outside these isles, not more than ten
millions, or one in thirty - seven, have any real self-
government for purposes of legislation and administration.

Political freedom, and civil freedom, so far as it rests
upon the other, are simply non-existent for the overwhelming majority of British subjects.   In the self-

---

[1] "The British Empire is a galaxy of free States," said Sir W. Laurier
in a speech, July 8, 1902.

governing colonies of Australasia and North America
alone is responsible representative government a reality,
and even there considerable populations of outlanders, as
in West Australia, or servile labour, as in Queensland,
temper the genuineness of democracy.   In Cape Colony
and Natal recent events testify how feebly the forms
and even the spirit of the free British institutions have
taken root in States where the great majority of the
population were always excluded from political rights.
The franchise and the rights it carries will remain
virtually a white monopoly in so-called self-governing
colonies, where the coloured population is to the white
as four to one and ten to one respectively.

In certain of our older Crown colonies there exists
a representative element in the government.   While
the administration is entirely vested in a governor
appointed by the Crown, assisted by a council nominated by him, the colonists elect a portion of the
legislative assembly.   The following colonies belong to
this order: Jamaica, Barbados, Trinidad, Bahamas, British
Guiana, Windward Islands, Bermudas, Malta, Mauritius,
Ceylon.

· The representative element differs considerably in
size and influence in these colonies, but nowhere does it
outnumber the non-elected element.   It thus becomes
an advisory rather than a really legislative factor.   Not
merely is the elected always dominated in numbers by
the non-elected element, but in all cases the veto of the
Colonial Office is freely exercised upon measures passed
by the assemblies.   To this it should be added that in
nearly all cases a fairly high property qualification is
attached to the franchise, precluding the coloured people
from exercising an elective power proportionate to their
numbers and their stake in the country.

The entire population of these modified Crown colonies amounted to 5,700,000 in 1898.[1]

The overwhelming majority of the subjects of the British Empire are under Crown colony government, or under protectorates. In neither case do they enjoy any of the important political rights of British citizens; in neither case are they being trained in the arts of free British institutions. In the Crown colony the population exercises no political privileges. The governor, appointed by the Colonial Office, is absolute, alike for legislation and administration; he is aided by a council of local residents usually chosen by himself or by home authority, but its function is merely advisory, and its advice can be and frequently is ignored. In the vast protectorates we have assumed in Africa and Asia there is no tincture of British representative government; the British factor consists in arbitrary acts of irregular interference with native government. Exceptions to this exist in the case of districts assigned to Chartered Companies, where business men, animated avowedly by business ends, are permitted to exercise arbitrary powers of government over native populations under the imperfect check of some British Imperial Commissioner.

Again, in certain native and feudatory States of India our Empire is virtually confined to government of foreign relations, military protection, and a veto upon grave internal disorder, the real administration of the countries being left in the hands of native princes or headmen. However excellent this arrangement may be, it lends little support to the general theory of the British Empire as an educator of free political institutions.

Where British government is real, it does not carry

---

[1] In all essential features India and Egypt are to be classed as Crown colonies.

freedom or self-government; where it does carry a certain amount of freedom and self-government, it is not real. Not five per cent. of the population of our Empire are possessed of any appreciable portion of the political and civil liberties which are the basis of British civilisation. Outside the ten millions of British subjects in Canada, Australia, and New Zealand, no considerable body is endowed with full self-government in the more vital matters, or is being "elevated from the position of inferiority to that of association."

This is the most important of all facts for students of the present and probable future of the British Empire. We have taken upon ourselves in these little islands the responsibility of governing huge aggregations of lower races in all parts of the world by methods which are antithetic to the methods of government which we most value for ourselves.

The question just here is not whether we are governing these colonies and subject races well and wisely, better than they could govern themselves if left alone, or better than another imperial European nation could govern them, but whether we are giving them those arts of government which we regard as our most valuable possessions.

The statement in the passage which we quoted, that underneath the fluctuations of our colonial policy throughout the nineteenth century lay the "fixed rule" of educating the dependencies for self-government, is so totally and manifestly opposed to historical records and to the testimony of loyal colonial politicians in all our colonies as to deserve no further formal refutation. The very structure of our party government, the ignorance or open indifference of colonial ministers of the elder generations, the biassed play of colonial cliques and interests reduced

the whole of our colonial government for many decades
to something between a see-saw and a game of chance:
the nearest approach to any "fixed rule" was the steady
prolonged pressure of some commercial interest whose
political aid was worth purchase.   That any such "beneficent spirit" as is recorded consciously presided over
the policy applied to any class of colonies during the
larger half of the nineteenth century is notoriously false.
To those statesmen to whom the colonies were not a
tiresome burden, they were a useful dumping-ground for
surplus population, including criminals, paupers and
ne'er-do-weels, or possible markets for British trade.   A
few more liberal-minded politicians, such as Sir W.
Molesworth and Mr. Wakefield, regarded with sympathetic interest the rising democracies of Australasia and
Canada.   But the idea of planning a colonial policy in-
spired by the motive of teaching the arts of free representative self-government not merely was not the "fixed
rule," but was not present as a rule at all in any responsible Colonial Secretary in Great Britain.

When the first dawn of the new Imperialism in the
seventies gave fuller political consciousness to "empire,"
it did indeed become a commonplace of Liberal thought
that England's imperial mission was to spread the arts
of free government, and the examples of Australia and
Canada looming big before all eyes suggested that we
were doing this.   The principles and practices of representative government were "boomed"; Liberal pro-consuls set on foot imposing experiments in India and in
the West Indies; the progress of the South African
colonies suggested that by fairly rapid degrees the
various populations of the Empire might attain substantial measures of self-government; and the larger vision
of a British Empire, consisting in the main or altogether

of a union of self-governing States, began to dazzle politicians.

Some persons—though a diminishing number—still entertain these notions and believe that we are gradually moulding the British Empire into a set of substantially self-governing States. Our position in India and in Egypt is justified, they think, by the training we are giving the natives in good government, and when they hear of "representative" elements in the government of Ceylon or of Jamaica they flatter themselves that the whole trend of imperial government is directed to this end. Admitting the facts regarding the small proportion of present political liberty throughout the Empire, they urge that this arises from the necessary regard we have to the mode of educating lower races: the vast majority of our subjects are "children" and must be trained slowly and carefully in the arts of responsible self-government.

Now such persons are suffering from a great and demonstrable delusion if they suppose that any appreciable number of the able energetic officials who practically administer our Empire from Downing Street, or on the spot, either believe that the populations which they rule are capable of being trained for effective free self-government, or are appreciably affected in their policy by any regard to such a contingency in the near or remote future. Very few British officials any longer retain the notion that we can instruct or are successfully instructing the great populations of India in the Western arts of government. The general admission or conviction is that experiments in municipal and other government conducted under British control on British lines are failures. The real success of our Indian Government admittedly consists in good order and justice administered autocratically by able British officials. There is some training of native officials for subordinate, and in rare instances for high offices, but there is no pretence that this is the chief or an important aim or end, nor is there the least intention that these native officials shall in the future become the servants of the free Indian nation rather than of the bureaucratic Imperial Government.

In other instances, as in Egypt, we are using natives for certain administrative work, and this training in lower offices is doubtless not without its value. Our practical success in preserving order, securing justice and developing the material resources of many of our colonies is largely due to the fact that we have learnt to employ native agents wherever possible for detailed work of administration, and to adapt our government, where it can be safely done, to native conditions. The retention of native laws and customs or of the foreign system of jurisprudence imposed by earlier colonists of another race,[1] while it has complicated government in the final court of the Privy Council, has greatly facilitated the detailed work of administration upon the spot.

Indeed the variety, not only of laws but of other modes of government in our Empire, arouses the enthusiastic admiration of many students of its history. " The British Empire," we are told, " exhibits forms and methods of government in almost exuberant variety. The several

---

[1] "Every country conquered or ceded to the Crown of England retains such laws and such rules of law (not inconsistent with the general law of England affecting dependencies) as were in force at the time of the conquest or cession, until they are repealed by competent authority. Now, inasmuch as many independent States and many dependent colonies of other States have become English dependencies, many of the English dependencies have retained wholly or in part foreign systems of jurisprudence. Thus Trinidad retains much of the Spanish law ; Demerara, Cape of Good Hope, and Ceylon retain much of Dutch law ; Lower Canada retains the French civil law according to the 'coutume de Paris'; St. Lucia retains the old French law as it existed when the island belonged to France " (Lewis, "Government of Dependencies," p. 198).

colonies at different times of their history have passed
through various stages of government, and in 1891 there
are some thirty or forty different forms operating simultaneously within our Empire alone. At this moment there
are regions where government of a purely despotic kind
is in full exercise, and the Empire includes also colonies
where the subordination of the colonial government has
become so slight as to be almost impalpable." [1]

Whether this is a striking testimony to the genius for
" elasticity " of our colonial policy, or an instance of hap-
hazard opportunism, one need not here discuss.[2]

The point is that an examination of this immense
variety of government disposes entirely of the suggestion
that by the extension of our Empire we are spreading the
type of free government which is distinctively British.

The present condition of the government under
which the vast majority of our fellow-subjects in the
Empire live is eminently un-British in that it is based,
not on the consent of the governed, but upon the will
of imperial officials; it does indeed betray a great

[1] Caldecott, "English Colonisation and Empire," p. 121.
[2] What "elasticity" actually signifies in Colonial Office government
may be illustrated by the following testimony of Miss Kingsley in regard
to West Africa. "Before taking any important steps the West African
governor is supposed to consult the officials at the Colonial Office, but as
the Colonial Office is not so well informed as the governor himself is, this
can be no help to him if he is a really able man, and no check on him
if he is not an able man. For, be he what he may, he is the representative of the Colonial Office; he cannot, it is true, persuade the Colonial
Office to go and involve itself in rows with European continental Powers,
because the Office knows about them; but if he is a strong-minded man
with a fad, he can persuade the Colonial Office to let him try that fad on
the natives or the traders, because the Colonial Office does not know the
natives nor the West African trade. You see, therefore, you have in the
governor of a West African possession a man in a bad position. He is
aided by no council worth having, no regular set of experts; he is held in
by another council equally non-expert, except in the direction of continental politics. . . . In addition to the governor there are the other
officials, medical, legal, secretarial, constabulary, and customs. The
majority of them are engaged in looking after each other and clerking.

variety of forms, but they agree in the essential of un-freedom. Nor is it true that any of the more enlightened methods of administration we employ are directed towards undoing this character. Not only in India, but in the West Indies, and wherever there exists a large preponder-ance of coloured population, the trend, not merely of ignorant, but of enlightened public opinion, is against a genuinely representative government on British lines. It is perceived to be incompatible with the economic and social authority of a superior race.

When British authority has been forcibly fastened upon large populations of alien race and colour, with habits of life and thought which do not blend with ours, it is found impossible to graft the tender plants of free representative government, and at the same time to preserve good order in external affairs. We are obliged in practice to make a choice between good order and justice administered autocratically in accordance with British standards, on the one hand, and delicate, costly, doubtful, and disorderly experiments in self-government

Clerking is the breath of the Crown colony system, and customs what it feeds on. Owing to the climate it is practically necessary to have a double staff in all these departments—that is what the system would have if it were perfect ; as it is, some official's work is always being done by a subordinate ; it may be equally well done, but it is not equally well paid for, and there is no continuity in policy in any department, except those which are entirely clerk, and the expense of this is necessarily great. The main evil of this want of continuity is, of course, in the governors—a governor goes out, starts a new line of policy, goes home on furlough leaving in charge the colonial secretary, who does not by any means always feel enthusiastic towards that policy, so it languishes. The governor comes back, goes at it again like a giant refreshed, but by no means better acquainted with local affairs for having been away ; then he goes home again or dies, or gets a new appointment ; a brand-new governor comes out, he starts a new line of policy, perhaps has a new colonial secretary into the bargain ; anyhow the thing goes on wavering, not advancing. The only description I have heard of our policy in West African colonies that seems to me to do it justice is that given by a medical friend of mine, who said it was a coma accompanied by fits " (" West African Studies," pp. 328–330).

on British lines upon the other, and we have practically everywhere decided to adopt the former alternative. A third and sounder method of permitting large liberty of self-government under a really loose protectorate, adopted in a few instances, as in Basutoland, part of Bechuanaland, and a few Indian States, meets with no great favour and in most instances seems no longer feasible. It cannot be too clearly recognised that the old Liberal notion of our educating lower races in the arts of popular government is discredited, and only survives for platform purposes when some new step of annexation is urged upon the country.

The case of Egypt is a *locus classicus.* Here we entered the country under the best auspices, as deliverers rather than as conquerors ; we have undoubtedly conferred great economic benefits upon large sections of the people, who are not savages, but inheritors of ancient civilised traditions. The whole existing machinery of government is virtually at our disposal, to modify it according to our will. We have reformed taxation, improved justice, and cleansed the public services of many corruptions, and claim in many ways to have improved the condition of the fellaheen. But are we introducing British political institutions in such wise as to graft them on a nation destined for progress in self-government ?

The following statement of Lord Milner may be regarded as typical, not of the fossilised, old-world official, but of the modern, more enlightened, practical Imperialist :—

"I attach much more importance, in the immediate future of Egypt, to the improvement of the character and intelligence of the official class than I do to the development of the representative institutions with which we endowed the country in 1883. As a true-born Briton,

I

I, of course, take off my hat to everything that calls
itself Franchise, Parliament, Representation of the People,
the Voice of the Majority, and all the rest of it.   But, as
an observer of the actual condition of Egyptian society,
I cannot shut my eyes to the fact that popular
government, as we understand it, is for a longer time
than any one can foresee at present out of the question.
The people neither comprehend it nor desire it.   They
would come to singular grief if they had it.   And
nobody, except a few silly theorists, thinks of giving it
to them." [1]

Yet here we went into this country upon the
express understanding that we should do precisely what
Lord Milner says we have no intention of doing, viz. teach
the people to govern themselves within the space of a few
years and then leave them to work their government.

I am not here, however, concerned to discuss either
the value of the governmental work which we are doing
or our right to impose our authority upon weaker populations.   But the fact is plain that the British Empire is
not to any appreciable extent a training ground in the
British arts of free government.

In the light of this inquiry, directed to the Empire
as a whole, how do we regard the new Imperialism?
Almost the whole of it, as we have seen, consists of
tropical or sub-tropical territory, with large populations
of savages or "lower races"; little of it is likely, even
in the distant future, to increase the area of sound
colonial life.   In the few places where English colonists
can settle, as in parts of the new South African States,
they will be so largely outnumbered by dark populations
as to render the adoption of free representative government impracticable.

[1] "England in Egypt," pp. 378, 379.

In a single word, the new Imperialism has increased the area of British despotism, far outbalancing the progress in population and in practical freedom attained by our few democratic colonies.

It has not made for the spread of British liberty and for the propagation of our arts of government. The lands and populations which we have annexed we govern, in so far as we govern these at all, by distinctively autocratic methods, administered chiefly from Downing Street, but partly from centres of colonial government, in cases where self-governing colonies have been permitted to annex.

II

Now this large expansion of British political despotism is fraught with reactions upon home politics which are deserving of most serious consideration. A curious blindness seems to beset the mind of the average educated Briton when he is asked to picture to himself our colonial Empire. Almost instinctively he visualises Canada, Australasia, and only quite recently South Africa—the rest he virtually ignores. Yet the Imperialism which is our chief concern, the expansion of the last quarter of a century, and the further expansion to which we may be tempted in the early future, has nothing in common with Canada and Australasia, and very little with " white man's Africa."

When Lord Rosebery uttered his famous words about " a free, tolerant and unaggressive Empire," he can scarcely have had in mind our vast recent encroachments in West and Central Africa, in the Soudan, on the Burmese frontier, or in Matabeleland. But the distinction between genuine Colonialism and Imperialism, important in itself, is vital when we consider their respective relations to domestic policy.

Modern British colonialism has been no drain upon our material and moral resources, because it has made for the creation of free white democracies, a policy of informal federation, of decentralisation, involving no appreciable strain upon the governmental faculties of Great Britain. Such federation, whether it remains informal with the slight attachment of imperial sovereignty which now exists, or voluntarily takes some more formal shape, political or financial, may well be regarded as a source of strength, political and military.

Imperialism is the very antithesis of this free, wholesome colonial connection, making, as it ever does, for greater complications of foreign policy, greater centralisation of power, and a congestion of business which ever threatens to absorb and overtax the capacity of parliamentary government.

The true political nature of Imperialism is best seen by confronting it with the watchwards of progress accepted in the middle of the nineteenth century by moderate men of both great parties in the State, though with interpretations varying in degree—peace, economy, reform, and popular self-government. Even now we find no formal abandonment of the principles of government these terms express, and a large section of professed Liberals believe or assert that Imperialism is consistent with the maintenance of all these virtues.

This contention, however, is belied by facts. The decades of Imperialism have been prolific in wars; most of these wars have been directly motived by aggression of white races upon "lower races," and have issued in

the forcible seizure of territory. Every one of the steps
of expansion in Africa, Asia, and the Pacific has been
accompanied by bloodshed; each imperialist Power keeps
an increasing army available for foreign service; rectification of frontiers, punitive expeditions, and other
euphemisms for war are in incessant progress. The *pax
Britannica*, always an impudent falsehood, has become
of recent years a grotesque monster of hypocrisy; along
our Indian frontiers, in West Africa, in the Soudan, in
Uganda, in Rhodesia fighting has been well-nigh incessant. Although the great imperialist Powers have kept
their hands off one another, save where the rising
empire of the United States has found its opportunity
in the falling empire of Spain, the self-restraint has been
costly and precarious. Peace as a national policy is
antagonised not merely by war, but by militarism, an
even graver injury. Apart from the enmity of France
and Germany, the main cause of the vast armaments
which are draining the resources of most European
countries is their conflicting interests in territorial and
commercial expansion. Where thirty years ago there
existed one sensitive spot in our relations with France,
or Germany, or Russia, there are a dozen now; diplomatic strains are of almost monthly occurrence between
Powers with African or Chinese interests, and the
chiefly business nature of the national antagonisms
renders them more dangerous, inasmuch as the policy
of Governments passes more under the influence of
distinctively financial juntos.

The contention of the *si pacem vis para bellum* school,
that armaments alone constitute the best security for
peace, is based upon the assumption that a genuine
lasting antagonism of real interests exists between the

various peoples who are called upon to undergo this monstrous sacrifice.

Our economic analysis has disclosed the fact that it is only the interests of competing cliques of business men—investors, contractors, export manufacturers, and certain professional classes—that are antagonistic; that these cliques, usurping the authority and voice of the people, use the public resources to push their private businesses, and spend the blood and money of the people in this vast and disastrous military game, feigning national antagonisms which have no basis in reality. It is not to the interest of the British people, either as producers of wealth or as tax-payers, to risk a war with Russia and France in order to join Japan in preventing Russia from seizing Corea; but it may serve the interests of a group of commercial politicians to promote this dangerous policy. The South African war, openly fomented by gold speculators for their private purposes, will rank in history as a leading case of this usurpation of nationalism.

War, however, represents not the success, but the failure of this policy; its normal and most perilous fruit is not war, but militarism. So long as this competitive expansion for territory and foreign markets is permitted to misrepresent itself as "national policy" the antagonism of interests seems real, and the peoples must sweat and bleed and toil to keep up an ever more expensive machinery of war.

Were logic applicable in such cases, the notion that the greater the preparation for war the smaller the probability of its occurrence might well appear a *reductio ad absurdum* of militarism, implying, as it does, that the only way to secure an eternal world peace is to concentrate the entire energy of all nations upon the art of war, which is thus rendered incapable of practice!

With such paradoxes, however, we need not concern ourselves. The patent admitted fact that, as a result of imperial competition, an ever larger proportion of the time, energy, and money of " imperialist " nations is absorbed by naval and military armaments, and that no check upon further absorption is regarded as practicable by Imperialists, brings " militarism " into the forefront of practical politics. Great Britain and the United States, which have hitherto congratulated themselves on escaping the militarism of continental Europe, are now rapidly succumbing. Why? Does any one suggest that either nation needs a larger army for the protection of its own lands or of any of its genuine white settlements in other lands? Not at all. It is not pretended that the militarisation of England is required for such protective work. Australia and New Zealand are not threatened by any Power, nor could a British army render them adequate assistance if they were; equally impotent would British land forces be against the only Power which could conceivably attack our Canadian Dominion; even South Africa, which lies on the borderland between colony and tropical dependency, cannot ultimately be secured by the military power of England. It is our mistaken annexation of tropical and sub-tropical territories, and the attempt to govern " lower races," that is driving us down the steep road to militarism.

If we are to hold all that we have taken since 1870 and to compete with the new industrial nations in the further partition of empires or spheres of influence in Africa and Asia, we must be prepared to fight. The enmity of rival empires, openly displayed throughout the

South African war, is admittedly due to the policy by which we have forestalled, and are still seeking to forestall, these rivals in the annexation of territory and of markets throughout the world. The theory that we may be compelled to fight for the very existence of our Empire against some combination of European Powers, which is now used to scare the nation into a definite and irretrievable reversal of our military and commercial policy, signifies nothing else than the intention of the imperialist interests to continue the reckless career of annexation. In 1896 Lord Rosebery gave a vivid description of the policy of the last two decades, and put forth a powerful plea for peace.

"The British Empire . . . needs peace. For the last twenty years, still more during the last twelve, you have been laying your hands, with almost frantic eagerness, on every tract of territory adjacent to your own or desirable from any other point of view which you thought it desirable to take. That has had two results. I dare say it has been quite right, but it has had two results. The first result is this, that you have excited to an almost intolerable degree the envy of other colonising (*sic!*) nations, and that, in the case of many countries, or several countries rather, which were formerly friendly to you, you can reckon—in consequence of your colonial policy, whether right or wrong—not on their active benevolence, but on their active malevolence. And, secondly, you have acquired so enormous a mass of territory that it will be years before you can settle it or control it, or make it capable of defence or make it amenable to the acts of your administration. . . . In twelve years you have added to the Empire, whether in the shape of actual annexation or of dominion, or of what is called a sphere of influence, 2,600,000 square miles of territory

. . . to the 120,000 square miles of the United Kingdom, which is part of your Empire, you have added
during the last twelve years twenty-two areas as large
as that United Kingdom itself. I say that that marks
out for many years a policy from which you cannot
depart if you would. You may be compelled to draw
the sword—I hope you may not be; but the foreign
policy of Great Britain, until its territory is consolidated, filled up, settled, civilised, must inevitably be a
policy of peace."[1]

Since these words were uttered, vast new tracts of
undigested empire have been added in the Soudan, in
East Africa, in South Africa, while Great Britain is busily
entangling herself in obligations of incalculable magnitude and peril in the China seas, and the prophet
who spoke this warning has himself been an active
instrument in the furtherance of the very folly he de-
nounced.

Imperialism—whether it consists in a further policy
of expansion or in the rigorous maintenance of all those
vast tropical lands which we have lately ear-marked as
British spheres of influence—implies militarism now and
ruinous wars in the near future. This truth is now
for the first time brought sharply and nakedly before
the mind of the nation. The kingdoms of the earth
are to be ours on condition that we fall down and
worship Moloch.

Militarism approaches Great Britain with the following dilemma. If the army needed for defence and
expansion of the Empire is to remain upon a voluntary
basis, consisting of selected material obtained by application of economic inducements, a considerable increase
either of the regular forces or the militia can only be

[1] Edinburgh, October 9, 1896.

obtained by a rise of pay so large as to tempt men, not from the unskilled labour market or the agricultural districts as heretofore, but from the skilled artisan classes of the towns. It requires but slight consideration to perceive that every fresh increment of the army will involve an appeal to a class accustomed to a higher standard of wage, and that the pay for the entire army must be regulated by the rate of pay needed to secure this last increment. Recruiting in time of war is always brisker than in time of peace, other motives blending with the distinctively economic motive. Every increase of our forces on a peace footing will involve a far more than proportionate increase in the rate of pay—how large an increase experiment alone can teach. It seems quite likely that in a period of normally good trade our voluntary army could only be increased 50 per cent. by doubling the former rate of pay, or by other improved conditions of employment involving an equivalent rise of cost, and that, if we required to double the size of our standing army, we should have to quadruple the rate of pay. If, on the other hand, the prospect of some such enormous increase of military expenditure should lead us to abandon the purely voluntary basis, and have recourse to conscription or some other form of compulsory service, we could not fail to suffer in average fighting calibre. Such selection of physique and morale as prevailed under the voluntary system would now disappear, and the radical unfitness of a nation of town-dwellers for arduous military service would be disclosed. The fatuous attempt to convert ineffective slum-workers and weedy city clerks into tough military material, fit for prolonged foreign service, or even for efficient home defence, would be detected, it may be hoped, before the trial by combat with a military Power drawing its soldiers from the soil. A nation, 70 per cent. of whose inhabitants are denizens of towns, cannot afford to challenge its neighbours to trials of physical force, for in the last resort war is determined neither by generalship nor superiority of weapons, but by those elements of brute endurance which are incompatible with the life of industrial towns.

The full danger of the dilemma of militarism is only perceived when the indirect is added to the direct expenditure. An army, volunteer or conscript, formed out of town material would take longer training or more frequent exercise than a peasant army; the waste of labour power, by withdrawing the youth of the nation from their early training in the productive arts in order to prepare them for the destructive art, would be greater, and would impair more grievously the skilled industries than in nations less advanced in the specialised trades and professions. The least of these economic injuries would be the actual loss of labour time involved in the withdrawal; far graver would be the damage to industrial skill and character by withdrawing youths at the period of best docility and aptitude for skilled work and subjecting them to a distinctively mechanical discipline, for though the slum-dweller and the clodhopper may gain in smartness and alertness by military training, the skilled labouring classes will lose more by the crushing of individual initiative which professional militarism always involves.

At a time when the call for free, bold initiative and individual enterprise and ingenuity in the assimilation of the latest scientific and technical knowledge for the arts of industry, for improved organisation and methods of business, becomes most urgent to enable us to hold our own in the new competition of the world—at such a time to subject the youth of our nation to the barrack system, or to any form of effective military training, would be veritable suicide. It is to no purpose to reply that some of our keen commercial competitors, notoriously Germany, are already saddled with this burden; the answer is that, if we can hardly hold our own with Germany while she bears this burden, we shall hand over to her an easy victory if we assume a still heavier one. Whatever virtues are attributed to military discipline by its apologists, it is admitted that this training does not conduce to industrial efficiency. The economic cost of militarism is therefore twofold; the greatly increased expense of the army must be defrayed by an impoverished people.

So far, I have regarded the issue on its narrowly economic side. Far most important are the political implications of militarism. These strike at the very root of popular liberty and the ordinary civic virtues. A few plain reflections serve to dispel the sophistical vapours which are used to form a halo round the life of the soldier. *Respice finem.* There exists an absolute antagonism between the activity of the good citizen and that of the soldier. The end of the soldier is not, as is sometimes falsely said, to die for his country; it is to kill for his country. In as far as he dies he is a failure; his work is to kill, and he attains perfection as a soldier when he becomes a perfect killer. This end, the slaughter of one's fellow-men, forms a professional character, alien from, and antagonistic to, the character of our ordinary citizen, whose work conduces to the preservation of his fellow-men. If it be contended that this final purpose, though informing and moulding the structure and functions of an army, operates but seldom and slightly upon the consciousness of the individual soldier, save upon the battlefield, the answer is that, in the absence from consciousness of this end, the entire routine of the soldier's life, his drill, parades, and whole military exercise, is a useless, purposeless activity, and that these qualities exercise a hardly less degrading influence on character than the conscious intention of killing his fellow-men.

The psychical reactions of military life are indeed notorious; even those who defend the utility of an army do not deny that it unfits a man for civil life. Nor can it be maintained that a shorter general service, such as suffices for a citizen army, escapes these reactions. If the service is long and rigorous enough to be effective, it involves these psychical reactions, which are, indeed, part and parcel of military efficiency. How clearly this is set forth by Mr. March-Phillips in his admirable appreciation of the common soldier's life!

"Soldiers as a class (I take the town-bred, slum-bred majority, mind) are men who have discarded the civil standard of morality altogether. They simply ignore it. This is, no doubt, why civilians fight shy of them. In the game of life they don't play the same rules, and the consequence is a good deal of misunderstanding, until finally the civilian says he won't play with the Tommy any more. In soldiers' eyes lying, theft, drunkenness, bad language, &c., are not evils at all. They steal like jackdaws. As to language, I used to think the language of a merchant ship's fo'c'sle pretty bad, but the language of Tommies, in point of profanity, quite equals, and, in point of obscenity, beats it hollow. This department is a speciality of his. Lying he treats with the same large charity. To lie like a trooper is quite a sound metaphor. He invents all sorts of elaborate lies for the mere pleasure of inventing them. Looting, again, is one of his perpetual joys. Not merely looting for profit, but looting for the sheer fun of the destruction, &c." [1] The fidelity of this description is attested by the sympathy which the writer displays with the soldierly attributes that accompany, and, in his opinion, atone for, these breaches of the civilian rules.

"Are thieving and lying and looting and bestial talk very bad things? If they are, Tommy is a bad man. But, for some reason or other, since I got to know him, I have thought rather less of the iniquity of these things than I did before."

This judgment is itself a striking comment on militarism. The fact that it should be given by a man of sterling character and culture is the most convincing testimony to the corrupting influence of war.

To this informal witness may be added the significant evidence of Lord Wolseley's "Soldier's Pocket-book."

"As a nation, we are brought up to feel it a disgrace to succeed by falsehood; the word 'spy' conveys in it something as repulsive as slave. We will keep hammering away with the conviction that honesty is the best policy, and that truth always wins in the long run. These pretty little sentences do well enough for a child's copy-book, but the man who acts upon them in war had better sheathe his sword for ever."

The order and progress of Great Britain during the nineteenth century has been secured by the cultivation and practice of the ordinary civic and industrial virtues, assisted by certain advantages of natural resources and historical contingencies. Are we prepared to substitute the military code of ethics or to distract the national mind and conduct by a perpetual conflict of two warring principles, the one making for the evolution of the

[1] "With Remington," by L. March-Phillips, pp. 131, 132.

good citizen, the other for the evolution of the good soldier ?

Ignoring, for the present, the distinctively moral degradation of this reversion from industrial to military ethics, we cannot but perceive that the damage done to commercial morality must react disastrously upon the wealth-producing power of the nation, and sap the roots of imperial expenditure.

But one loophole of escape from this dilemma presents itself, an escape fraught with still graver peril. The new Imperialism is, we have seen, chiefly concerned with tropical and sub-tropical countries where large "lower races" are brought under white control. Why should Englishmen fight the defensive or offensive wars of this Empire when cheaper, more numerous, and better-assimilated fighting material can be raised upon the spot, or transferred from one tropical dominion to another ? As the labour of industrial development of tropical resources is put upon the "lower races" who reside there, under white superintendence, why should not militarism be organised upon the same basis, black or brown or yellow men, to whom military discipline will be "a wholesome education," fighting for the British Empire under British officers ? Thus can we best economise our own limited military material, keeping most of it for home defence. This simple solution—the employment of cheap foreign mercenary armies—is no new device. The organisation of vast native forces, armed with "civilised" weapons, drilled on "civilised" methods, and commanded by "civilised" officers, formed one of the most conspicuous features of the latest stages of the great Eastern Empires, and afterwards of the Roman Empire. It has proved one of the most perilous devices of parasitism, by which a metropolitan population entrusts the defence of its lives and possessions to the precarious fidelity of " conquered races," commanded by ambitious pro-consuls.

One of the strangest symptoms of the blindness of Imperialism is the reckless indifference with which Great Britain, France, and other imperial nations are embarking on this perilous dependence.   Great Britain has' gone farthest.   Most of the fighting by which we have won our Indian Empire has been done by natives; in India, as more recently in Egypt, great standing armies are placed under British commanders; almost all the fighting associated with our African dominions, except in the southern part, has been done for us by natives.   How strong the pressure is to reduce the proportion of British soldiers employed in these countries to a bare minimum of safety is amply illustrated in the case of India, when the South African emergency drove us to reduce the accepted minimum by more than fifteen thousand men, while in South Africa itself we established a precedent which will cost us dear in the future, by employing large numbers of armed natives to fight against another white race.

Those best acquainted with the temper of the British people and of the politicians who have the direct determination of affairs will understand how readily we may be drawn along this perilous path.   Nothing short of the fear of an early invasion of these islands will induce the British people to undergo the onerous experience of a really effective system of compulsory military service ; no statesman except under the shadow of a serious menace of invasion will dare to press such a plan.   A regular provision for compulsory foreign service will never be adopted when the alternative of mercenary native armies remains.   Let these " niggers " fight for

the Empire in return for the services we render them by
annexing and governing them and teaching them " the
dignity of labour," will be the prevailing sentiment, and
" imperialist " statesmen will be compelled to bow before
it, diluting with British troops ever more thinly the
native armies in Africa and Asia.

This mode of militarism, while cheaper and easier in
the first instance, implies less and less control from Great
Britain. Though reducing the strain of militarism upon
the population at home, it enhances the risks of wars,
which become more frequent and more barbarous in proportion as they involve to a less degree the lives of
Englishmen. The expansion of our Empire under the
new Imperialism has been compassed by setting the
" lower races " at one another's throats, fostering tribal
animosities, and utilising for our supposed benefit the
savage propensities of the peoples to whom we have a
mission to carry Christianity and civilisation.

That we do not stand alone in this ignominious
policy does not make it better, rather worse, offering
terrible prophetic glimpses into a not distant future, when
the horrors of our eighteenth century struggle with
France in North America and India may be revived
upon a gigantic scale, and Africa and Asia may furnish
huge cock-pits for the struggles of black and yellow
armies representing the imperialist rivalries of Christendom. The present tendencies of Imperialism plainly
make in this direction, involving in their recoil a degradation of Western States and a possible *débâcle* of
Western civilisation.

In any event Imperialism makes for war and for
militarism, and has brought a great and limitless increase
of expenditure of national resources upon armaments.
It has impaired the independence of every nation which

K

has yielded to its false glamour. Great Britain no longer possesses a million pounds which it can call its own ; its entire financial resources are mortgaged to a policy to be dictated by Germany, France, or Russia. A move from any of these Powers can force us to expend upon more battleships and military preparations the money we had designed to use for domestic purposes. The priority and reckless magnitude of our imperial expansion has made the danger of an armed coalition of great Powers against us no idle chimera. The recent development of their resources along the lines of the new industrialism, on the one hand, by driving them to seek foreign markets, brings them in all parts of the world against the vexatious barriers of British possessions; on the other, has furnished them with ample means of public expenditure. The spread of modern industrialism tends to place our "rivals" on a level with ourselves in their public resources. Hence, at the very time when we have more reason to fear armed coalition than formerly, we are losing that superiority in finance which made it feasible for us to maintain a naval armament superior to any European combination.

All these perils in the present and the near future are the fruits of the new Imperialism, which is thus exposed as the implacable and mortal enemy of Peace and Economy. How far the military aspect of Imperialism has already eaten into the resources of modern European States may be judged by the following table showing the growth of expenditure of the various great European States on military equipment in the last generation :—

MILITARY EXPENDITURE OF GREAT EUROPEAN POWERS.

	1869-1870.	1897-1898.
	£	£
Great Britain	22,440,000	40,094,000
France	23,554,000	37,000,000
Russia	15,400,000	35,600,000
Germany	11,217,000	32,800,000
Austria	9,103,000	16,041,000
Italy	7,070,000	13,510,000
Totals .	88,784,000	175,045,000

For the whole body of European States the increase has been from £105,719,000 in 1869-1870 to £208,877,000 in 1897-1898.

III

There are those who deny the antagonism of Imperialism and social reform. "The energy of a nation like ours, they urge, is not to be regarded as a fixed quantity, so that every expenditure upon imperial expansion implies a corresponding restriction for purposes of internal progress; there are various sorts of energy demanding different outlets, so that the true economy of British genius requires many domestic and external fields of activity; we are capable at one and the same time of imperial expansion in various directions, and of a complex energy of growth in our internal economy. The inspiration of great achievements throughout the world reacts upon the vitality of the British nation, rendering it capable of efforts of internal progress which would have been precluded by the ordinary course of smug insular self-development."

Now it is needless to argue the incompatibility of social reform with Imperialism on any abstract principle regarding the quantity of national energy. Though limits of quantity exist underneath the finest economy of division of labour, as indeed is illustrated on the military plane by the limits which population imposes upon the combination of aggressive expansion and home defence, these limits are not always easy to discover and are sometimes capable of great elasticity. It cannot, therefore, be contended that the sound intellectual stuff which goes into our Indian Civil Service involves a corresponding loss to our home professions and official services, or that the adventurous energy of great explorers, missionaries, engineers, prospectors, and other pioneers of empire could and would have found as ample a field and as sharp a stimulus for their energies within these islands. The issue we are considering —that of Imperialism—does not in its main political and social effects turn upon any such exact considerations of quantitative economy of energy, nor does the repudiation of Imperialism imply a confinement within rigid territorial limits of any individual or co-operative energy which may find better scope abroad. We are concerned with economy of governmental power, with Imperialism as a public policy. Even here the issue is not primarily one of quantitative economy, though, as we shall see, that is clearly involved. The antagonism of Imperialism and social reform is an inherent opposition of policy involving contradictory methods and processes of government. Some of the more obvious illustrations of this antagonism are presented by considerations of finance. Most important or popular measures of social reform, the improvement of the machinery of public education, any large handling of the land and housing questions in town and country, the public control of the drink traffic, old-age pensions, legislation for improving the condition of the workers, involve con-

siderable outlay of public money raised in taxation
by the central or local authorities. Now Imperialism,
through the ever-growing military expenditure it involves, visibly drains the public purse of the money
which might be put to such purposes. Not only has
the Exchequer not sufficient money to expend on public
education, old-age pensions, or other State reforms; the
smaller units of local government are similarly crippled,
for the tax-payers and the rate-payers are in the main
the same persons, and when they are heavily mulcted
by taxes for unproductive State purposes they cannot
easily bear increased rates.

Every important social reform, even if it does
not directly involve large public expenditure, causes
financial disturbances and risks which are less tolerable at times when public expenditure is heavy and
public credit fluctuating and embarrassed. Every
social reform involves some attack on vested interests,
and these can best defend themselves when active
Imperialism absorbs public attention. When legislation
is involved, economy of time and of governmental
interest is of paramount importance. Imperialism, with
its "high politics," involving the honour and safety of
the Empire, claims the first place, and, as the Empire
grows, the number and complexity of its issues, involving
close, immediate, continuous attention, grow, absorbing
the time of the Government and of Parliament. It
becomes more and more impossible to set aside parliamentary time for the full unbroken discussion of matters
of most vital domestic importance, or to carry through
any large serious measure of reform.

It is needless to labour the theory of this antagonism
when the practice is apparent to every student of politics.
Indeed, it has become a commonplace of history how

Governments use national animosities, foreign wars and the glamour of empire-making, in order to bemuse the popular mind and divert rising resentment against domestic abuses. The vested interests, which, on our analysis, are shown to be chief prompters of an imperialist policy, play for a double stake, seeking their private commercial and financial gains at the expense and peril of the commonwealth. They at the same time protect their economic and political supremacy at home against movements of popular reform. The city ground landlord, the country squire, the banker, the usurer, and the financier, the brewer, the mine-owner, the ironmaster, the shipbuilder, and the shipping trade, the great export manufacturers and merchants, the clergy of the State Church, the universities and great public schools, the legal trade unions and the services have, both in Great Britain and on the Continent, drawn together for common political resistance against attacks upon the power, the property, and the privileges which in various forms and degrees they represent. Having conceded under pressure the form of political power in the shape of elective institutions and a wide franchise to the masses, they are struggling to prevent the masses from gaining the substance of this power and using it for the establishment of equality of economic opportunities. The collapse of the Liberal party upon the Continent, and now in Great Britain, is only made intelligible in this way. Friends of liberty and of popular government so long as the new industrial and commercial forces were hampered by the economic barriers and the political supremacy of the *noblesse* and the landed aristocracy, they have come to temper their " trust " of the people by an ever-growing quantity of caution, until within the last two decades they have

either sought political fusion with the Conservatives or
have dragged on a precarious existence on the strength
of a few belated leaders with obsolescent principles.
Where Liberalism preserves any real strength, it is
because the older struggle for the franchise and the
primary liberties has been delayed, as in Belgium and
in Denmark, and a *modus vivendi* has been possible with
the rising working-class party. In Germany, France,
and Italy the Liberal party, as a factor in practical
politics, has either disappeared or is reduced to im-
potence; in England it now stands convicted of a gross
palpable betrayal of the first conditions of liberty, feebly
fumbling after programmes as a substitute for principles.
Its leaders, having sold their party to a confederacy of
stock gamblers and jingo sentimentalists, find themselves
impotent to defend Free Trade, Free Press, Free Schools,
Free Speech, or any of the rudiments of ancient Liberalism.
They have alienated the confidence of the people. For
many years they have been permitted to conduct a sham
fight and to call it politics; the people thought it real
until the South African war furnished a decisive dramatic
test, and the unreality of Liberalism became apparent.
It is not that Liberals have openly abandoned the old
principles and traditions, but that they have rendered
them of no account by dallying with an Imperialism
which they have foolishly and futilely striven to distinguish from the firmer brand of their political
opponents. This surrender to Imperialism signifies that
they have preferred the economic interests of the possessing and speculative classes, to which most of their
leaders belong, to the cause of Liberalism. That they
are not conscious traitors or hypocrites may be readily
conceded, but the fact remains that they have sold
the cause of popular reform, which was their rightful

heritage, for an Imperialism which appealed to their business interests and their social prepossessions. The mess of potage has been seasoned by various sweeter herbs, but its "stock" is class selfishness. The majority of the influential Liberals fled from the fight which was the truest test of Liberalism in their generation because they were "hirelings," destitute of firm political principle, gladly abandoning themselves to whatever shallow and ignoble defences a blear-eyed, raucous "patriotism" was ready to devise for their excuse.

It is possible to explain and qualify, but this remains the naked truth, which it is well to recognise. A Liberal party can only survive as a discredited or feeble remnant in England, unless it consents definitely to dissever itself from that Imperialism which its past leaders, as well as their opponents, have permitted to block the progress of domestic reforms.

There are individuals and sections among those who have comprised the Liberal party whose deception has been in large measure blind and involuntary, because they have been absorbed by their interest in some single important issue of social reform, whether it be temperance, land tenure, education, or the like. Let these men now recognise, as in honesty they can scarcely fail to do, that Imperialism is the deadly enemy of each of these reforms, that none of them can make serious advance so long as the expansion of the Empire and its satellite (militarism) absorb the time, the energy, the money of the State. Thus alone is it still possible that a strong rally of Liberals might, by fusion or co-operation with the political organisations of the working classes, fight Imperialism with the only effectual weapon, social reconstruction on the basis of democracy.

IV

The antagonism with democracy drives to the very roots of Imperialism as a political principle. Not only is Imperialism used to frustrate those measures of economic reform now recognised as essential to the effectual working of all machinery of popular government, but it operates to paralyse the working of that machinery itself. Representative institutions are ill adapted for empire, either as regards men or methods. The government of a great heterogeneous medley of lower races by departmental officials in London and their nominated emissaries lies outside the scope of popular knowledge and popular control. The Foreign, Colonial, and Indian Secretaries in Parliament, the permanent officials of the departments, the governors and staff who represent the Imperial Government in our dependencies, are not, and cannot be, controlled directly or effectively by the will of the people. This subordination of the legislative to the executive, and the concentration of executive power in an autocracy, are necessary consequences of the predominance of foreign over domestic politics. The process is attended by a decay of party spirit and party action, and an insistence on the part of the autocracy, whether it be a Kaiser or a Cabinet, that all effective party criticism is unpatriotic and verges on treason. An able writer, discussing the new foreign policy of Germany, summarises the point of view of the expansionists: " It is claimed by them that in foreign affairs the nation should stand as one man, that policies once entered upon by the Government should not be repudiated, and that criticism should be avoided as weakening the influence of the nation abroad. . . . It is evident that, when the most important concerns of a nation are thus withdrawn from the field of party difference, party government itself must grow weak, as dealing no longer with vital affairs. . . . Thus, as the importance of the executive is enhanced, that of the legislative is lowered, and parliamentary action is looked down upon as the futile and irritating activity of unpractical critics.   If the governmental measures are to be adopted inevitably, why not dispense with the irritating delay of parliamentary discussion ?"[1]

The Kaiser's speech at Hamburg, October 19, 1899, condenses the doctrine thus : "The face of the world has changed greatly during the last few years.   What formerly required centuries is now accomplished in a few months.   The task of Kaiser and Government has consequently grown beyond measure, and a solution will only be possible when the German people renounce party divisions.   Standing in serried ranks behind the Kaiser, proud of their great fatherland, and conscious of their real worth, the Germans must watch the development of foreign States.   They must make sacrifices for their position as a world-power, and, abandoning party spirit, they must stand united behind their prince and emperor."

Autocratic government in imperial politics naturally reacts upon domestic government.   The intricacy of the departmental work of the Home Office, the Board of Trade, of Education, and other important offices has favoured this reaction, which has taken shape in government by administrative orders in accordance with large powers slipped into important statutes and not properly challenged or safeguarded amid the chaotic hurry in

---

[1] "World Politics," by P. S. Reinsch, pp. 300, 301 (Macmillan & Co.).

which most governments are driven in legislation. It is noticeable that in America a still more dangerous practice has sprung up, entitled "government by injunction," in which the judiciary is virtually empowered to issue decrees having the effect of laws with attendant penalties for specific acts.

In Great Britain the weakening of "party" is visibly attended by a decline of the reality of popular control. Just in proportion as foreign and colonial policy bulks more largely in the deliberative and administrative work of the State is government necessarily removed from the real control of the people. It is no mere question of economy of the time and energy of Parliament, though the dwindling proportion of the sessions devoted to consideration of domestic questions represents a corresponding decline of practical democracy. The wound to popular government penetrates far deeper. Imperialism, and the military, diplomatic, and financial resources which feed it, have become so far the paramount considerations of recent Governments that they mould and direct the entire policy, give point, colour and character to the conduct of public affairs, and overawe by continual suggestions of unknown and incalculable gains and perils the nearer and more sober processes of domestic policy. The effect on parliamentary government has been great, quick, and of palpable import, making for the diminution of the power of representative institutions. At elections the electorate is no longer invited to exercise a free, conscious, rational choice between the representatives of different intelligible policies; it is invited to endorse, or to refuse endorsement, to a difficult, intricate, and hazardous imperial and foreign policy, commonly couched in a few well-sounding general phrases, and supported by an appeal to the necessity of solidarity and continuity of national conduct—virtually a blind vote of confidence. In the deliberations of the House of Commons the power of the Opposition to oppose has been seriously and progressively impaired: partly by alteration in the rules of the House, which have diminished the right of full discussion of legislative measures in their several stages, and impaired the privileges of the Commons, viz. the right of discussing grievances upon motions of Supply, and of questioning ministers regarding the conduct of their offices; partly by a forcible encroachment of the Government upon the rights and privileges formerly enjoyed by private members in moving resolutions and in introducing bills. This diminution of the power of opposition is only the first of a series of processes of concentration of power. The Government now claims for its measures the complete disposal of the time of the House whenever it judges such monopoly to be desirable.

Within the Government itself the same centripetal forces have been operative. "There can," writes Mr. Bryce, "be no doubt that the power of the Cabinet as against the House of Commons has grown steadily and rapidly, and it appears (1901) to be still growing."[1]

So the Cabinet absorbs the powers of the House, while the Cabinet itself has been deliberately and consciously expanded in size so as to promote the concentration of real power in an informal but very real "inner Cabinet," retaining some slight selective elasticity, but virtually consisting of the Prime Minister and the Foreign and Colonial Secretaries and the Chancellor of the Exchequer. This process of centralisation of power, which tends to

---

[1] "Studies in History and Jurisprudence," vol. i. p. 177.

destroy representative government, reducing the House of Commons to be little more than a machine for the automatic registration of the decrees of an unelected inner Cabinet, is manifestly attributable to Imperialism.[1] The consideration of delicate, uncertain intelligence affecting our relations with foreign Powers, the accepted necessity of secrecy in diplomacy, and of expeditious, unobtrusive action, seem to favour and even to necessitate a highly centralised autocratic and bureaucratic method of government.

Amid this general decline of parliamentary government the "party system" is visibly collapsing, based as it was on plain cleavages in domestic policy which have little significance when confronted with the claims and powers of Imperialism. If the party system is destined to survive in British politics, it can only do so by the consolidation of all sections opposed to the "imperialist" practices to which Liberal as well as Conservative ministries have adhered during recent years. So long as Imperialism is allowed to hold the field, the only real political conflict is between groups representing the divergent branches of Imperialism, the men upon the spot and the Home Government, the Asiatic interests of

---

[1] An experienced observer thus records the effect of these changes upon the character and conduct of members of Parliament: "For the most part, as in the country, so in the House, the *political* element has waned as a factor. The lack of interest in constitutional matters has been conspicuous. . . . The 'Parliament man' has been disappearing ; the number of those desirous of furthering social and industrial reforms has been waning. On the other hand, those who have been anxious to grasp such opportunities of various kinds outside its work and duties as are afforded by membership of the House of Commons, and who are willing to support the Government in the division lobby without being called upon to do much more, came up in large numbers in 1895 and 1900, and now form a very large proportion, if not the majority, of the House of Commons" (Mr. John E. Ellis, M.P., *The Speaker*, June 7, 1902).

India and China and the forward policy in Africa, the advocates of a German alliance or a Franco-Russian alliance.

V

Imperialism and popular government have nothing in common: they differ in spirit, in policy, in method. Of policy and method I have already spoken; it remains to point out how the spirit of Imperialism poisons the springs of democracy in the mind and character of the people.   As our free self-governing colonies have furnished hope, encouragement, and leading to the popular aspirations in Great Britain, not merely by practical successes in the arts of popular government, but by the wafting of a spirit of freedom and equality, so our despotically ruled dependencies have ever served to damage the character of our people by feeding the habits of snobbish subservience, the admiration of wealth and rank, the corrupt survivals of the inequalities of feudalism.   This process began with the advent of the East Indian Nabob and the West Indian planter into English society and politics, bringing back with his plunders of the slave trade and the gains of corrupt and extortionate officialism the acts of vulgar ostentation, domineering demeanour and corrupting largesse to dazzle and degrade the life of our people.   Cobden, writing in 1860 of our Indian Empire, put this pithy question: "Is it not just possible that we may become corrupted at home by the reaction of arbitrary political maxims in the East upon our domestic politics, just as Greece and Rome were demoralised by their contact with Asia?"[1]

Not merely is the reaction possible, it is inevitable. As the despotic portion of our Empire has grown in

[1] Morley, "Life of Cobden," vol. ii. p. 361.

area, a larger and larger number of men, trained in the temper and methods of autocracy as soldiers and civil officials in our Crown colonies, protectorates, and Indian Empire, reinforced by numbers of merchants, planters, engineers, and overseers, whose lives have been those of a superior caste living an artificial life removed from all the healthy restraints of ordinary European society, have returned to this country, bringing back the characters, sentiments, and ideas imposed by this foreign environment. The South and South-West of England is richly sprinkled with these men, many of them wealthy, most of them endowed with leisure, men openly contemptuous of democracy, devoted to material luxury, social display, and the shallower arts of intellectual life. The wealthier among them discover political ambitions, introducing into our Houses of Parliament the coarsest and most selfish spirit of "Imperialism," using their imperial experience and connections to push profitable companies and concessions for their private benefits, and posing as authorities so as to keep the yoke of Imperialism firmly fixed upon the shoulders of the "nigger." The South African millionaire is the brand most in evidence: his methods are the most barefaced, and his success, social and political, the most redoubtable. But the practices which are writ large in Rhodes, Beit, and their parliamentary confederates are widespread on a smaller scale; the South of England is full of men of local influence in politics and society whose character has been formed in our despotic Empire, and whose incomes are chiefly derived from the maintenance and furtherance of this despotic rule. Not a few enter our local councils, or take posts in our constabulary or our prisons: everywhere they stand for coercion and for resistance to reform. Could the incomes expended in the Home

Counties and other large districts of Southern Britain be traced to their sources, it would be found that they were in large measure wrung from the enforced toil of vast multitudes of black, brown, or yellow natives, by arts not differing essentially from those which supported in idleness and luxury imperial Rome.

It is, indeed, a nemesis of Imperialism that the arts and crafts of tyranny, acquired and exercised in our unfree Empire, should be turned against our liberties at home. Those who have felt surprise at the total disregard or the open contempt displayed by the aristocracy and the plutocracy of this land for infringements of the liberties of the subject and for the abrogation of constitutional rights and usages have not taken sufficiently into account the steady reflux of this poison of irresponsible autocracy from our "unfree, intolerant, aggressive" Empire.

The political effects, actual and necessary, of the new Imperialism, as illustrated in the case of the greatest of imperialist Powers, may be thus summarised. It is a constant menace to peace, by furnishing continual temptations to further aggression upon lands occupied by lower races, and by embroiling our nation with other nations of rival imperial ambitions; to the sharp peril of war it adds the chronic danger and degradation of militarism, which not merely wastes the current physical and moral resources of the nations, but checks the very course of civilisation. It consumes to an illimitable and incalculable extent the financial resources of a nation by military preparation, estopping the expenditure of the current income of the State upon productive public purposes and burdening posterity with heavy loads of debt. Absorbing the public money, time, interest and energy on costly and unprofitable work of territorial aggrandisement, it thus wastes those energies of public life in the governing classes and the nations which are needed for internal reforms and for the cultivation of the arts of material and intellectual progress at home. Finally, the spirit, the policy, and the methods of Imperialism are hostile to the institutions of popular self-government, favouring forms of political tyranny and social authority which are the deadly enemies of effective liberty and equality.

CHAPTER II

THE SCIENTIFIC DEFENCE OF IMPERIALISM

I

THOUGH it can hardly be denied that the ambitions of individuals or nations have been the chief conscious motives in Imperialism, it is possible to maintain that here, as in other departments of human history, certain larger hidden forces operate towards the progress of humanity. The powerful hold which biological conceptions have obtained over the pioneers in the science of sociology is easily intelligible. It is only natural that the laws of individual and specific progress so clearly discerned in other parts of the animal kingdom should be rigorously applied to man; it is not unnatural that the deflections or reversals of the laws of lower life by certain other laws, which only attain importance in the higher psychical reaches of the *genus homo*, should be underrated, misinterpreted, or ignored. The biologist who enters human history often finds himself confronted by intellectual antagonists who regard him as an interloper, and seek to raise a barrier between human and animal development. Indeed, from the ranks of the biological profession itself, scientists of such eminence as Huxley and A. R. Wallace have lent themselves to this separatism, distinguishing the ethical or spiritual progress of the human race from the general cosmic process, and endowing men with qualities and with laws of action different in kind from those which obtain in the rest of the animal kingdom. A reaction against the abrupt dogmatism of this position has led many others to an equally abrupt and equally dogmatic assertion of the laws of the lower forms of physical struggle and selection which explain or describe progress in lower animals as sufficient for all purposes of sociology.

Sociologists have shown themselves in some cases eager to accept this view, and apply it to defend the necessity, the utility, and even the righteousness of maintaining to the point of complete subjugation or extermination the physical struggle between races and types of civilisation.

Admitting that the efficiency of a nation or a race requires a suspension of intestine warfare, at any rate *à l'outrance*, the crude struggle on the larger plane must, they urge, be maintained. It serves, indeed, two related purposes. A constant struggle with other races or nations is demanded for the maintenance and progress of a race or nation; abate the necessity of the struggle and the vigour of the race flags and perishes. Thus it is to the real interest of a vigorous race to be "kept up to a high pitch of external efficiency by contest, chiefly by way of war with inferior races, and with equal races by the struggle for trade routes and for the sources of raw material and of food supply." "This," adds Professor Karl Pearson, "is the natural history view of mankind, and I do not think you can in its main features subvert it."[1]

Others, taking the wider cosmic standpoint, insist that the progress of humanity itself requires the maintenance of a selective and destructive struggle between

[1] "National Life from the Standpoint of Science," p. 44 (Black, 1901).

races which embody different powers and capacities, different types of civilisation. It is desirable that the earth should be peopled, governed, and developed, as far as possible, by the races which can do this work best, *i.e.* by the races of highest "social efficiency"; these races must assert their right by conquering, ousting, subjugating, or extinguishing races of lower social efficiency. The good of the world, the true cause of humanity, demands that this struggle, physical, industrial, political, continue, until an ideal settlement is reached whereby the most socially efficient nations rule the earth in accordance with their several kinds and degrees of social efficiency. This principle is clearly enunciated by M. Edmond Demolins, who describes it as being "as indisputable as the law of gravitation."

"When one race shows itself superior to another in the various externals of domestic life, it *inevitably* in the long run gets the upper hand in public life and establishes its predominance. Whether this predominance is asserted by peaceable means or feats of arms, it is none the less, when the proper time comes, officially established, and afterwards unreservedly acknowledged. I have said that this law is the only thing which accounts for the history of the human race and the revolutions of empires, and that, moreover, it explains and justifies the appropriation by Europeans of territories in Asia, Africa, and Oceania, and the whole of our colonial development."[1]

The western European nations with their colonies represent the socially efficient nations, in various degrees. Some writers, American and English, such as Professor Giddings and Mr. Kidd, believe that the Teutonic races, and in particular the Anglo-Saxon branches, represent

---

[1] "Boers or British?" p. 24.

the highest order of efficiency, in which notion they are supported by a little group of Anglophil Frenchmen.

This genuine and confident conviction about "social efficiency" must be taken as the chief moral support of Imperialism. "Human progress requires the maintenance of the race struggle, in which the weakest races shall go under, while the 'socially efficient' races survive and flourish: we are the 'socially efficient' race." So runs the imperialist argument.

Now, thus closely stated, the meaning of the term "socially efficient" becomes evident. It is simply the antithesis of "weak," and is equivalent to "strong in the struggle of life." Taken at the first blush it suggests admitted moral and intellectual virtues of some broad general kind, and is afterwards taken to imply such qualities. But applied in the present "natural history" sense it signifies nothing more or less than capacity to beat other races, who, from their failure, are spoken of as "lower." It is merely a repetition of the phrase "survival of the fittest," the meaning of which is clear when the question is put, "Fittest to do what?" and the answer follows, "Fittest to survive."

It is true that "social efficiency" seems to imply much more than mere fighting capacity in war and trade, and, if we were to take into account all qualities which go to make a good society, we should include much more; but from our present "natural history" standpoint it is evident that these must be excluded and only those included which aid directly in the struggle.

Giving, then, the proper value to the terms, it simply comes to this. "In the history of man, as throughout nature, stronger races have continually trampled down, enslaved, and exterminated other races." The biologist says: "This is so rooted in nature, including human

nature, that it must go on." He adds: "It has been
the prime condition and mode of progress in the past,
therefore it is desirable it should go on. It must go on,
it ought to go on."

So easily we glide from natural history to ethics, and
find in utility a moral sanction for the race struggle.
Now, Imperialism is nothing but this natural history
doctrine, regarded from the standpoint of one's own
nation. We represent the socially efficient nation, we
have conquered and acquired dominion and territory in
the past: we must go on, it is our destiny, one which
is serviceable to ourselves and to the world, our duty.

Thus, emerging from natural history, the doctrine
soon takes on a large complexity of ethical and religious
finery, and we are wafted into an elevated atmosphere
of "imperial Christianity," a "mission of civilisation,"
in which we are to teach "the arts of good government"
and "the dignity of labour."

II

That the power to do anything constitutes a right
and even a duty to do it is perhaps the commonest,
the most "natural" of temperamental fallacies. Even
Professor Pearson does not avoid it, when, after an
able vindication of the necessity of intra-race selection
and of race struggle, he speaks of "our right to work
the unutilised resources of earth, be they in Africa or
in Asia."[1]

This belief in a "divine right" of force, which teachers
like Carlyle, Kingsley, Ruskin did so much to foster, is
primarily responsible for the transmutation of a natural
history law into a moral enthusiasm.

[1] "National Life," p. 46.

Elsewhere I have dwelt with so much insistence on the more sordid and calculating motives which direct Imperialism that I am anxious here to do justice to the nobler aspects of the sentiment of Imperialism, interpreted through a naïve rendering of science into a gospel of arduous chivalry. Such a revelation is conveyed in the charming nature and buoyant career of Hubert Hervey, of the British South African Chartered Company, as rendered by his fellow-adventurer, Earl Grey. In his career we have Imperialism at its best in action, and what is better for our purpose, a most ingenuous and instructive attempt to set forth the gist of the imperialist philosophy.

"Probably every one would agree that an Englishman would be right in considering his way of looking at the world and at life better than that of the Maori or Hottentot, and no one will object in the abstract to England doing her best to impose her better and higher view on those savages. But the same idea will carry you much farther. In so far as an Englishman differs in essentials from a Swede or Belgian, he believes that he represents a more perfectly developed standard of general excellence. Yes, and even those nations nearest to us in mind and sentiment—German and Scandinavian—we regard on the whole as not so excellent as ourselves, comparing their typical characteristics with ours. Were this not so, our energies would be directed to becoming what they are. Without doing this, however, we may well endeavour to pick out their best qualities ¡and add them to ours, believing that our compound will be superior to the foreign stock.

"It is the mark of an independent nation that it should feel thus. How far such a feeling is, in any particular case, justified, history alone decides. But it is essential that each claimant for the first place should put forward his whole energy to prove his right. This is the moral justification for international strife and for war, and a great change must come over the world and over men's minds before there can be any question of everlasting universal peace, or the settlement of all international differences by arbitration. More especially must the difficulty caused by the absence of a generally recognised standard of justice be felt in the case of contact between civilised and uncivilised races. Is there any likelihood of the gulf between the white and the black man being bridged within any period of time that we can foresee ? Can there be any doubt that the white man must, and will, impose his superior civilisation on the coloured races ? The rivalry of the principal European countries in extending their influence over other continents should lead naturally to the evolution of the highest attainable type of government of subject races by the superior qualities of their rulers." [1]

Here is the undiluted gospel of Imperialism, the fact of physical struggle between white races, the fact of white subjugation of lower races, the necessity based upon these facts, the utility based upon the necessity, and the right or duty upon the utility. As a revelation of the purer spirit of Imperialism it is not to be bettered. The Englishman believes he is a more excellent type than any other man; he believes that he is better able to assimilate any special virtues others may have; he believes that this character gives him a right to rule which no other can possess. Mr. Hervey admits that the patriotic Frenchman, the German, the Russian feels in the same way his sense of superiority and the rights it confers on him; so much the better

---

[1] "Memoir of Hubert Hervey," by Earl Grey (Arnold, 1899).

(and here he is in line with Professor Pearson), for this cross-conviction and these cross-interests intensify the struggle of white races, and ensure the survival and progressive fitness of the fittest.

So long as we regard this Imperialism exclusively from the standpoint of the English, or any other single nation, its full *rationale* escapes us. It is essential to the maintenance of the struggle of nations, which is to quicken vigour and select the fittest or most efficient, that each competitor shall be stimulated to put forth his fullest effort by the same feelings regarding the superiority, the destiny, the rights and imperial duties of his country as the English imperialist entertains regarding England. And this is just what we seem to find.

The Englishman is genuinely confident in the superior fitness of England for any work she may essay in the civilisation of the world. This is the supreme principle of the imperialist statesmen, so well expressed in Lord Rosebery's description of the British Empire as "the greatest secular agency for good the world has ever seen," and in Mr. Chamberlain's conviction[1] that "the Anglo-Saxon race is infallibly destined to be the predominant force in the history and civilisation of the world." Of the superior competence of Englishmen for all purposes of government, quite irrespective of climatic, racial, or any other conditions, there is no touch of doubt in the average man. "Why, I suppose you imagine we could undertake to govern France better than Frenchmen can govern her?" I heard put as an ironical poser in a discussion on British capacity. The triumphant retort, "Why, of course I do," was no rhetorical paradox, but a perfectly genuine expression of the real conviction of most Englishmen.

[1] "Foreign and Colonial Speeches," p. 6.

Now, the French Chauvinist, the German colonialist, the Russian Pan-Slavist, the new American expansionist, entertain the same general conviction, with the same intensity, regarding the capacity, the destiny, the rights of their own nation. These feelings have, perhaps, come more clearly into the forefront of our national conscious- ness than in the case of any other nation, but events are rapidly educating the same imperial aspirations in all our chief industrial and political competitors.

"In our own day Victor Hugo declares France 'the saviour of nations,' and bursts out, 'Non, France, l'univers a besoin que tu vives! Je le redis, la France est un besoin des hommes.' Villari, echoing the illus- trious Gioberti, claims for Italy the primacy among nations. The Kaiser tells his people, 'Der alte gute Gott has always been on our side.' M. Podyedonostseff points to the freedom of Russia from the shibboleths of a decadent civilisation, and looks to the young and vigorous Slavonic stock as the residuary legatee of the treasures and conquests of the past. The Americans are not less confident than in the days of Martin Chuzzlewit that it is their mission to 'run this globe.'"[1]

Nor are these barren sentiments; in various parts of the world they are inspiring young soldiers, politicians, and missionaries to a practical direction of the resources of France, Germany, Italy, Russia, the United States towards territorial expansion.

We are now in a position to restate and test the scientific basis of Imperialism regarded as a world-policy. The maintenance of a military and industrial struggle for life and wealth among nations is desirable in order to quicken the vigour and social efficiency of the several competitors, and so to furnish a natural process of

[1] G. P. Gooch in "The Heart of the Empire," p. 333.

selection, which shall give an ever larger and intenser control over the government and the economic exploitation of the world into the hands of the nation or nations representing the highest standard of civilisation or social efficiency, and by the elimination or subjugation of the inefficient shall raise the standard of the government of humanity.

This statement withdraws the issue from the purely national, political, and from the distinctively ethical standpoints, referring it back to its scientific basis in the laws or analogies of biology.

Here we can profitably start from a statement of Professor K. Pearson. " History shows me one way, and one way only, in which a high state of civilisation has been produced, namely, the struggle of race with race, and the survival of the physically and mentally fitter race. If men want to know whether the lower races of man can evolve a higher type, I fear the only course is to leave them to fight it out among themselves, and even then the struggle for existence between individual and individual, between tribe and tribe, may not be supported by that physical selection due to a particular element, on which, probably, so much of the Aryans' success depended."

Now, assuming that this is a true account of the evolution of civilisation during the past, is it essential that the same methods of selection must dominate the future? or are there any forces which have been coming into play during the later periods of human history that deeply modify, suspend, and even reverse the operations of selective forces that dominate the rest of nature?

In the very work from which I quote, Professor Pearson furnishes a complete answer to his own contention for the necessity of this physical struggle between races.

In the last sentence of the passage given above, he seems to recognise the utility in lower races of the physical struggle for life between "individuals" in the same tribe. But his general position as a "socialist" is very different. In order that a tribe, a nation, or other society may be able to compete successfully with another society, the individual struggle for life within the society itself must be suspended. The competitive vigour, the social efficiency, of the nation requires a saving of the friction of individual competition for life or for the means of life. Now this is in itself a reversal of the generally recognised law of progress throughout the animal world, in which the struggle for food and other livelihood is held to be essential to the progress of the species, and this though every species is engaged in more or less direct competition for food, &c., with other species. Co-operation, social solidarity, is indeed recognised as an adjunct of progress in many of the higher species, but the struggle between individuals for a restricted supply of food or other necessaries is maintained as a leading instrument of progress by rejection of the physically unfit.

Now Professor Pearson justly recognises and boldly admits the danger which attends the humanitarianism that has in large measure suspended the "struggle for life" among individuals, and has incited modern civilised nations to secure for all individuals born in its midst the food, shelter, and other necessaries enabling them to grow to maturity and to propagate their kind.

He sees quite clearly that this mere suspension of the individual struggle for life not only is not essential to the solidarity and efficiency of the nation, but that it impairs those virtues by burdening society with a horde of physical and moral weaklings, who would have been eliminated under earlier forms of the struggle for life. He rightly enforces the doctrine that a nation which is reproduced from its bad stock more than from its better stock is doomed to deterioration of physique and morale. It is as essential to the progress of man as to that of any other animal, as essential in the future as in the past, that reproduction shall be from the better stock and that the worst stock shall be eliminated. Humanitarianism and the sense of social solidarity by no means recognise, or even admit, that this condition should be sacrificed; they merely impose new methods on the process of selection.

Irrational nature selects wastefully and with the maximum of pain and misery, requiring innumerable individuals to be born in order that they may struggle and perish. Rational humanity would economise and humanise the struggle by substituting a rational, social test of parenthood for the destruction of children by starvation, disease, or weakness.

To prevent reproduction from bad stock, however difficult and dangerous it may be, is obviously the first duty of an organised society, acting alike in its own self-defence and for the interests of its individual members. It is not necessary for the safety and progress of society that "unfit" children should die, it is necessary that they should not be born, and ultimately the society which prospers most in the character of its members will be the one which best fulfils this preventive duty.

Yet, when Professor Pearson passes from a society of individuals to the society of nations, which we call humanity, he insists upon retaining the older, cruder, irrational method of securing progress, the primitive struggle for physical existence. Why? If it is profitable and consistent with progress to put down the primitive struggle for life among individuals with one another, the family and tribal feuds which survive even in fairly developed societies, and to enlarge the area of social internal peace until it covers a whole nation, may we not go farther and seek, with hope, to substitute international peace and co-operation, first among the more civilised and more nearly related nations, and finally throughout the complete society of the human race? If progress is helped by substituting rational selection for the struggle for life within small groups, and afterwards within the larger national groups, why may we not extend the same mode of progress to a federation of European States, and finally to a world-federation? I am not now concerned with the grave practical difficulties besetting such an achievement, but with the scientific theory.

Although a certain sort of individual efficiency is sacrificed by repressing private war within a tribe or nation, it is rightly judged that the gain in tribal or national unity and efficiency outweighs that loss. May not a similar biological and rational economy be subserved by substituting government for anarchy among nations? We admit that a nation is strengthened by putting down internecine tribal warfare; what finality attaches to the arbitrary social group we term a "nation" which obliges us to reverse the economy applicable to tribes when we come to deal with nations?

Two objections are raised against this idea of internationalism. One is historical in its nature; it consists in a denial that a society of nations does or can exist at the present time or in any future which concerns us. The physical and psychical relations which exist between nations, it is urged, have no real analogy with those existing between individuals or tribes within a nation. Society is dependent on a certain homogeneity of character, interests, and sympathies of those who form it. In the ancient world this was seldom found of sufficient strength save among close neighbours, and the city-state was the true social type: the actual and positive relations of these city-states with one another were commonly those of war, modified by transitory compacts, which rarely led them into any truly national unity. In such a condition close-welded co-operation of citizens was essential as a condition of civic survival and progress, and a struggle for life between the several city-states was a means of progress in accordance with the biological law. The nation-state stands now where the city-state stood in ancient Greece or mediæval Italy; there remains the same historical and even ethical necessity to retain the struggle between nations now as to retain the inter-civic struggle in earlier times.

Social psychologists attempt to fortify this position by laying emphasis upon the prime psychical condition of a national life. The possible area of a genuine society, a nation, is determined by the extension of a " consciousness of kind," an "ethical like-mindedness."[1] This may be applied as a limiting condition by a " little Englander " or as an expansive principle to justify imperial expansion, according to the quantity and quality of like-mindedness taken as the basis of social unity in a "nation" or an "empire." The most precise statement of this doctrine in its application as a barrier to ethical and political internationalism is that of Dr. Bosanquet. " The nation-state is the widest organisation which has the common experience necessary to found a common life."[2] He

[1] Professor Giddings, "Empire and Democracy," pp. 10, 51.
[2] "The Philosophical Theory of the State," p. 320.

carries the finality of the national type of society so far
as virtually to repudiate the ethical fact and the utility
of the conception of humanity. "According to the
current ideas of our civilisation, a great part of the lives
which are being lived and have been lived by mankind
are not lives worth living, in the sense of embodying
qualities for which life seems valuable to us. This being
so, it seems to follow that *the object of our ethical idea of
humanity is not really mankind as a single community.*
Putting aside the impossibilities arising from succession
in time, we see that no such identical experience can be
pre-supposed in all mankind as is necessary to effective
membership of a common society and exercise of a
general will."[1] Though a subtle qualification follows,
based on the duty of States to recognise humanity, not
as a fact but as a type of life, "and in accordance with it
to recognise and deal with the rights of alien individuals
and communities," the real upshot of this line of thought
is to emphasise the ethical self-sufficiency of a nation and
to deny the validity of any practical standard of the
conduct of nations towards one another, at any rate so
far as the relations between higher and lower, or Eastern
and Western, nations are concerned.

This view is stoutly supported by some sociologists
and statesmen from the juridical standpoint. There can,
we are told, be no real "rights" of nations because there
exists no "sanction," no recognised tribunal to define and
enforce rights. The legal rigour of this position I am
not greatly concerned to question. It may here suffice
to say that the maintenance under ordinary conditions
of treaty relations, international credit and exchange, a
common postal, and within narrower limits, a common
railway system, not to mention the actual machinery of

[1] *Op. cit.*, p. 329.

conventions and conferences for concerted international action, and the whole unwritten law of war and international courtesies, embassies, consulates, and the like—all these things rest upon a basis of recognition of certain reciprocal duties, the neglect or violation of which would be punished by forfeiture of most favoured nations' treatment in the future, and by the reprobation and the possibly combined intervention of other States.

III

We have here at least a real beginning of effective international federation, with the rudiments of legal sanction for the establishment and enforcement of rights.

The studied ignoring of those vital facts in the more recent statecraft, and the reversion, alike of legal theorists and high politicians of the Bismarck school, to a nationalism which emphasises the exclusive rather than the inclusive aspect of patriotism and assumes the antagonism of nations as an all-important and a final fact, form the most dangerous and discreditable factor of modern politics. This conduct in politics we have already in part explained in our analysis of the economic driving forces that exhibit certain sectional interests and orders within the nation usurping the national will and enforcing their private advantages, which rest upon international antagonism, to the detriment of the national advantage, which is identical with that of other nations.

This obstinate halt in the evolution of such relations at the limit of political nationality now reached will be recognised as the most difficult of all present political phenomena for the future historian to explain. The

M

community of interests between nations is so great, so
multifarious, and so obvious, the waste, pain, and damage
of conflicts so gross and palpable, that to those who do
not understand the strong sectional control in every
modern State it may well appear that some natural barriers
of race, boundaries, or colour make any real extension of
" society " outside the area of nationality impossible.

But to ascribe finality to nationalism upon the
ground that members of different nations lack " the
common experience necessary to found a common life "
is a very arbitrary reading of modern history. Taking
the most inward meaning of experience, which gives
most importance to the racial and traditional characters that mark the divergences of nationality, we
are obliged to admit that the fund of experience
common to peoples of different nationality is growing
with great rapidity under the numerous, swift, and
accurate modes of intercommunication which mark
the latest phases of civilisation. It is surely true
that the dwellers of large towns in all the most advanced European States, an ever-growing proportion of
the total population, have, not merely in the externals
of their lives, but in the chief formative influences
of their reading, their art, science, recreation, a larger
community of experience than existed a century ago
among the more distant members of any single
European nation, whether dwelling in country or in
town. Direct intercommunication of persons, goods,
and information is so widely extended and so rapidly
advancing that this growth of " the common experience
necessary to found a common life " beyond the area
of nationality is surely the most markworthy feature
of the age. Making, then, every due allowance for
the subjective factors of national character which

temper or transmute the same external phenomena, there surely exists, at any rate among the more conscious and more educated sections of the chief European nations, a degree of true "like-mindedness," which forms the psychical basis of some rudimentary internationalism in the field of politics. Indeed it is curious and instructive to observe that while some of those most insistent upon "like-mindedness" and "common experience," as the tests of a true social area, apply them in defence of existing nationalities and in repudiation of attempts to absorb alien nationalities, others, like Professor Giddings, apply them in the advocacy of expansion and Imperialism.

Surely there is a third alternative to the policy of national independence on the one hand, and of the right of conquest by which the more efficient nation absorbs the less efficient nation on the other, the alternative of experimental and progressive federation, which, proceeding on the line of greatest common experience, shall weave formal bonds of political attachment between the most "like-minded" nations, extending them to others as common experience grows wider, until an effective political federation is established, comprising the whole of "the civilised world," *i.e.* all those nations which have attained a considerable fund of that "common experience" comprised under the head of civilisation.

This idea does not conflict with the preservation of what is really essential and valuable in nationalism, nor does it imply a suspension or abolition of any form of struggle by which the true character of a nation may express itself, in industry, in politics, in art or literature.

If it be objected that the requisite amount of "like-mindedness" or "common experience" does not exist

even among the nations most subjected to modern as-
similative influences, that the forces of racial and national
antagonism even there preclude any truly effective union,
I can only repeat that this is a matter for experiment
and that the experiment has never been tried. Racial
and national antagonisms have been so fed, fostered, and
inflamed, for the class and personal ends and interests
which have controlled politics, that the deeper underlying
sympathies and community of different peoples have
never been permitted free expression, much less political
assertion. The most potent and pervasive forces in the
industrial, intellectual, and moral life of most European
races, so far as the masses of the peoples are concerned,
have so rapidly and closely assimilated during the last
century as of necessity to furnish a large common body
of thought and feeling, interests and aspirations which
furnish a "soul" for internationalism.

The main economic conditions affecting the working
life of the masses of the peoples, both in town and
country, on the one hand, the matter and methods of
education through the school, the church, the press
upon the other, show features of similarity so much
stronger and more numerous than those of difference as
to make it a safe assertion that the "peoples" of Europe
are far closer akin in actual interests than their governments, and that this common bond is already so
strong as to furnish a solid and stable foundation for
political federal institutions, if only the obstruction of
class governments could be broken down and the real
will of the peoples set in the seat of authority. To
take the commonest of concrete instances, it is at least
probable that the body of the workers in different
countries who fight and pay for wars would refuse to
fight and pay in the future if they were allowed to

understand the real nature of the issues used to inflame them.

If this view is correct, the mere facts that wars still occur and that national animosities are continually flaring up must not be taken as proof that sufficient common sympathy and experience does not exist between the different nations to render impossible a suspension of physical conflict and the establishment of a political machinery required to maintain peace.

To hold this position it is not necessary to exaggerate the extent of this international community of interests. If any considerable amount of real community exists, it furnishes the spirit which should and might inform a body of political institutions. Here is the significance of the recent Hague Conference, alike in its success and its failure. Its success, the mere fact that it was held and the permanent nucleus of internationalism it created, attests a real and felt identity of interests among different nations in the maintenance of peace; its failure and the open derision expressed by many politicians merely indicate the presence in high places of cliques and classes opposed in their interests and feelings to those of the peoples, and the necessity of dethroning these enemies of the people if the new cause of internationalism is to advance. Secure popular government, in substance and in form, and you secure internationalism: retain class government, and you retain military Imperialism and international conflicts.

IV

In following out the psychical argument against regarding nations as final social areas, I seem to have wandered very far from the biological basis, the alleged necessity of maintaining conflicts between nations for

purposes of "natural selection." In reality I have come
round precisely to the point of divergence. Assuming
it were possible to enthrone the will of the peoples and
so to secure institutions of internationalism with a
suspension of war, would the individuality of a nation
suffer, would it lose vigour, become less efficient and
perish? Is the maintenance of physical conflict essential
to the "natural selection" of nations?

Turn to the suspension of the cruder physical
struggle which takes place in the evolution of tribal
or national solidarity. As such national organisation
becomes stronger and more skilful the ravages of intestine strife, starvation, and certain diseases cease to
be selective instruments, and the kind of individual
fitness which was tested by them is superseded; the vast
expenditure of individual energy formerly engaged in
protecting life and in securing necessaries of life is
reduced to insignificant dimensions; but the struggle
for individual life is not abated, it is simply shifted on
to higher planes than that of bare animal existence,
nourishment, and propagation. Instead of struggling
for these simpler vital ends, individuals now struggle
with all the extra energy spared from the earlier struggles
for other ends of an enlarged and more complex life,
for comfort and wealth, for place and personal honour,
for skill, knowledge, character, and even higher forms
of self-expression, and for services to their fellow-men,
with whom they have identified themselves in that expanded individuality we term altruism or public spirit.

Individuality does not suffer but greatly gains by
the suppression of the lower struggle; there is more
energy, greater scope for its expression, a wider field
of close competitors; and higher and more varied forms
of fitness are tested and evoked. It is not even true

that the struggle ceases to be physical; the strain and the support of the higher forms of struggle, even in the topmost intellectual and moral planes, are largely physical; the health and nervous energy which take part in the struggles of the law or literature or on any intellectual arena are chief requisites if not the supreme determinant of success. In all the higher forms of struggle an elimination of the physically unfit is still maintained, though the criteria of physical unfitness are not quite the same as in the primitive human struggles. How arbitrary are the convenient distinctions between physical, intellectual, and moral qualities and defects is nowise better illustrated than in the elaborate methods which modern complex civilisation evolves for the detection, degradation, and final extinction of bad stock whose "degeneracy" is attested not less by physical than by mental and moral stigmata. The struggle for physical fitness never flags, but the physical forms part of a higher and more complex test of character determined by a higher standard of social utility. The point is this: national government, or State socialism, using the term in its broad sense, as a coercive and educative force, does not, in so far as it is wisely exercised, diminish the individual struggle, repress individual vigour, reduce the arena for its display. It does just the opposite; it quickens and varies the struggle; by equalising certain opportunities it keeps a fairer ring, from which chance or other factors alien to personal fitness are excluded; it admits on more equal terms a larger number of competitors, and so furnishes a better test of fitness and a more reliable selection of the fittest.

Professor Pearson rightly urges that truly enlightened national government will insist on mending the slow

painful, and irregular elimination of bad stock which
goes on through progressive degeneracy by substituting
some rational control of parentage, at least to the extent
of preventing through public education, or if necessary by
law, the propagation of certain surely recognised unfit-
nesses.

Does a nation thus firmly planted in rational self-
government, with individual competition within its ranks
conducted most keenly upon a wide variety of different
fields, furnishing the keenest incentive to the education
and display of every kind of personal originality, really
require a maintenance of the crude form of physical
struggle with other nations in order to maintain its
character and progress? If individuality does not disappear with the removal of the cruder struggle for life
within the nation, why should the valid force of nationality disappear if a corresponding change takes place
in the nature of international conflict?

Biology furnishes no reason for believing that the
competition among nations must always remain a crude
physical struggle, and that the substitution of "rational"
for "natural" selection among individual members of a
nation cannot be extended to the selection of nations
and of races.

V

The history of past nations indeed gives an appearance of natural necessity to imperial expansion and to the
military policy which is its instrument, and many who
deplore this necessity accept it. A recent American
writer in a brilliant monograph[1] argues the perpetual
necessity of wars of conquest and of the Imperialism

[1] "War and Economics," by Professor E. van Dyke Robinson,
Political Science Quarterly, Dec. 1900.

which such wars express, as following from "the law of decreasing returns." A population on a limited area of land not only tends to grow but actually grows faster than the food supply that is available; improvement in the arts of cultivation does not enable a people to obtain full subsistence for its growing population, hence a natural and necessary pressure for access to new rich land, and conflicts with and victories over neighbours who seek to hold their own, or are even actuated by the same needs of territorial expansion. Hunger is a necessary spur to migration, and where emigrants, planting themselves successfully upon new fertile lands, formerly unoccupied or occupied by people whom they have subjugated, desire to retain the political union with the mother country, an unlimited expansion of national areas ensues. Whether such expansion takes shape in genuine colonisation or in what is here properly distinguished as Imperialism, involving centralised government and forcible control of "inferior races," matters little to this wide argument. The essence of this policy is the acquisition of an expanding area for food supply. A nation with growing population must either send a constant flow of population into other lands to grow food for themselves, or, failing this, it must produce at home an ever-growing surplus of manufactures which evade the law of decreasing returns and find markets for them, so as to obtain payment in food from foreign lands, which, in their turn, are thus forced more quickly to experience the pinch of the same natural law. As more nations pursue this course they either realise directly the pressure of the law driving them to find new lands for their surplus population, or they find themselves embroiled in an ever fiercer competition with rival manufacturing nations seeking a share in an over-stocked or too slowly expanding market for manufactures. Imperialism lies in both directions, and cannot be avoided. "The cause of war is as permanent as hunger itself, since both spring from the same source, the law of diminishing returns. So long as that persists, war must remain, in the last analysis, a national business undertaking, designed to procure or preserve foreign markets, that is, the means of continued growth and prosperity. 'Chacun doit grandir ou mourir.'"[1]

Now the finality of this alleged necessity has often been subjected to incidental criticism, so far as Great Britain is concerned. Imperialism, it has been shown, is not in fact necessitated in order to obtain by trade an increased food supply which should keep pace with the growth of British population, nor has it chiefly been engaged in forwarding such trade; still less is it engaged in finding land upon which our surplus population may subsist and multiply.

But the validity of the whole argument from natural history is contestable. As man grows in civilisation, i.e. in the art of applying reason to the adjustment of his relations with his physical and social environment, he obtains a corresponding power to extricate himself from the necessity which dominates the lower animal world. He can avoid the necessity of war and expansion in two ways, by a progressive mitigation of the law of diminishing returns in agriculture and the extractive arts, and by limiting the rate of growth of population. The tendency of rational civilisation is to employ both methods. It may fairly be maintained that reason is educated in individual men, and is applied to further a co-operative policy, chiefly by acts of choice which are directed to avoid the hardships and perils of war and the expansive practices. In animal life, and in man just so far as he resembles

---

[1] Robinson, *Political Science Quarterly*, p. 622.

other animals, war and extension of territory form the only means of providing for a growth of population which is determined by a mere interaction of sexual instincts and physical conditions of environment. But from very early times this dominion of irrational forces, which finds direct expression in "the law of diminishing returns," is qualified by two sets of checks. On the one hand, improvements in agriculture and the beginnings of trade increase the quantity of human life which a given piece of land is able to support; on the other, customs relating to marriage and maintenance of children, often of a degraded character, such as exposure or infanticide, are added to the "natural" checks upon increase of population. Both forces represent the crude beginnings of "reason" or conscious human policy in its struggle to overcome the play of the non-rational forces of nature. Throughout history, so far as it is known, these rational forces have been so slow and feeble in their application as only to moderate or postpone the operation of "the law of decreasing returns." But this need not always continue to be the case. There is some ground to believe that both sets of rational checks may in the future be amply adequate to suspend or overcome the limitations of matter so far as the food supply of a nation on a given area is concerned. Progress in agriculture even of the most progressive nations of the past was very slow: modern science, which has achieved such marvels in revolutionising the manufacturing and transport industries, is beginning more and more to concentrate its power on agriculture in such wise that the pace of progress in this art may be vastly accelerated. When the sciences of agricultural chemistry and botany are adequately reinforced by mechanics, scientific method being duly guided and enriched by garnering the empirical

wisdom of great agricultural races whose whole practical
genius has been centred for countless ages on minute cultivation, like the Chinese, and when to such improved
knowledge of agricultural arts is added a perfection of
co-operative labour for those processes where this yields
a true economy, the possibilities of intensive cultivation
are virtually unlimited.   These new conditions of a
national policy of agriculture are themselves so important
as to make it easily conceivable that a nation keenly set
upon utilising them might for a long time to come
reverse the operation of " the law of diminishing returns,"
extracting from its own proper lands an increasing stock
of food to meet its " natural " growth of population without a more than proportionate increase of labour engaged
in agriculture.   In face of recent experiments in intensive
and scientific agriculture and the practical substitution of
skilled gardening for unskilled farming, it is impossible
to deny that such a triumph of the laws of mind over the
laws of matter is probable in the most highly intelligent
peoples.   There are already manifested throughout Great
Britain certain signs of such a set towards agriculture as
took place in England during the middle of the eighteenth
century, and led then to relatively great improvements
in crop growing and stock breeding.   If a brief fashion
and sportive interest on the part of a small well-to-do
class could then produce what is not wrongly described
as an " agricultural revolution," what might not be
achieved now by vastly greater numbers, capital, and intelligence directed in a public policy and wielding the
accumulated knowledge of modern science ?   Many causes
consciously contribute towards such a brilliant revival of
British agriculture.   The growing sense of the hygienic
and military perils which attend a nation of town dwellers,
whose powers of forcible resistance are impaired in just

proportion as their dependence upon precarious foreign supplies of food increases, is driving the issue of restoring a people to the land into the forefront of politics. Modern scientific transport, hitherto centripetal in its main economy, now seems to tend more to become centrifugal, while the wider spread of culture does something, and may do much, to cause a moral and æsthetic revolt against the life and work of towns. A careful and drastic system of land reform which should aim at the net economy of individual enterprise and co-operative aid for agriculture is of course in Great Britain a prior condition to all rapid and effective progress. All these conditions are within the power of man, and belong to rational policy; once secured, it is at least probable that private incentives to gain, bringing brain and capital to bear upon the land, might in this or any other industrial country produce so vast an increase of the productiveness of the soil as to destroy completely all speciousness which history attaches to the necessity of expansion for purposes of food supply.

It is not necessary here to discuss the part played respectively by public policy and private initiative in the development of this economy of intensive cultivation. It is sufficient to insist that it furnishes the larger half of a complete answer to the alleged natural necessity of expansion. The other half has reference to a rational control of the growth of population, which must in any sound national economy tend more and more to replace the wasteful and cruel prodigality which nature unchecked by reason here as elsewhere displays. However difficult it may be, rational control of the quantity and quality of population is quite essential to the physical and moral progress of a species which has striven successfully to suspend or stay the cruel and wasteful checks which disease, famine, pestilence, internecine warfare, and early savage usages employed in the struggle for existence. To stay the "natural" checks, and to refuse to substitute "rational" checks, is to promote not merely the unrestricted growth of population, but the survival and multiplication of the physically and morally unfit, the least effective portion of the population, which is able to be born, reared, and to propagate its kind. How far the operation of the great public policy of preventing the propagation of certain definite forms of unfitness can best be left to the free play of individual interest and discretion, illuminated by the growing knowledge of biological science, or how far such private determination must be reinforced by public pressure, is a matter with which we need not here concern ourselves. But there is every reason to believe that both quantitative and qualitative checks upon the "natural" growth of population are already operative in modern civilised communities, that they are already appreciably affecting the general growth of population, and that their operation is likely to continue in the future. With the spread of biological and moral education the methods of moderating the growth of population may be expected to come more truly "rational," and in particular the increasing economic liberty and enlightenment of women will contribute to the efficacy of this reasonable self-restraint. This second check upon the false necessity assigned to the law of decreasing returns is not unrelated to the first. It is in fact its true complement. Taken by itself the improvement in methods of obtaining food might not suffice to do more than to postpone or hold in check for a period the law of limitation of the food supply obtainable from a national area. But if the same forces of human reason which substitute intensive for extensive cultivation of the soil are at work imposing the same substitution in the cultivation of the species, checking the merely quantitative increase in order to secure a higher quality of individuation, this mutual reinforcement may secure the triumph of rational policy over the untamed forces of natural history.

I have laboured this issue at some length because it is required in order to bring home the distinctively rational character of that choice of national life against which Imperialism sins so fatally. There is no natural necessity for a civilised nation to expand the area of its territory, in order either to increase its production of food and other forms of material wealth, or to find markets for its increased products. Progress, alike for the nation and for the individual, consists in substituting everywhere an intensive or qualitative for an extensive or quantitative economy. The low-skilled farmer is given to spread his capital and labour over a large area of poorly cultivated land, wherever a large quantity of free or cheap land is available; the skilled, competent farmer obtains a larger net return by concentrating his productive power upon a smaller area scientifically cultivated, recognising that the best use of his productive resources imposes a limit to the size of his farm. So with the economy of national resources—the craving and the necessity of expansion are signs of barbarism; as civilisation advances and industrial methods become more highly skilled and better differentiated, the need for expansion of territory is weakened, the progress of the nation concerns itself more and more with the intensive or qualitative development of its national resources. Size of territory can never be eliminated as a condition of progress, but it becomes relatively less important with each step from barbarism to civilisation, and the idea of indefinite expansion as necessary or good is opposed to reason and sane policy. This was recognised by the most profound of ancient thinkers. "There is," wrote Aristotle, "a certain degree of greatness fit for States as for all other things, living creatures, plants, instruments, for each has its proper virtue and faculty, when neither very little nor yet excessively great."[1] That the tendency has ever been to excess is the commonplace of history. The true greatness of nations has been educated by the concentrated skill in the detailed development of limited national resources which the contracted area of the State has developed in them. "It is to the burning vitality of compact, independent nations, the strong heart in the small body, to Judæa and to Athens, to Rome the republic, to the free cities of Italy, Germany, and Flanders, to France, to Holland, and to England the island, that we owe the highest achievements in the things that make life most worth living."[2]

If imperial expansion were really nothing other than a phase of the natural history of a nation it would be as idle to protest against it as to argue with an earthquake. But the policy of civilised States differs from that of un-civilised States in resting more largely upon deliberate conscious choice, partaking more definitely of the character of conduct. The same growth of collective reason which makes it technically possible for a nation to subsist and prosper by substituting an intensive for an extensive economy of national resources enables it by deliberate exercise of will to resist the will of the older "destiny" by which nations attaining a certain degree of development were led by a debilitating course of Imperialism to final collapse.

[1] "Politics," vii. 4.
[2] *Imperium et Libertas*, by Bernard Holland, p. 12.

VI

Thus met, the biological argument is sometimes turned on to another track.

" If these nations," it is argued, " are no longer called upon to struggle for food, and check their growth of population while they increase their control over their material supplies, they will become effete for purposes of physical struggle; giving way to an easy and luxurious life, they will be attacked by lower races multiplying freely and maintaining their military vigour, and will succumb in the conflict." This is the danger indicated by Mr. C. H. Pearson in his interesting book " National Life and Character."

The whole argument, however, rests on a series of illusions regarding actual facts and tendencies.

It is not true that the sole object and result of the stoppage of individual warfare has been to increase the efficiency of the nation for the physical struggle with other nations. As man has grown from barbarism towards civilisation, the struggle to adapt his material and social environment to purposes of better livelihood and life has continuously tended to replace the physical struggle for the land and food supply of other nations. This is precisely the triumph of intensive over extensive cultivation: it implies a growing disposition to put that energy which formerly went to war into the arts of industry, and a growing success in the achievement. It is the need of peaceful, steady, orderly co-operation for this work, as the alternative to war, and not the needs of war itself, that furnishes the prime motive towards a suspension of internecine struggles, at any rate in most societies. This is a matter of pivotal importance in

N

understanding social evolution. If the sole or main purpose of suspending individual conflict was to strengthen the purely military power of a tribe or nation, and the further evolution of society aimed at this sort of social efficiency, it might well be attended by the decay of individual freedom and initiative, by the sacrifice of individuality to a national life. The fact that this result has not occurred, that in modern civilised nations there exists far more individual freedom, energy, and initiative than in more primitive societies, attests the truth that military efficiency was not the first and sole object of social organisation. In other words, the tendency of growing civilisation on the national scale has been more and more to divert the struggle for life from a struggle with other nations to a struggle with environment, and so to utilise the fruits of reason as to divert a larger and larger proportion of energy to struggles for intellectual, moral, and æsthetic goods rather than for goods which tax the powers of the earth, and which, conforming to the law of diminishing returns, are apt to bring them into conflict with other nations.

As nations advance towards civilisation it becomes less needful for them to contend with one another for land and food to support their increasing numbers, because their increased control of the industrial arts enables them to gain what they want by conquering nature instead of conquering their fellow-men.

This truth does not indeed disclose itself readily with its full brilliancy to the eyes of modern civilised peoples, whose greed for foreign wealth and foreign lands seems as fruitful a source of war as in more primitive times. The illusion that it is necessary and advantageous to fight for new territory and distant markets, while leaving most imperfectly developed the land and markets of

their own nation, is slow to be dispelled. Its sources
have been already explored ; it has been traced to the
dominance of class interests in national politics. Democracy alone, if it be attainable, will serve to fasten on the
national mind the full economy of substituting the inner
struggle with the natural environment for the outer
struggle with other nations.

If, as seems possible, the civilised white nations,
gradually throwing off the yoke of class governments
whose interests make for war and territorial expansion,
restrict their increase of population by preventing reproduction from bad stock, while they devote their energies
to utilising their natural resources, the motives of international conflict will wane, and the sympathetic motives
of commerce and friendly intercourse will maintain permanent peace on a basis of international union.

Such a national economy would not only destroy the
chief motives of war, it would profoundly modify the
industrial struggle in which governments engage. Democracies chiefly concerned with developing their own
markets would not need to spend men and money in
fighting for the chance of inferior and less stable foreign
markets. Such rivalry as was retained would be the
rivalry not of nations but of individual manufacturers
and merchants within the nation ; the national aspect
of industrial warfare, by tariffs and bounties and commercial treaties, would disappear. For the dangers and
hostilities of national commercial policies are due, as
we have seen, almost entirely to the usurpation of the
authority and political resources of the nations by
certain commercial and financial interests. Depose these
interests, and the deep, true, underlying harmonies of
interest between peoples, which the prophets of Free
Trade dimly perceived, will manifest themselves, and

the necessity of permanent industrial warfare between
nations will be recognised as an illusion analogous in
nature and origin to the illusion of the biological
necessity of war.

The struggle for life is indeed a permanent factor
in social progress, selection of the physically fit is a
necessity, but as men become more rational they rationalise the struggle, substituting preventive for destructive
methods of selection, and raising the standard of fitness
from a crudely physical robustness to one which main-
tains physical endurance as the raw material of higher
psychical activities. Thus, while men no longer fight
for food, their personal fitness is maintained, the struggle
and the fitness are both raised to a higher plane. If this
can take place in the struggle of individuals, it can take
place in the struggle of nations. The economy of internationalism is the same as that of nationalism. As
individuality does not disappear but is raised and
quickened by good national government, so nationality
does not disappear but is raised and quickened by internationalism.

War and commercial tariffs are the crudest and most
wasteful forms of national struggles, testing the lowest
forms of national fitness. Let international government
put down wars and establish Free Trade, the truly vital
struggles of national expression will begin. As in the
case of individuals, so now of nations, the competition
will be keener upon the higher levels; nations having
ceased to compete with guns and tariffs will compete
with feelings and ideas.

Whatever there is of true original power and interest
in the Celtic, the Teutonic, the various blends of Latin
and Slavonic races can only bear its fruit in times of
peace.

So far as nationality or race has any distinct character or value for itself and for the world, that value and character are expressed through work. Hitherto the absorption of so much national energy upon military, and in later times rude industrial occupations, has checked the higher forms of national self-expression; while the permanent hostility of international relations has chilled the higher intercourse and prevented what is really great and characteristic in the national achievements of art, literature, and thought from penetrating other nations, and so by subtle educative processes laying the foundation of true feelings of humanity, based, as such feelings must be, not on vague imaginative sympathy, but upon common experience of life and a common understanding. Peaceful intercourse between nations is thus not merely the condition, but the powerful stimulus of national energy and achievement in the higher arts of life; for the self-appreciation of national pride can never furnish so wholesome an incentive or so sound a criterion of human excellence as the impartial judgment of civilised humanity, no longer warped by baser patriotic prejudices, but testing what is submitted to it by the impartial universal standard of humanity. A few rare individual men of genius in art and literature, a few more in science and in religion, have broken the barriers of nationality and have become fertilising, humanising forces in other nations—such men as Jesus, Buddha, Mahomet, Homer, Shakspere, Plato, Aristotle, Kant, Copernicus, Newton, Darwin. A larger number of great men have exercised some real and abiding influence upon the little world of science and letters which in the middle ages had attained an internationalism lost in the rise of militant nationalism and being slowly rediscovered in our own age.

But outside these conquests of personal genius the broad streams of national influence and achievement which might have fertilised the wide plains of the intellectual world have been confined within their narrow national channels. Nationalism as a restrictive and exclusive force, fostering political and industrial enmities and keeping down the competition of nationalities and races to the low level of military strife, has everywhere checked the free intercourse requisite for the higher kinds of competition, the struggle of languages, literatures, scientific theories, religious, political, and social institutions, and all the arts and crafts which are the highest and most important expressions of national as of individual life.

VII

This thought unearths the lowest root fallacy of the crude biological sociology, the assumption that there is one sort of national efficiency and that it is tested by a contest of military or commercial power. The only meaning that can be given to the "social efficiency" of a nation identifies it with the power it displays of adapting itself to its physical environment and of altering that environment to help the adaptation; the attainments in religion, law, politics, intellectual life, industry, &c., are the expressions of this social efficiency. Bearing this in mind, it is evident that for concrete purposes of comparison there are many kinds of social efficiency, and that the notion that civilisation is a single beaten track, upon which every nation must march, and that social efficiency, or extent of civilisation, can be measured by the respective distances the nations have gone, is a mischievous delusion.

The true social efficiency, or civilisation, of a nation

only shows itself in its more complex achievements and activities. The biologist who understood his science would recognise that a true test of the efficiency of nations demanded that the conflict of nations should take place not by the more primitive forms of fight and the ruder weapons in which nations are less differentiated, but by the higher forms of fight and the more complex intellectual and moral weapons which express the highest degree of national differentiation. This higher struggle, conducted through reason, is none the less a national struggle for existence, because in it ideas and institutions which are worsted die, and not human organisms. The civilisation of the world can only proceed upon the higher planes on condition that this struggle of national ideals and institutions is waged by a free field of competitors, and this struggle cannot be effectively maintained unless the lower military and industrial struggles cease.

Biology always demands as a condition of progress the competition of individuals, but as reason grows in the nation it closes the ring and imposes laws, not to stop the struggle, but to make it a fairer test of a fuller form of individual fitness. Biology demands as a condition of world-progress that the struggle of nations or races continue; but as the world grows more rational it will in similar fashion rationalise the rules of that ring, imposing a fairer test of forms of national fitness.

The notion of the world as a cock-pit of nations in which round after round shall eliminate feebler fighters and leave in the end one nation, the most efficient, to lord it on the dung-hill, has no scientific validity. Invoked to support the claims of militant nationalism, it begins by ignoring the very nature and purposes of national life, assuming that uniformity of character and environment which are the negation of nationalism.

The belief that with the stoppage of war, could it be achieved, national vigour must decay, is based on a complete failure to recognise that the lower form of struggle is stopped for the express purpose and with the necessary result that the higher struggle shall become possible. With the cessation of war, whatever is really vital and valuable in nationality does not perish; on the contrary, it grows and thrives as it could not do before, when the national spirit out of which it grows was absorbed in baser sorts of struggle.

Internationalism is no more opposed to the true purposes of nationalism than socialism within the nation, rightly guided, is hostile to individualism. The problem and its solution are the same. We socialise in order that we may individuate; we cease fighting with bullets in order to fight with ideas.

All the essentials of the biological struggle for life are retained, the incentive to individual vigour, the intensity of the struggle, the elimination of the unfit and the survival of the fittest.

The struggle has become more rational in mode and purpose and result, and reason is only a higher form of nature.

VIII

The shortsightedness of this school of biological sociologists is nowhere more strikingly displayed than by the exclusive attention they pay to the simpler form of struggle, the direct conflict of individuals and species, to the exclusion of the important part played by " crossing " as a means of progress throughout organic life.

The law of the fertility of "crosses" as applied to

civilisation or "social efficiency" alike on the physical and psychical plane requires, as a condition of effective operation, internationalism. It is of course true that throughout history the "crossing" of national types has been largely achieved by means of war, conquest, and subjugation. But this, though subserving progress in the long run, has been a most wasteful, indirect, and unsafe method, the selection being determined by no clear view of the future or of any higher purpose of social efficiency. Just in proportion as internationalism promotes free intercourse between nations for higher purposes of peaceful interest, will blending of races by intermarriage be determined on grounds of affinity more fruitful of improved racial efficiency, and new modifications of species more numerous and more novel will compete with one another as factors in the civilisation of the world, raising the character and intensity of the competition and enhancing the pace of human progress.

Nay, we may carry the biological analogy still farther, following the insistence of Professor Pearson regarding the necessity of bringing direct social pressure, of public opinion or of law, to prevent the fatal process of breeding from "bad stock." If the ordinary processes of physical degeneracy within the nation do not suffice for the elimination of bad stock, but must be supplemented by some direct prohibition of bad parentage, it might be necessary in the interests of humanity that similar measures should be enforced upon the larger scale by the mandates of organised humanity. As lower individuals within a society perish by contact with a civilisation to which they cannot properly assimilate themselves, so "lower races" in some instances disappear by similar contact with higher races whose diseases and physical vices prove too strong for them. A rational stirpiculture in the wider social interest might, however, require a repression of the spread of degenerate or unprogressive races, corresponding to the check which a nation might place upon the propagation from bad individual stock. With the other moral and practical issues involved in such a proposal we need not here concern ourselves; regarded exclusively from a biological standpoint, that course would seem to follow from the application of direct rational rejection of bad stock upon the smaller scale of national life. The importance of this consideration rests upon the fact that this rejection of unsound racial stock implies the existence of an international political organisation which has put down war and has substituted this rational for the cruder national selection and rejection of races.

Whether a nation or a society of nations will ever proceed as far as this, or, going farther, will attempt the fuller art of stirpiculture, encouraging useful "crosses" of families or races, may be matter of grave doubt; but if the maintenance and improvement of the national stock ever warranted such experiments, we are entitled to insist that logic would justify the application of the same rule in the society of nations.

Again, while it is questionable how far the law of the utility of cross-fertilisation is transferable from the world of physical organisms to the psychical realm in its literal bearing, the more general applicability cannot be disputed. That scientific theories, religious, social, and political arts and institutions gain by free, friendly, vital intercourse with other theories, arts, and institutions, undergoing serviceable accretions, excretions, and modifications, is a commonplace of intellectual life. Whether, therefore, we regard the contact of ideas and feelings and the arts they animate as a direct struggle for existence, in which the worse or falser perish and the better and truer survive, or as a friendly intercourse in which each selects and assimilates something from the others, internationalism is as essential to the efficiency of these processes as nationalism itself.

It is only when we realise the true nature of this spread and fertilisation of ideas, arts, and institutions, the riper fruits of the spirit of a nation, that we realise the legitimate as distinguished from the illegitimate expansion, the valid significance of empire. When nations compete to take one another's lives or land or trade, the dominion which the conqueror establishes has no element of permanence; another turn of the military or commercial tide wipes out the victory and leaves scarce a ripple in the sands. But the influence exerted through acts of peace is more lasting, more penetrating, and more glorious. Shakspere, Byron, Darwin, and Stevenson have done incomparably more for the influence of England in the history of the world than all the statesmen and soldiers who have won victories or annexed new provinces. Macaulay has well said it, "There is an empire exempt from all natural sources of decay—that empire is the imperishable empire of our art and our morals, our literature and our law." This antagonism between the extensive empire and the intensive empire is not rhetorical, it is grounded upon biological necessities.

The essential conditions of the lower struggle for the life and land and trade of others preclude the higher and more profitable competition of ideas by which the empire of the national mind is extended: it is not merely the economy of energy which determines that the national vigour cannot at the same time engage effectively in both struggles; but, far more important, the very nature of the lower struggle drives each nationality to feed upon itself in insolent, exclusive pride, inhibiting the receptivity of other nations.

Effective internationalism is the only sound basis of competition and rational selection among nations. In the cruder form of the human struggle, accident, or numbers, or some primitive force or cunning, may secure the success of a people whose "social efficiency" is of a low order, impermanent and unproductive, while it stamps out or checks the growth of a people whose latent powers of achievement and capacities of progress are far superior. Only in proportion as racial or national selection is rationally guided and determined does the world gain security against such wastes and such calamities. An international government alone can furnish adequate protection to weak but valuable nationalities, and can check the insolent brutality of powerful aggressors, preserving that equality of opportunities for national self-expression which is as essential to the commonwealth of nations as to the welfare of the several nations.

Only by raising the crude, fragmentary, informal, often insincere beginnings of international government into a stronger, more coherent, and more complex authority can the struggle for life proceed upon the highest arena of competition, selecting the finest forms of social efficiency.

One further objection to the final efficacy of a federation of civilised nations demands consideration. Suppose a federal government of European nations and their colonial offspring to be possible in such wise that internal conflicts were precluded, this peace of Christendom would be constantly imperilled by the "lower races," black and yellow, who, adopting the arms and military tactics now discarded by the "civilised races," would overwhelm them in barbarian incursions, even as

the ruder European and Asiatic races overwhelmed the
Roman Empire. We cannot get the whole world to the
level of civilisation which will admit it into the alliance;
the Powers outside will be a constant menace, and if the
main purpose of federation is to eliminate militarism
from the economy of national life, the attainment of
this purpose will render effective resistance to such
invaders no longer possible. This has been the universal fate of Empires in the past; what talisman could
this latest federal Empire possess enabling it to escape?
To this objection we may make this preliminary answer.
Two factors in the older Empires have primarily contributed to weaken their powers of resistance against
outside "barbarians," and to strengthen and stimulate
the zeal of the invaders. There is first the habit of
economic parasitism, by which the ruling State has used
its provinces, colonies, and dependencies in order to
enrich its ruling class and to bribe its lower classes
into acquiescence. This bleeding of dependencies, while
it enfeebles and atrophies the energy of the imperial
people, irritates and eventually rouses to rebellion the
more vigorous and less tractable of the subject races;
each repression of rebellion rankles in the blood, and
gradually a force of gathering discontent is roused which
turns against the governing Power.

The second factor, related to the first, consists in
that form of "parasitism" known as employment of mercenary forces. This is the most fatal symptom of imperial infatuation, whereby the oppressor at once deprives
himself of the habit and instruments of effective self-protection and hands them over to the most capable and
energetic of his enemies.

This fatal conjunction of folly and vice has always
contributed to bring about the downfall of Empires in

the past.   Will it prove fatal to a federation of European States ?

Obviously it will, if the strength of their combination is used for the same parasitic purposes, and the white races, discarding labour in its more arduous forms, live as a sort of world-aristocracy by the exploitation of " lower races," while they hand over the policing of the world more and more to members of these same races. These dangers would certainly arise if a federation of European States were simply a variant of the older Empires, using a *pax Europœa* for similar purposes and seeking to maintain it by the same methods as those employed under the so-called *pax Romana*.   The issue is a great one, furnishing, in fact, the supreme test of modern civilisation.

Is it possible for a federation of civilised States to maintain the force required to keep order in the world without abusing her power by political and economic parasitism ?

CHAPTER III

MORAL AND SENTIMENTAL FACTORS

I

ANALYSIS of the actual course of modern Imperialism has laid bare the combination of economic and political forces which fashions it. These forces are traced to their sources in the selfish interests of certain industrial, financial, and professional classes, seeking private advantages out of a policy of imperial expansion, and using this same policy to protect them in their economic, political, and social privileges against the pressure of democracy. It remains to answer the question, " Why does Imperialism escape general recognition for the narrow, sordid thing it is ? " Each nation, as it watches from outside the Imperialism of its neighbours, is not deceived; the selfish interests of political and commercial classes are seen plainly paramount in the direction of the policy. So every other European nation recognises the true outlines of British Imperialism and charges us with hypocrisy in feigning blindness. This charge is false; no nation sees its own shortcomings; the charge of hypocrisy is seldom justly brought against an individual, against a nation never. Frenchmen and Germans believe that our zeal in promoting foreign missions, putting down slavery, and in spreading the arts of civilisation is a false disguise conveniently assumed to cover naked national self-assertion. The actual case is somewhat different.

There exists in a considerable though not a large proportion of the British nation a genuine desire to spread Christianity among the heathen, to diminish the cruelty and other sufferings which they believe exist in countries less fortunate than their own, and to do good work about the world in the cause of humanity. Most of the churches contain a small body of men and women deeply, even passionately, interested in such work, and a much larger number whose sympathy, though weaker, is quite genuine. Ill-trained for the most part in psychology and history, these people believe that religion and other arts of civilisation are portable commodities which it is our duty to convey to the backward nations, and that a certain amount of compulsion is justified in pressing their benefits upon people too ignorant at once to recognise them.

Is it surprising that the selfish forces which direct Imperialism should utilise the protective colours of these disinterested movements? Imperialist politicians, soldiers, or company directors, who push a forward policy by portraying the cruelties of the African slave raids or the infamous tyranny of a Prempeh or a Thebaw, or who open out a new field for missionary enterprise in China or the Soudan, do not deliberately and consciously work up these motives in order to incite the British public. They simply and instinctively attach to themselves any strong, genuine elevated feeling which is of service, fan it and feed it until it assumes fervour, and utilise it for their ends. The politician always, the business man not seldom, believes that high motives qualify the political or financial benefits he gets: it is certain that Lord Salisbury really believes that the South African war, for which his Government is responsible, has been undertaken for the benefit of the people of South Africa and will result in increased liberty and happiness; it is quite likely that Earl Grey thinks that the Chartered Company which he directs is animated by a desire to improve the material and moral condition of the natives of Rhodesia and that it is attaining this object.

So Leopold, King of the Belgians, has claimed for his government of the Congo—"Our only programme is that of the moral and material regeneration of the country." It is difficult to set any limit upon the capacity of men to deceive themselves as to the relative strength and worth of the motives which affect them: politicians, in particular, acquire so strong a habit of setting their projects in the most favourable light that they soon convince themselves that the finest result which they think may conceivably accrue from any policy is the actual motive of that policy. As for the public, it is only natural that it should be deceived. All the purer and more elevated adjuncts of Imperialism are kept to the fore by religious and philanthropic agencies: patriotism appeals to the general lust of power within a people by suggestions of nobler uses, adopting the forms of self-sacrifice to cover domination and the love of adventure. So Christianity becomes "imperialist" to the Archbishop of Canterbury, a "going out to all the world to preach the gospel"; trade becomes "imperialist" in the eyes of merchants seeking a world market.

It is precisely in this falsification of the real import of motives that the gravest vice and the most signal peril of Imperialism reside. When, out of a medley of mixed motives, the least potent is selected for public prominence because it is the most presentable, when issues of a policy which was not present at all to the minds of those who formed this policy are treated as chief causes, the moral currency of the nation is de-

o

based. The whole policy of Imperialism is riddled with
this deception. Although no candid student of history
will maintain for a moment that the entrance of British
power into India, and the chief steps leading to the
present British Empire there, were motived by considerations other than our own political and commercial
aggrandisement, nothing is more common than to hear
the gains which it is alleged the natives of the country
have received from British rule assigned as the moral
justification of our Indian Empire. The case of Egypt
is a still more striking one. Though the reasons openly
assigned for the British occupation of Egypt were military
and financial ones affecting our own interests, it is now
commonly maintained that we went there in order to
bestow the benefits which Egyptians have received from
our sway, and that it would be positively wicked of us
to keep the pledge we gave to withdraw within a short
term of years from the country. When the ordinary
Englishman reads how " at no previous period of his
history has the fellah lived under a Government so
careful to promote his interests or to preserve his
rights," [1] he instinctively exclaims, " Yes, that is what
we went to Egypt for," though, in point of fact, the
play of "Imperialism" which carried us there was determined by quite other considerations. Even if one
supposes that the visible misgovernment of Egypt, in
its bearing on the life of the inhabitants, did impart
some unselfish element to our conduct, no one would
suggest that as an operative force in the direction of
our imperial policy such motive has ever determined
our actions. [2] Not even the most flamboyant Imperialist

[1] "England in Egypt," p. 97.

[2] How far the mystification of motives can carry a trained thinker
upon politics may be illustrated by the astonishing argument of Professor
Giddings, who, in discussing "the consent of the governed" as a condi-

contends that England is a knight-errant, everywhere in search of a quest to deliver oppressed peoples from oppressive governments, regardless of her own interests and perils. Though perhaps not so inefficient, the Russian tyranny is quite as oppressive and more injurious to the cause of civilisation than the government of the Khedive, but no one proposes that we should coerce Russia, or rescue Finland from her clutches. The case of Armenia, again, attests the utter feebleness of the higher motives. Both the Government and the people of Great Britain were thoroughly convinced of the atrocious cruelties of Turkey, public opinion was well informed and thoroughly incensed, Great Britain was expressly pledged by the Cyprus Convention to protect Armenia; but the "cause of humanity" and the "mission of civilisation" were powerless either for interference or for effective protest.

Aggressive Imperialism, as our investigation has shown, is virtually confined to the coercion by stronger or better-armed nations of nations which are, or seem to be, weaker and incapable of effective resistance; everywhere some definite economic or political gain is sought

---

tion of government, argues that "if a barbarous people is compelled to accept the authority of a State more advanced in civilisation, the test of the rightfulness or wrongfulness of this imposition of authority is to be found, not at all in any assent or resistance at the moment when the government begins, but only *in the degree of probability* that, after full experience of what the government can do to raise the subject population to a higher plane of life, *a free and rational consent will be given* by those who have come to understand all that has been done" ("Empire and Democracy," p. 265). Professor Giddings does not seem to recognise that the entire weight of the ethical validity of this curious doctrine of retrospective consent is thrown upon the act of judging *the degree of probability that a free and rational consent will be given*, that his doctrine furnishes no sort of security for a competent, unbiassed judgment, and that, in point of fact, it endows any nation with the right to seize and administer the territory of any other nation on the ground of a self-ascribed superiority and self-imputed qualifications for the work of civilisation.

by the imperial aggressor. The chivalrous spirit of
Imperialism leads neither Great Britain nor any other
Western nation to assail a powerful State however
tyrannous or to assist a weak State reputed to be
poor.

The blending of strong interested with weak disinterested forces is indeed characteristic of the age. It
is the homage which Imperialism pays to humanity.
But just as the mixture known as "philanthropy and
5 per cent." is distrusted in the ordinary business world,
so in the larger policy of nations the same combination
is by right suspect. When business is harnessed with
benevolence the former is commonly allowed to determine the direction and to set the pace. Doubtless it
says something for the moral sensibility of a nation that
a gainful course is rendered more attractive by a tincture
of disinterestedness. But the theory and the practice
in modern history often border so closely on hypocrisy that we cannot feel surprise that unfriendly
foreigners apply the term to them. What, for example, can we say of the following frank description
of Imperialism by Sir George Baden-Powell? "The
ultimate unit, the taxpayer—whether home or colonial
—looks for two groups of results as his reward. On
the one hand, he hopes to see Christianity and civilisation *pro tanto* extended; and, on the other, to see
some compensating development of industry and trade.
Unless he, or 'his servants the Government,' secure
either or both these results, the question must be plainly
asked, Has he the right, and is he right, to wage such
wars ? " [1]

What is the mode of equating the two groups of
results? how much Christianity and civilisation balance

[1] Addendum to "The Downfall of Prempeh."

how much industry and trade? are curious questions which seem to need an answer. Is not the ultimate unit in his capacity of taxpayer liable to lay more stress upon the asset which admits of momentary measurement and to undervalue the one that evades arithmetic?

"To combine the commercial with the imaginative" was the aim which Mr. Rhodes ascribed to himself as the key of his policy. The conjunction is commonly described by the word "speculation," a word whose meaning becomes more sinister when politics and private business are so inextricably interwoven as they were in the career of Mr. Rhodes, who used the legislature of Cape Colony to support and strengthen the diamond monopoly of De Beers, while from De Beers he financed the Raid, debauched the constituencies of Cape Colony, and bought the public press, in order to engineer the war, which was to win him full possession of his great "thought" the North.[1]

II

It may safely be asserted that, wherever "the commercial" is combined with "the imaginative" in any shape or sort, the latter is exploited by the former. There is a brand of "Christian Imperialist" much commended in certain quarters, the "industrial missionary," who is designed to float Christianity upon an ocean of profitable business, inculcating theological dogmas in the intervals of teaching the material arts and crafts. "To the sceptical Chinese the interest manifested by a missionary in business affairs would go far towards dispelling the suspicions which now attach to the presence in their midst of men whose motives they are unable

[1] "The North is my thought" ("Cecil Rhodes: His Political Life and Speeches," p. 613).

to appreciate, and therefore condemn as unholy." "Immense services might be rendered to our commercial interests if only the members of the various missions in China would co-operate with our Consuls in the exploitation of the country, and the introduction of commercial as well as of purely theological ideas to the Chinese intelligence." [1] This revelation of the mercantile uses of Christianity by a British Consul leaves little to be desired in point of frankness. Its full significance is, however, only perceived when it is reinforced by the naïve confession of Lord Hugh Cecil.[2] "A great many people were most anxious to go with their whole hearts into what might be called the imperial movement of the day, but had, as it were, a certain uneasiness of conscience whether, after all, this movement was quite as unpolluted by earthly considerations as they would desire it to be. He thought that by making prominent to our own minds the importance of missionary work we should to some extent sanctify the spirit of Imperialism."

We are well aware that most British missionaries are quite untainted with admixture of political and commercial motives, and that they set about their work in a single spirit of self-sacrifice, eager to save the souls of the heathen, and not a whit concerned to push British trade or "sanctify the spirit of Imperialism." Indeed, it is quite evident that, just in proportion as the suspicions of worldly motives appear in missionary work, so the genuinely spiritual influence evaporates. The whole history of missionary work in China is one long commentary on this text. The early Catholic missionaries, relying on the authority of their holy lives and teaching,

[1] Passages from a recent report of the British Consul at Canton.

[2] An address at the annual meeting of the Society for Propagation of the Gospel, May 4, 1900.

won not only security, but wide influence, both among the masses and in the governing circles, introducing not only Christianity, but the elements of Western science. Though they made no large numbers of converts, they constituted a peaceful factor in the civilisation of the great Eastern Empire. But the introduction in the nineteenth century of national and sectarian competition in missionary enterprise, each mission using freely the diplomatic and even the military resources of some European State for its defence or propagation, has inhibited the play of spiritual forces, generating suspicions which, only too well grounded, have changed the early receptiveness into a temper of fanatical hostility.

"It must be very difficult," writes an educated Chinaman, "for the mandarins to dissociate the missionaries from the secular power, whose gunboats seem ever ready to appear on behalf of their respective Governments. . . . The Chinese have watched with much concern the sequence of events—first the missionary, then the Consul, and at last the invading army. They had scarcely forgotten the loss of Annam in this way when the German action in Shan-tung created a profound sensation amongst all classes of the literati." "We cannot wonder that the Chinese officials should hate the missionaries. Their Church is an *imperium in imperio*, propagating a strange faith and alienating the people from that of their ancestors. The missionaries are not amenable to Chinese laws, and in some cases have acted in a high-handed manner in the protection of their convents. In this lies one of the secrets of the mysterious hatred entertained against 'the friends of China,' as the missionaries call themselves." [1]

[1] "The Chinese Crisis from Within," by Wen Ching, pp. 10, 12, 14 (Grant Richards).

How injurious to the cause "whose kingdom is not of this earth" is this alliance with politics and armaments might appear too obvious for discussion.   Yet it is quite evident that sincere men are prepared to support the use of political and military force in order to open fields for missionary enterprise, and that the missionary, who is by turns trader, soldier, and politician, seems a most desirable instrument of civilisation.

How close in motive and in conduct this combination really is may be thus illustrated from the recent history of the Soudan.

"Detachments of officers and men from every regiment, British and Egyptian, were conveyed across the Nile in the gunboats to take part in the Gordon memorial service, and to witness the hoisting of the British flag on the ruins of Khartoum. . . . Surrounded by the soldiers he had directed with terrible and glorious effect, the successful general ordered the flags to be hoisted. . . . The officers saluted, the men presented arms, and the band played the Egyptian National Anthem and our own.   Then the Sirdar called for three cheers for Her Majesty. . . . The memorial service followed, and the solemn words of the English Prayer-book were read in that distant garden. . . . The bands played their dirge and Gordon's favourite hymn, 'Abide with Me'; a gunboat on the river crashed out the salute. . . . The Highlanders played a long lament, and .thus the ceremony was duly fulfilled.   Nine thousand of those who would have prevented it lay dead on the plain of Omdurman.   Other thousands were scattered in the wilderness, or crawled wounded to the river for water."[1]   While the writer of this passage omits the final touch, the deliberate shooting of wounded

---

[1] "The River War," by Winston Churchill, vol. ii. pp. 204–206.

crawlers by troops under British commanders, the picture is profoundly suggestive, with its strange amalgam of the British flag, "Abide with Me," and the avenging of Gordon.

Yet it is evident that those who ascend to the misty heights of Imperialism are able to unite these diverse jarring factors in "a higher synthesis," and while deploring, often in earnest, the necessity of the Maxim and the gunboat, find a glorious justification in the higher ends of a civilisation promoted by such means. The Western nations are, according to this gospel, rapidly realising a beneficent control of the earth which will, in the near future, secure general peace and the industrial, scientific, and moral supremacy of Western arts.

> "Fly, happy, happy sails, and bear the Press,
> Fly, happy with the mission of the Cross,
> Knit land to land, and blowing heavenward,
> Enrich the markets of the golden year."

This is the benevolent theory. Let Sir Charles Dilke's estimate of our recent acquisitions in tropical Africa serve for commentary.

"If we cannot make the most fertile of the West India Islands pay, how can we expect to make countries which are far less healthy and less fertile in the very heart of Africa, return a profit? Our people have been interested in Africa through their traditional desire to suppress the evils of the slave trade, and to pay conscience money in these days for the sins, in connection with slavery, of their predecessors; but it is probable that we have done more harm by promoting the partition of Africa and the creation, in the name of liberty, of such governments as that of the Congo

Free State than the harm which our grandfathers did
to Africa by their participation in African slavery and
the slave trade."[1]

III

The psychical problem which confronts us in the
advocates of the mission of Imperialism is certainly
no case of hypocrisy, or of deliberate conscious simu-
lation of false motives. It is partly the dupery of
imperfectly realised ideas, partly a case of psychical
departmentalism. Imperialism has been floated on a
sea of vague, shifty, well-sounding phrases which are
seldom tested by close contact with fact. "It is not
in size and variety alone that English dominion is
unique. Its crowning glory is its freedom,"[2] writes
Mr. Henley, doubtless believing what he says. The
suggestion of these words is that the "freedom" we
enjoy in these isles is common to our fellow-subjects
throughout the British Empire. This suggestion is
false, as we have seen, but phrase-mongering Imperialism does not recognise its falsehood. The largest
and most essential facts of Imperialism, political,
economic, moral, are commonly unknown to the
average "educated" Briton. To him our Empire is
composed of a number of free, self-governing States,
which are in close and growing industrial relations
with us; individual and racial freedom and equal
justice prevail everywhere; Christianity and British
moral ideals are rapidly winning their way over the
vast populations of the lower races, which gladly recognise the superiority of our ideas and characters
and the benefits which they receive from British rule.
These vague, hasty notions are corrected by no close

[1] "The British Empire," p. 114.   [2] "Imperialism," p. 7.

study of facts and figures: the only substance which they commonly possess is the assertion of some friends or relatives who are "on the spot" in some British possessions and whose individual testimony is made to sustain a pile of imperialist notions. How many persons, during the South African war, based their convictions regarding the "outlander grievances" and the character and motives of the Boer Government upon the impassioned statement of some single dweller in Johannesburg, who had virtually no contact with Boers and knew nothing of grievances, excepting through the Rhodesian press, which fashioned them!

To what extent Imperialism lives upon "masked words"[1] it is difficult to realise unless we turn to the language of diplomacy, the verbal armoury of Imperialism. Paramount power, effective autonomy, emissary of civilisation, rectification of frontier, and a whole sliding scale of terms from "hinterland" and "sphere of interest" to "effective occupation" and "annexation" will serve as ready illustrations of a phraseology devised for purposes of concealment and encroachment. The Imperialist who sees modern history through these masks never grasps the "brute" facts, but always sees them at several removes, refracted, interpreted, and glossed by convenient renderings. Some measure of responsibility for his ignorance he retains, for he must often be aware that the truth is not told him and that he is refusing

[1] "There are masked words droning and skulking about us in Europe just now which nobody understands, but which everybody uses and most people will also fight for, live for, or even die for, fancying they mean this or that or the other of things dear to them. There never were creatures of prey so mischievous, never diplomatists so cunning, never poisons so deadly, as these masked words; they are the unjust stewards of all men's ideas; whatever fancy or favourite instinct a man most cherishes he gives to his favourite masked word to take care of for him; the word at last comes to have an infinite power over him, and you cannot get at him but by its ministry" (Ruskin, "Sesame and Lilies," p. 29).

to penetrate the disguises. This persistent evasion of naked truth endows him sometimes with an almost preternatural power of self-deceit. Mr. Lecky writes: "Of all forms of prestige, moral prestige is the most valuable, and no statesman should forget that one of the chief elements of British power is the moral weight that is behind it."[1] The vast majority of "educated" Englishmen genuinely believe that England's greatest gain from the Boer war is an enhancement of her "moral prestige"!

An error so monstrous is only made intelligible by reference to another curious psychical factor. Nowhere is the distrust of what is termed "logic," as a guide for public conduct, so firmly rooted as in England: a course of conduct which stands out sharply "logical" is in itself suspect. The practice of "party" government has so commonly made "compromises" a necessity that we have come to believe that our national progress is due to this necessity, and that if the sharper and more rapid application of "ideas" had been feasible, we should, by following them, have been led into false paths involving much trouble of retracing steps, or over the brink of some revolutionary peril. Though sound "compromise" is nowise illogical, but is simply logic applied within certain limits of time and environment, it easily degenerates into the opportunism of an idle policy of short-range utility. The complexity of modern politics in such a country as Great Britain, reacting on the exigencies and temptations of a party system, has driven the habit of "compromise" to such foolish extremes as to corrupt the political intelligence of the nation. Elsewhere the same tendency has been operative, but has been checked or modified by a narrow and more consciously definite policy

----

[1] "The Map of Life."

on the part of a ruling monarch or a ruling class, by the limits of a written constitution, and, in some of the Latin nations, by an inherent and widespread belief in the value of ideas as operative forces in politics. In England, and indeed throughout Anglo-Saxondom, a sort of cheery optimism has commonly usurped the seat of intelligent direction, a general belief in "national destiny," which enables us "somehow to muddle through," and advises us "to do the best we can and not look too far ahead." Now, with the disdain of history and the neglect of sociological laws which this implies I am not here so much concerned as with the injurious reaction wrought upon the mind of the citizen confronted with some new event which challenges his judgment. Our rough-and-ready, hand-to-mouth, "take-what-you-can-get" politics have paralysed judgment by laming the logical faculty of comparison. Not being required to furnish to ourselves or others clear, consistent reasons for our short-range expediencies of public conduct, we have lost all habit of mental consistency, or, putting it conversely, we have developed a curious and highly dangerous aptitude for entertaining incompatible and often self-contradictory ideas and motives.

One or two extreme concrete instances will serve as illustrations of the damage done to the public intelligence by the absence of all sense of clear logical order in the conduct of affairs. At the beginning of the South African war the numerical insignificance of the Boers was regarded as an aggravation of their insolence in entering upon strife with the greatest Empire of the world. But the numerical smallness did not in the least interfere with the equally genuine belief and feeling that we were contending with a Power as large, numerically, as ourselves, which were required to support the sense of tri-

umph when we won a victory, or to turn the edge of
shame when our tiny adversary inflicted a defeat upon
us. The shifts of detailed mendacity and curious invention to which we were driven in the course of the war by
the necessity of keeping up this double and contradictory
belief will doubtless attract the attention of the psychological historian, how the numbers alternately and automatically expanded and contracted according as it was
sought to impress upon the nation the necessity of voting
large supplies of troops and money, or else to represent the war as "nearly over" and as having lapsed into
a trifling guerilla struggle. Or take another instance.
It was possible for informed politicians to maintain at
one and the same time that our conduct in providing
food and shelter to the families whose property we had
destroyed in South Africa was an act of unprecedented
generosity, and to defend the right to sell by public auc-
tion their farms in order to defray the very cost of keep
which was the ground for our self-commendation. These
two contentions could be uttered in the House of Commons by the same minister and accepted by the nation
without any recognition of their inconsistency. Why?
Simply from a practical inhibition of the faculty of comparison. A line of action is pursued from the felt pressure of some close expediency: afterwards some "reasons"
must be found for it, some justification given: no attempt
is made before or after the action to see it as a whole with
its causes and its consequences, and so there is no clear
comparison of actual motives and results. This genius
of inconsistency, of holding conflicting ideas or feelings
in the mind simultaneously, in watertight compartments,
is perhaps peculiarly British. It is, I repeat, not hypocrisy; a consciousness of inconsistency would spoil the
play: it is a condition of the success of this conduct that

it should be unconscious. For such inconsistency has its uses. Much of the brutality and injustice involved in "Imperialism" would be impossible without this capacity. If, for example, the British mind had been sufficiently consistent to have kept clearly before it the fact that 400 millions of people were contending with a body less than a quarter of a million, whatever view was held as to the necessity and justice of the war, much of its detailed barbarism and all the triumphant exultation on success would have been impossible.

There is of course much more than this in the psychology of Imperialism, but there are two main factors, the habit and capacity of substituting vague and decorative notions, derived through "masked" words, for hard naked facts, and the native or acquired genius of inconsistency. Great Britain would be incapable of this policy if she realised in clear consciousness the actual play of motives and their results. Most of the men who have misled her have first been obliged to mislead themselves. There is no enthusiasm in hypocrisy, and even bare-faced greed furnishes no adequate stimulus to a long policy. Imperialism is based upon a persistent misrepresentation of facts and forces chiefly through a most refined process of selection, exaggeration, and attenuation, directed by interested cliques and persons so as to distort the face of history.

The gravest peril of Imperialism lies in the state of mind of a nation which has become habituated to this deception and which has rendered itself incapable of self-criticism.

For this is the condition which Plato terms "the lie in the soul"—a lie which does not know itself to be a lie. One of the marks of this diseased condition is a fatal self-complacency. When a nation has succumbed to it, it easily and instinctively rejects all criticism of other nations as due to envy and malice, and all domestic criticism is attributed to the bias of anti-patriotism.   In more primitive nations the lusts of domination and material acquisition which underlie Imperialism express themselves freely and unconsciously: there is little self-complacency because there is little self-consciousness. But nations which have grown in self-consciousness as far as the Western European nations seek to stimulate and feed their instinctive lusts by conscious reflection. Hence the elaborate weaving of intellectual and moral defences, the ethics and sociology of empire which we have examined.

The controlling and directing agent of the whole process, as we have seen, is the pressure of financial and industrial motives, operated for the direct, short-range, material interests of small, able, and well-organised groups in a nation.   These groups secure the active co-operation of statesmen and of political cliques who wield the power of "parties" partly by associating them directly in their business schemes, partly by appealing to the conservative instincts of members of the possessing classes, whose vested interests and class dominance are best preserved by diverting the currents of political energy from domestic on to foreign politics.   The acquiescence, even the active and enthusiastic support, of the body of a nation in a course of policy fatal to its own true interests is secured partly by appeals to the mission of civilisation, but chiefly by playing upon the primitive instincts of the race.

The psychology of these instincts is not easy to explore, but certain prime factors easily appear.   The passion which a French writer describes as kilometritis,[1] or milo-mania, the instinct for control of land, drives

[1] M. Novicow, *La Federation de l'Europe*, p. 158.

back to the earliest times when a wide range of land was necessary for a food supply for men or cattle, and is linked on to the "trek" habit, which survives more powerfully than is commonly supposed in civilised peoples. The "nomadic" habit bred of necessity survives as a chief ingredient in the love of travel, and merges into "the spirit of adventure" when it meets other equally primitive passions. This "spirit of adventure," especially in the Anglo-Saxon, has taken the shape of "sport," which in its stronger or "more adventurous" forms involves a direct appeal to the lust of slaughter and the crude struggle for life involved in pursuit. The animal lust of struggle, once a necessity, survives in the blood, and just in proportion as a nation or a class has a margin of energy and leisure from the activities of peaceful industry, it craves satisfaction through "sport," in which hunting and the physical satisfaction of striking a blow are vital ingredients. The leisured classes in Great Britain, having most of their energy liberated from the necessity of work, naturally specialise on "sport," the hygienic necessity of a substitute for work helping to support or coalescing with the survival of a savage instinct. As the milder expressions of this passion are alone permissible in the sham or artificial encounters of domestic sports, where wild game disappears and human conflicts more mortal than football are prohibited, there is an ever stronger pressure to the frontiers of civilisation in order that the thwarted "spirit of adventure" may have strong, free play. These feelings are fed by a flood of the literature of travel and of imaginative writing, the security and monotony of the ordinary civilised routine imparting an ever-growing fascination to the wilder portions of the earth. The milder satisfactions afforded by sport to the

P

upper classes in their ample leisure at home are imitated by the industrial masses, whose time and energy for recreation have been growing, and who, in their passage from rural to town conditions, have never abandoned the humbler sports of feudal country life to which from time immemorial they had been addicted. "Football is a good game, but better than it, better than any other game, is that of man-hunting."[1]

The sporting and military aspects of Imperialism form, therefore, a very powerful basis of popular appeal. The desire to pursue and kill either big game or other men can only be satisfied by expansion and militarism. It may indeed be safely said that the reason why our army is so inefficient in its officers, as compared with its rank and file, is that at a time when serious scientific preparation and selection are required for an intellectual profession, most British officers choose the army and undertake its work in the spirit of "sport." While the average "Tommy" is perhaps actuated in the main by similar motives, "science" matters less in his case, and any lack of serious professional purpose is more largely compensated by the discipline imposed on him.

But still more important than these supports of militarism in the army is the part played by "war" as a support of Imperialism in the non-combatant body of the nation. Though the active appeal of "sport" is still strong, even among townsmen, clear signs are visible of a degradation of this active interest of the participant into the idle excitement of the spectator. How far sport has thus degenerated may be measured by the substitution everywhere of a specialised professionalism for a free amateur exercise, and by the growth of the attendant vice of gambling, which everywhere expresses the worst

[1] Baden-Powell, "Aids to Scouting," p. 124.

form of sporting excitement, drawing all disinterested sympathy away from the merits of the competition, and concentrating it upon the irrational element of chance in combination with covetousness and low cunning. The equivalent of this degradation of interest in sport is Jingoism in relation to the practice of war. Jingoism is merely the lust of the spectator, unpurged by any personal effort, risk, or sacrifice, gloating in the perils, pains, and slaughter of fellow-men whom he does not know, but whose destruction he desires in a blind and artificially stimulated passion of hatred and revenge. In the Jingo all is concentrated on the hazard and blind fury of the fray. The arduous and weary monotony of the march, the long periods of waiting, the hard privations, the terrible tedium of a prolonged campaign, play no part in his imagination; the redeeming factors of war, the fine sense of comradeship which common personal peril educates, the fruits of discipline and self-restraint, the respect for the personality of enemies whose courage he must admit and whom he comes to realise as fellow-beings—all these moderating elements in actual war are eliminated from the passion of the Jingo. It is precisely for these reasons that some friends of peace maintain that the two most potent checks of militarism and of war are the obligation of the entire body of citizens to undergo military service and the experience of an invasion.

Whether such expensive remedies are really effectual or necessary we are not called on to decide, but it is quite evident that the spectatorial lust of Jingoism is a most serious factor in Imperialism. The dramatic falsification both of war and of the whole policy of imperial expansion required to feed this popular passion forms no small portion of the art of the real organisers of im-

perialist exploits, the small groups of business men and
politicians who know what they want and how to get it.

Tricked out with the real or sham glories of military
heroism and the magnificent claims of empire-making,
Jingoism becomes a nucleus of a sort of patriotism which
can be moved to any folly or to any crime.

IV

Where this spirit of naked dominance needs more
dressing for the educated classes of a nation, the requisite
moral and intellectual decorations are woven for its
use ; the church, the press, the schools and colleges, the
political machine, the four chief instruments of popular
education, are accommodated to its service. From the
muscular Christianity of the last generation to the
imperial Christianity of the present day it is but a single
step; the temper of growing sacerdotalism and the
doctrine of authority in the established churches well
accord with militarism and political autocracy. Mr. Goldwin Smith has rightly observed how "force is the
natural ally of superstition, and superstition knows it
well." [1] As for the most potent engine of the press, the
newspaper, so far as it is not directly owned and operated
by financiers for financial purposes (as is the case to
a great extent in every great industrial and financial
centre), it is always influenced and mostly dominated by
the interests of the classes which control the advertisements upon which its living depends ; the independence
of a paper with a circulation so large and firm as to
"command" and to retain advertisements in the teeth of
a policy disliked by the advertising classes is becoming
rarer and more precarious every year, as the cluster of

[1] Letter in *The Manchester Guardian*, 14th October 1900.

interests which form the business nucleus of Imperialism becomes more consolidated and more conscious in its politics. The political machine is an hireling, because it is a machine, and needs constant repair and lubrication from the wealthy members of the party; the machinist knows from whom he takes his pay, and cannot run against the will of those who are in fact the patrons of the party, the tightening of whose purse-strings will automatically stop the machine. The recent Imperialism both of Great Britain and America has been materially assisted by the lavish contributions of men like Rockefeller, Hanna, Rhodes, Beit to party funds for the election of " imperialist " representatives and for the political instruction of the people.

Most serious of all is the persistent attempt to seize the school system for Imperialism masquerading as patriotism. To capture the childhood of the country, to mechanise its free play into the routine of military drill, to cultivate the savage survivals of combativeness, to poison its early understanding of history by false ideals and pseudo-heroes and by a consequent disparagement and neglect of the really vital and elevating lessons of the past, to establish a "geocentric" view of the moral universe in which the interests of humanity are subordinated to that of the " country " (and so, by easy, early, natural inference, that of the " country " to that of the " self "), to feed the always overweening pride of race at an age when self-confidence most commonly prevails, and by necessary implication to disparage other nations, so starting children in the world with false measures of value and an unwillingness to learn from foreign sources—to fasten this base insularity of mind and morals upon the little children of a nation and to call it patriotism is as foul an abuse of

education as it is possible to conceive. Yet the power
of Church and State over primary education is being
bent consistently to this purpose, while the blend of
clericalism and autocratic academicism which dominates
the secondary education of this country pours its enthusiasm into the same evil channel.[1]   Finally, our
centres of highest culture, the universities, are in peril
of a new perversion from the path of free inquiry and
expression, which is the true path of intellectual life.
A new sort of "pious founder" threatens intellectual
liberty.   Our colleges are, indeed, no longer to be the
subservient defenders of religious orthodoxy, repressing science, distorting history, and moulding philosophy
to conserve the interests of Church and King.   The
academic studies and their teachers are to employ the
same methods, but directed to a different end: philosophy, the natural sciences, history, economics, sociology,
are to be employed in setting up new earthworks against
the attack of the disinherited masses upon the vested
interests of the plutocracy.   I do not of course represent
this perversion as destructive of the educational work of
the colleges: the services rendered in defence of "conservatism" may even be regarded in most cases as incidental: only perhaps in philosophy and economics is
the bias a powerful and pervasive one, and even there
the individuality of strong independent natures may
correct it.   Moreover, it is needless to charge dishonesty
against the teachers, who commonly think and teach
according to the highest that is in them.   But the actual
teaching is none the less selected and controlled, wherever it is found useful to employ the arts of selection
and control, by the business interests playing on the

---

[1] For striking illustrations cf. Spencer's "Facts and Comments," pp.
126, 127.

vested academic interests. No one can follow the history of political and economic theory during the last century without recognising that the selection and rejection of ideas, hypotheses, and formulæ, the moulding of them into schools or tendencies of thought, and the propagation of them in the intellectual world, have been plainly directed by the pressure of class interests. In political economy, as we might well suspect, from its close bearing upon business and politics, we find the most incontestable example. The " classical " economics in England were the barely disguised formulation of the mercantile and manufacturing interests as distinguished from, and opposed to, the landowning interest on the one hand, the labouring interest on the other, evoking in later years other class economics of " protection" and of " socialism " similarly woven out of sectional interests.

The real determinants in education are given in these three questions: " Who shall teach? What shall they teach? How shall they teach?" Where universities are dependent for endowments and incomes upon the favour of the rich, upon the charity of millionaires, the following answers will of necessity be given: " Safe teachers. Safe studies. Sound (*i.e.* orthodox) methods." The coarse proverb which tells us that " he who pays the piper calls the tune" is quite as applicable here as elsewhere, and no bluff regarding academic dignity and intellectual honesty must blind us to the fact.

The interference with intellectual liberty is seldom direct, seldom personal, though of late both in the United States and Canada some instances of the crudest heresy-hunting have occurred. The real danger consists in the appointment rather than in the dismissal of teachers, in the determination of what subjects shall be taught, what relative attention shall be given to each subject, and what text-books and other apparatus of instruction shall be used. The subservience to rank and money, even in our older English universities, has been of late evinced so nakedly, and the demands for monetary aid in developing new faculties necessarily looms so large in academic eyes, that the danger here indicated is an ever-growing one. It is not so much the weight of the "dead hand" that is to be feared as that of the living: a college so unfortunate as to harbour teachers who, in handling vital issues of politics or economics, teach truths deeply and obviously antagonistic to the interests of the classes from whom financial aid was sought, would be committing suicide. Higher education has never been economically self-supporting; it has hardly ever been fully organised from public funds; everywhere it has remained parasitic on the private munificence of wealthy persons. The peril is too obvious to need further enforcement: it is the hand of the prospective, the potential donor that fetters intellectual freedom in our colleges, and will do so more and more so long as the duty of organising public higher education for a nation out of public funds fails of recognition.

The area of danger is, of course, far wider than Imperialism, covering the whole field of vested interests. But, if the analysis of previous chapters is correct, Imperialism stands as a first defence of these interests: for the financial and speculative classes it means a pushing of their private businesses at the public expense, for the export manufacturers and merchants a forcible enlargement of foreign markets and a related policy of Protection, for the official and professional classes large openings of honourable and lucrative employment, for the Church it represents the temper and practice of authority and the assertion of spiritual control over vast multitudes of lower people, for the political oligarchy it means the only effective diversion of the forces of democracy and the opening of great public careers in the showy work of empire-making.

This being so, it is inevitable that Imperialism should seek intellectual support in our seats of learning, and should use the sinews of education for the purpose. The millionaire who endows Oxford does not buy its men of learning outright, need not even stipulate what should be taught. But the practical pressure of Imperialism is such that when a professional appointment is made in history it is becoming more difficult for a scholar with the intellectual outlook of a John Morley, a Frederick Harrison, or a Goldwin Smith to secure election, or for a political economist with strong views on the necessity of controlling capital to be elected to a chair in economics. No formal tests are necessary; the instinct of financial self-preservation will suffice. The price which universities pay for preferring money and social position to intellectual distinction in the choice of chancellors and for touting among the millionaires for the equipment of new scientific schools is this subservience to the political and business interests of their patrons : their philosophy, their history, their economics, even their biology must reflect in doctrine and method the consideration that is due to patronage, and the fact that this deference is unconscious enhances the damage done to the cause of intellectual freedom.

Thus do the industrial and financial forces of Imperialism, operating through the party, the press, the church, the school, mould public opinion and public policy by the false idealisation of those primitive lusts of struggle, domination, and acquisitiveness which have survived throughout the eras of peaceful industrial order

and whose stimulation is needed once again for the work
of imperial aggression, expansion, and the forceful exploitation of lower races.   For these business politicians
biology and sociology weave thin convenient theories of
a race struggle for the subjugation of the inferior peoples,
in order that we, the Anglo-Saxon, may take their lands
and live upon their labours; while economics buttresses
the argument by representing our work in conquering
and ruling them as our share in the division of labour
among nations, and history devises reasons why the
lessons of past empire do not apply to ours, while social
ethics paints the motive of "Imperialism" as the desire
to bear the "burden" of educating and elevating races
of "children." Thus are the "cultured" or semi-cultured
classes indoctrinated with the intellectual and moral
grandeur of Imperialism.   For the masses there is a cruder
appeal to hero-worship and sensational glory, adventure
and the sporting spirit: current history falsified in coarse
flaring colours, for the direct stimulation of the combative
instincts.   But while various methods are employed,
some delicate and indirect, others coarse and flamboyant,
the operation everywhere resolves itself into an incitation
and direction of the brute lusts of human domination
which are everywhere latent in civilised humanity, for
the pursuance of a policy fraught with material gain to
a minority of co-operative vested interests which usurp
the title of the commonwealth.

CHAPTER IV

IMPERIALISM AND THE LOWER RACES

I

THE statement, often made, that the work of imperial expansion is virtually complete is not correct. It is true that most of the "backward" races have been placed in some sort of dependence upon one or other of the "civilised" Powers as colony, protectorate, hinterland, or sphere of influence. But this in most instances marks rather the beginning of a process of imperialisation than a definite attainment of empire. The intensive growth of empire by which interference is increased and governmental control tightened over spheres of influence and protectorates is as important and as perilous an aspect of Imperialism as the extensive growth which takes shape in assertion of rule over new areas of territory and new populations.

The famous saying, attributed to Napoleon, that "great empires die of indigestion" serves to remind us of the importance of the imperialist processes which still remain after formal "expansion" has been completed. During the last twenty years Great Britain, Germany, France, and Russia have bitten off huge mouthfuls of Africa and Asia which are not yet chewed, digested, or assimilated. Moreover, great areas still remain whose independence, though threatened, is yet unimpaired.

Vast countries in Asia, such as Persia, Thibet, Siam, Afghanistan, are rapidly forging to the front of politics as likely subjects of armed controversy between European Powers with a view to subjugation; the Turkish dominions in Asia Minor, and perhaps in Europe, await a slow, precarious process of absorption; the paper partition of Central Africa teems with possibilities of conflict. The entrance of the United States into the imperial struggle throws virtually the whole of South America into the arena; for it is not reasonable to expect that European nations, with settlements and vast economic interests in the southern peninsula, will readily leave all this territory to the special protection or ultimate absorption of the United States, when the latter, abandoning her old consistent isolation, has plunged into the struggle for empire in the Pacific.

Beyond and above all this looms China. It is not easy to suppose that the present lull and hesitancy of the Powers will last, or that the magnitude and manifest risks of disturbing this vast repository of incalculable forces will long deter adventurous groups of profit-seekers from driving their Governments along the slippery path of commercial treaties, leases, railway and mining concessions, which must entail a growing process of political interference.

It is not my purpose to examine here the entanglement of political and economic issues which each of these cases presents, but simply to illustrate the assertion that the policy of modern Imperialism is not ended but only just begun, and that it is concerned almost wholly with the rival claims of Empires to dominate "lower races" in tropical and sub-tropical countries, or in other countries occupied by manifestly unassimilable races.

In asking ourselves what are the sound principles of world policy and of national policy in this matter, we may at first ignore the important differences which should affect our conduct towards countries inhabited by what appear to be definitely low-typed unprogressive races, countries whose people manifest capacity of rapid progress from a present low condition, and countries like India and China, where an old civilisation of a high type, widely differing from that of European nations, exists.

Before seeking for differences of policy which correspond to these conditions, let us try to find whether there are any general principles of guidance in dealing with countries occupied by "lower" or unprogressive peoples.

It is idle to consider as a general principle the attitude of mere *laissez faire*. It is not only impracticable in view of the actual forces which move politics, but it is ethically indefensible in the last resort.

To lay down as an absolute law that "the autonomy of every nation is inviolable" does not carry us very far. There can no more be absolute nationalism in the society of nations than absolute individualism in the single nation. Some measure of practical internationality, implying a "comity of nations," and some relations of "right" and "duty" between nations, are almost universally admitted. The rights of self-government, implied by the doctrine of autonomy, if binding in any sense legal or ethical on other nations, can only possess this character in virtue of some real international organisation, however rudimentary.

It is difficult for the strongest advocate of national rights to assert that the people in actual occupation or political control over a given area of the earth are entitled to do what they will with "their own," entirely disregarding the direct and indirect consequences of their actions upon the rest of the world.

It is not necessary to take extreme cases of a national policy which directly affects the welfare of a neighbouring State, as where a people on the upper reaches of a river like the Nile or the Niger might so damage or direct the flow as to cause plague or famine to the lower lands belonging to another nation. Few, if any, would question some right of interference from without in such a case. Or take another case which falls outside the range of directly other-regarding actions. Suppose a famine or flood or other catastrophe deprives a population of the means of living on their land, while unutilised land lies in plenty beyond their borders in another country, are the rulers of the latter entitled to refuse an entrance or a necessary settlement? As in the case of individuals, so of nations, it will be generally allowed that necessity knows no laws, which, rightly interpreted, means that the right of self-preservation transcends all other rights as the prime condition of their emergence and exercise.

This carries us on an inclined plane of logic to the real issue as ably presented by Mr. Kidd, Professor Giddings, and the "Fabian" Imperialists. It is an expansion of this plea of material necessity that constitutes the first claim to a control of the tropics by "civilised" nations. The European races have grown up with a standard of material civilisation based largely upon the consumption and use of foods, raw materials of manufacture, and other goods which are natural products of tropical countries. The industries and the trade which furnish these commodities are of vital importance to the maintenance and progress of Western civilisation. The large part played in our import trade by such typically tropical products as sugar, tea, coffee, india-rubber, rice, tobacco, indicates the dependence of

such countries as Great Britain upon the tropics. Partly
from sheer growth of population in temperate zones,
partly from the rising standard of material life, this
dependence of the temperate on the tropical countries
must grow. In order to satisfy these growing needs
larger and larger tracts of tropical country must be
cultivated, the cultivation must be better and more
regular, and peaceful and effective trade relations with
these countries must be maintained. Now the ease with
which human life can be maintained in the tropics
breeds indolence and torpor of character. The inhabitants of these countries are not "progressive people"; they
neither develop the arts of industry at any satisfactory
pace, nor do they evolve new wants or desires, the
satisfaction of which might force them to labour. We
cannot therefore rely upon the ordinary economic
motives and methods of free exchange to supply the
growing demand for tropical goods. The resources of
the tropics will not be developed voluntarily by the
natives themselves.

"If we look to the native social systems of the
tropical East, the primitive savagery of Central Africa,
to the West Indian Islands in the past in process of
being assisted into the position of modern States by
Great Britain, or the black republic of Hayti in the
present, or to modern Liberia in the future, the lesson
seems everywhere the same; it is that there will be no
development of the resources of the tropics under native
government." [1]

We cannot, it is held, leave these lands barren; it
is our duty to see that they are developed for the
good of the world. White men cannot " colonise " these
lands and, thus settling, develop the natural resources

[1] Kidd, "The Control of the Tropics," p. 53 (Macmillan & Co.).

by the labour of their own hands ; they can only organise and superintend the labour of the natives. By doing this they can educate the natives in the arts of industry and stimulate in them a desire for material and moral progress, implanting new " wants " which form in every society the roots of civilisation.

It is quite evident that there is much force in this presentation of the case, not only on material but on moral grounds ; nor can it be brushed aside because it is liable to certain obvious and gross abuses. It implies, however, two kinds of interference which require justification. To step in and utilise natural resources which are left undeveloped is one thing, to compel the inhabitants to develop them is another. The former is easily justified, involving the application on a wider scale of a principle whose equity, as well as expediency, is recognised and enforced in most civilised nations. The other interference, whereby men who prefer to live on a low standard of life with little labour shall be forced to harder or more continuous labour, is far more difficult of justification.

I have set the economic compulsion in the foreground, because in point of history it is the *causa causans* of the Imperialism that accompanies or follows.

In considering the ethics and politics of this interference, we must not be bluffed or blinded by critics who fasten on the palpable dishonesty of many practices of the gospel of " the dignity of labour " and " the mission of civilisation." The real issue is whether, and under what circumstances, it is justifiable for Western nations to use compulsory government for the control and education in the arts of industrial and political civilisation of the inhabitants of tropical countries and other so-called lower races. Because Rhodesian mine-owners or Cuban sugar-growers stimulate the British or American Government to Imperialism by parading motives and results which do not really concern them, it does not follow that these motives under proper guidance are unsound, or that the results are undesirable.

There is nothing unworthy, quite the contrary, in the notion that nations which, through a more stimulative environment, have advanced further in certain arts of industry, politics, or morals, should communicate these to nations which from their circumstances were more backward, so as to aid them in developing alike the material resources of their land and the human resources of their people. Nor is it clear that in this work some "inducement, stimulus, or pressure" (to quote a well-known phrase), or in a single word, "compulsion," is wholly illegitimate. Force is itself no remedy, coercion is not education, but it may be a prior condition to the operation of educative forces. Those, at any rate, who assign any place to force in the education or the political government of individuals in a nation can hardly deny that the same instrument may find a place in the civilisation of backward by progressive nations.

Assuming that the arts of "progress," or some of them, are communicable, a fact which is hardly disputable, there can be no inherent natural right in a nation to refuse that measure of compulsory education which shall raise it from childhood to manhood in the order of nationalities. The analogy furnished by the education of a child is *primâ facie* a sound one, and is not invalidated by the dangerous abuses to which it is exposed in practice.

The real issue is one of safeguards, of motives, and of methods. What are the conditions under which a nation may help to develop the resources of another,

Q

and even apply some element of compulsion in doing
so? The question, abstract as it may sound, is quite
the most important of all practical questions for this
generation. For, that such development will take place,
and such compulsion, legitimate or illegitimate, be exercised, more and more throughout this new century
in many quarters of this globe, is beyond the shadow
of a doubt. It is the great practical business of the
century to explore and develop, by every method which
science can devise, the hidden natural and human
resources of the globe.

That the white Western nations will abandon a quest
on which they have already gone so far is a view which
does not deserve consideration. That this process of
development may be so conducted as to yield a gain
to world-civilisation, instead of some terrible *débâcle* in
which revolted slave races may trample down their
parasitic and degenerate white masters, should be the
supreme aim of far-sighted scientific statecraft.

II

To those who utter the single cry of warning, " *laissez
faire*, hands off, let these people develop their resources
themselves with such assistance as they ask or hire, un-
disturbed by the importunate and arrogant control of
foreign nations," it is a sufficient answer to point out the
impossibility of maintaining such an attitude.

If organised Governments of civilised Powers re-
fused the task, they would let loose a horde of private
adventurers, slavers, piratical traders, treasure hunters,
concession mongers, who, animated by mere greed of gold
or power, would set about the work of exploitation under
no public control and with no regard to the future;

playing havoc with the political, economic, and moral institutions of the peoples, instilling civilised vices and civilised diseases, importing spirits and firearms as the trade of readiest acceptance, fostering internecine strife for their own political and industrial purposes, and even setting up private despotisms sustained by organised armed forces.   It is unnecessary to revert to the buccaneering times of the sixteenth century, when a "new world" was thrown open to the plunder of the old, and private gentlemen of Spain or England competed with their Governments in the most gigantic business of spoliation that history records.   The story of Samoa, of Hawaii, and a score of South Sea Islands in quite recent years, proves that, at a time when every sea is a highway, it is impossible for the most remote land to escape the intrusion of "civilised" nations, represented by precisely their most reckless and debased specimens, who gravitate thither in order to reap the rapid fruits of licence.   The contact with white races cannot be avoided, and it is more perilous and more injurious in proportion as it lacks governmental sanction and control.   The most gigantic modern experiment in private adventure is slowly yielding its full tale of horrors in the Congo Free State, while the handing over of large regions in Africa to the virtually unchecked government of Chartered Companies exposes everywhere the dangers of a contact based on private commercialism.[1]

[1] Chartered Company government is not necessarily bad in its direct results.   It is, in fact, little else than private despotism rendered more than usually precarious in that it has been established for the sake of dividends.   A "managing director" may be scrupulous and far-sighted, as Sir G. T. Goldie in the Niger Company, or unscrupulous and short-sighted, as Mr. Rhodes in the South African Chartered Company.   The unchecked tyranny of the managing director may be illustrated by the evidence of the Duke of Abercorn tendered to the South African Committee.   "Mr. Rhodes had received a power of attorney to do precisely what he liked without consultation with the Board, he simply notifying what was done."

To abandon the backward races to these perils of private exploitation, it is argued forcibly, is a barbarous dereliction of a public duty on behalf of humanity and the civilisation of the world. Not merely does it leave the tropics to be the helpless prey of the offscourings of civilised nations; it opens grave dangers in the future, from the political or military ambitions of native or imported rulers, who, playing upon the religious fanaticism or the combative instincts of great hordes of semi-savages, may impose upon them so effective a military discipline as to give terrible significance to some black or yellow "peril." Complete isolation is no longer possible even for the remotest island; absolute self-sufficiency is no more possible for a nation than for an individual: in each case society has the right and the need to safeguard its interests against an injurious assertion of individuality.

Again, though there is some force in the contention that the backward natives could and would protect themselves against the encroachments of private adventurers, if they had the assurance that the latter could not call upon their Government for assistance or for vengeance, history does not lead us to believe that these powers of self-protection, however adequate against forcible invasions, would suffice to meet the more insidious wiles by which traders, prospectors, and political adventurers insinuate their poisons into primitive societies like that of Samoa or Ashanti.

So far, we have established two tentative principles. First, that all interference on the part of civilised white nations with "lower races" is not *primâ facie* illegitimate. Second, that such interference cannot safely be left to private enterprise of individual whites. If these principles be admitted, it follows that civilised Governments *may* undertake the political and economic control of lower races—in a word, that the characteristic form of modern Imperialism is not under all conditions illegitimate.

What, then, are the conditions which render it legitimate? They may be provisionally stated thus: Such interference with the government of a lower race must be directed primarily to secure the safety and progress of the civilisation of the world, and not the special interest of the interfering nation. Such interference must be attended by an improvement and elevation of the character of the people who are brought under this control. Lastly, the determination of the two preceding conditions must not be left to the arbitrary will or judgment of the interfering nation, but must proceed from some organised representation of civilised humanity.

The first condition is deduced directly from the principle of social utility expanded to its widest range, so as to be synonymous with "the good of humanity." Regarding the conduct of one nation towards another we can find no other standard. Whatever uncertainty or other imperfection appertains to such a standard, regarded as a rule for international policy, any narrower standard is, of necessity, more uncertain and more imperfect. No purely legal contentions touching the misapplication of the term "right" to international relations, in the absence of any form of "sanction," affects our issue. Unless we are prepared to reaffirm in the case of nations, as the all-sufficient guide of conduct, that doctrine of "enlightened selfishness" which has been almost universally abandoned in the case of individuals, and to insist that the unchecked self-assertion of each nation, following the line of its own private present interest, is the best guarantee of the general progress of humanity, we must set up, as a supreme standard of moral appeal, some conception of the welfare of humanity regarded as an organic unity. It is, however, needless to insist upon the analogy between the relation of an individual to the other individuals of his society, and that of one society towards another in the commonwealth of nations. For, though cynical statesmen of the modern Macchiavelli school may assert the visible interest of their country as the supreme guide of conduct, they do not seriously suggest that the good of humanity is thus attained, but only that this wider end has no meaning or appeal for them. In the light of this attitude all discussion of general principles "justifying" conduct is out of place, for "just" and "justice" are ruled out *ab initio*. The standard here proposed would not, however, in point of fact be formally rejected by any school of political thinkers who were invited to find a general law for the treatment of lower races. No one would assert in so many words that we had a right to sacrifice the good of any other nation, or of the world at large, to our own private national gain.

In England, certainly, Lord Rosebery's declaration that the British Empire is "the greatest secular agency for good known to the world" would everywhere be adopted as the fundamental justification of empire.

Lord Salisbury expressly endorses the principle, asserting that "the course of events, which I should prefer to call the acts of Providence, have called this country to exercise an influence over the character and progress of the world such as has never been exercised in any Empire before"; while the Archbishop of Canterbury propounds a doctrine of "imperial Christianity" based upon the same assumptions. It may, then, fairly be understood that every act of "Imperialism" consisting of forcible interference with another people can only be justified by showing that it contributes to "the civilisation of the world."

Equally, it is admitted that some special advantage must be conferred upon the people who are the subject of this interference. On highest ground of theory, the repression, even the extinction, of some unprogressive or retrogressive nation, yielding place to another more socially efficient and more capable of utilising for the general good the natural resources of the land, might seem permissible, if we accepted unimpaired and unimproved the biological struggle for existence as the sole or chief instrument of progress. But, if we admit that in the highest walks of human progress the constant tendency is to substitute more and more the struggle with natural and moral environment for the internecine struggle of living individuals and species, and that the efficient conduct of this struggle requires the suspension of the lower struggle and a growing solidarity of sentiment and sympathy throughout entire humanity, we shall perceive two important truths. First, "expansion," in order to absorb for the more "progressive" races an ever larger portion of the globe, is not the "necessity" it once appeared, because progress will take place more and more upon the qualitative plane, with more intensive cultivation alike of natural resources and of human life. The supposed natural necessity for crowding out the lower races is based on a narrow, low, and purely quantitative analysis of human progress.

Secondly, in the progress of humanity, the services of nationality, as a means of education and of self-development, will be recognised as of such supreme importance that nothing short of direct physical necessity in self-defence can justify the extinction of a nation. In

a word, it will be recognised that " le grand crime inter-
nationnel est de détruire une nationalité." [1]   But even
those who would not go so far in their valuation of
the factor of nationality will agree that it is a sound
practical test of conduct to insist that interference with
the freedom of another nation shall justify itself by
showing some separate advantage conferred upon the
nation thus placed in an inferior position: partly,
because it seems obvious that the gain to the general
cause of civilisation will chiefly be contained in or compassed by an improvement in the character or condition
of the nation which is the subject of interference; partly,
because the maxim which recognises the individual person as an end, and requires State government to justify
itself by showing that the coercion it exercises does in
reality enlarge the liberty of those whom it restrains, is
applicable also to the larger society of nations.   Without
unduly pressing the analogy of individual and nation as
organisms, it may safely be asserted that imperial interference with a " lower race " must justify itself by showing that it is acting for the real good of the subject race.
Mr. Chamberlain is no sentimentalist, and his declaration
may rank as a *locus classicus* upon this matter.   " Our
rule over the territories [native] can only be justified if
we can show that it adds to the happiness and prosperity
of the people."

The moral defence of Imperialism is generally based
upon the assertion that in point of fact these two conditions are fulfilled, viz. that the political and economic
control forcibly assumed by " higher " over " lower races "
does promote at once the civilisation of the world and
the special good of the subject races.   The real answer,
upon which British Imperialists rely in defending ex-

[1] M. Brunetière, quoted *Edinburgh Review*, April 1900.

pansion, is to point to actual services rendered to India, Egypt, Uganda, &c., and to aver that other dependencies where British government is less successful would have fared worse if left either to themselves or to another European Power.

Before considering the practical validity of this position, and the special facts that determine and qualify the work of "civilising" other races, it is right to point out the fundamental flaw in this theory of "Imperialism," viz. the non-fulfilment of the third condition laid down above. Can we safely trust to the honour, the public spirit, and the insight of any of the competing imperial races the subordination of its private interests and ends to the wider interests of humanity or the particular good of each subject race brought within its sway?

No one, as we point out, contends that so perfect a natural harmony exists that every nation, consciously following its own chief interest, is "led" as "by an invisible hand" to a course of conduct which necessarily subserves the common interest, and in particular the interest of the subject race. What security, then, can possibly exist for the practices of a sound Imperialism fulfilling the conditions laid down? Does any one contend that the special self-interest of the expanding and annexing nation is not a chief, or indeed the chief conscious determinant in each step of practical Imperialism? *Primâ facie* it would seem reasonable to suppose that many cases would occur in which the special temporary interests of the expanding nation would collide with those of the world-civilisation, and that the former would be preferred. It is surely unreasonable to take as proof of the fulfilment of the conditions of sane Imperialism the untested and unverified *ipse dixit* of an interested party.

III

While it is generally agreed that the progress of world-civilisation is the only valid moral ground for political interference with "lower races," and that the only valid evidence of such progress is found in the political, industrial, and moral education of the race that is subjected to this interference, the true conditions for the exercise of such a "trust" are entirely lacking.

The actual situation is, indeed, replete with absurdity. Each imperialist nation claims to determine for itself what are the lower races it will take under its separate protection, or agrees with two or three neighbours to partition some huge African tract into separate spheres of influence; the kind of civilisation that is imposed is never based on any sober endeavour to understand the active or latent progressive forces of the subject race, and to develop and direct them, but is imported from Europe in the shape of set arts of industry, definite political institutions, fixed religious dogmas, which are engrafted on alien institutions. In political government progress is everywhere avowedly sacrificed to order, and both alike are subservient to the quick development of certain profitable trading industries, or to the mere lust of territorial aggrandisement. The recurrent quarrels of the armed white nations, each insisting on his claim to take up the white man's burden in some fresh quarter of the globe; the trading companies seeking to oust each other from a new market, the very missionaries competing by sects and nationalities for "mission fields," and using political intrigue and armed force to back their special claims, present a curious commentary upon the "trust for civilisation" theory.[1]

It is quite evident that this self-assertive sway lacks the first essentials of a trust, viz. security that the "trustee" represents fairly all the interested parties, and is responsible to some judicial body for the faithful fulfilment of the terms of the trust. Otherwise what safeguard exists against the abuse of the powers of the trustee? The notorious fact that half the friction between European nations arises from conflicting claims to undertake the office of "trustee for civilisation" over lower races and their possessions augurs ill alike for the sincerity of the profession and the moral capacity to fulfil it. It is surely no mark of cynicism to question closely this extreme anxiety to bear one another's burdens among the nations.

This claim to justify aggression, annexation, and forcible government by talk of duty, trust, or mission can only be made good by proving that the claimant is accredited by a body genuinely representative of civilisation, to which it acknowledges a real responsibility, and that it is in fact capable of executing such a trust.

In a word, until some genuine international council exists, which shall accredit a civilised nation with the duty of educating a lower race, the claim of a "trust" is nothing else than an impudent act of self-assertion.

[1] From the *Times*, 24th February 1902.

"Hong-Kong, 22nd February.

"The German missionaries who escaped after the mission house at Frayuen was destroyed by Chinese have returned. It is reported from Canton that the French bishop intends to protect the natives who destroyed the Berlin mission station. The first information showed that hostility existed on the part of the Catholics towards the native Protestants, but it is believed that the aggressors assumed Catholicism as a subterfuge. If the bishop defends them, the situation of the missions in Kwang-tung will become complicated."

One may well be sceptical about the early feasibility of any such representative council; but until it exists it would be far more honest for "expanding" nations to avow commercial necessity or political ambition as the real determinant of their protection of lower races than to feign a "trust" which has no reality. Even were international relations more advanced, and the movement begun at the Hague Conference had solidified in a permanent authoritative body, representative of all the Powers, to which might be referred not only the quarrels between nations, but the entire partition of this "civilising" work, the issue would still remain precarious. There would still be grave danger lest the "Powers," arrogating to themselves an exclusive possession of "civilisation," might condemn to unwholesome and unjust subjection some people causing temporary trouble to the world by slow growth, turbulence or obnoxious institutions, for which liberty might be the most essential condition of progress. Apart from such genuine misapprehensions, there would exist the peril of the establishment of a self-chosen oligarchy among the nations which, under the cloak of the civilising process, might learn to live parasitically upon the lower races, imposing upon them "for their own good" all the harder or more servile work of industry, and arrogating to themselves the honours and emoluments of government and supervision.

Clear analysis of present tendencies points indeed to some such collusion of the dominant nations as the largest and gravest peril of the early future. The series of treaties and conventions between the chief European Powers, beginning with the Berlin African Conference of 1885, which fixed a standard for the "amicable division" of West African territory, and the similar treaty in 1890, fixing boundaries for English, German, and Italian encroachments in East Africa, doubtless mark a genuine advance in the relations of the European Powers, but the objects and methods they embody throw a strange light upon the trust theory. If to the care of Africa we add that of China, where the European Powers have lately taken common action in "the interests of civilisation," the future becomes still more menacing. While the protection of Europeans was the object in the foreground, and imposed a brief genuine community of policy upon the diverse nations, no sooner was the immediate object won than the deeper and divergent motives of the nations became manifest. The entire history of European relations with China in modern times is little else than one long cynical commentary upon the theory that we are engaged in the civilisation of the Far East. Piratical expeditions to force trade upon a nation whose one principle of foreign policy was to keep clear of foreigners, culminating in a war to compel the reception of Indian opium; abuse of the generous hospitality given for centuries to peaceful missionaries by wanton insults offered to the religious and political institutions of the country, the forcible exaction of commercial and political "concessions" as punishment for spasmodic acts of reprisal, the cold-blooded barter of murdered missionaries for the opening of new treaty ports, territory at Kiao Chow, or a new reach of the Yang-Tse for British trading vessels; the mixture of menace, cajolery, and bribery by which England, Russia, Germany, France, and Japan have laboured to gain some special and separate railway or mining concessions, upon terms excluding or damaging the interest of the others; the definite assumption by Christian bishops and missionaries of political authority,

and the arrogant and extensive use of the so-called right
of "extra-territoriality," whereby they claim, not only
for themselves but for their alleged converts and protégés, immunity from the laws of the land—all these
things sufficiently expose the hollowness in actual history
of the claims that considerations of a trust for civilisation animate and regulate the foreign policy of Christendom, or of its component nations.   What actually
confronts us everywhere in modern history is selfish,
materialistic, short-sighted, national competition, varied
by occasional collusion.   When any common. international policy is adopted for dealing with lower races
it has partaken of the nature, not of a moral trust, but
of a business "deal."

It seems quite likely that this policy of "deals" may
become as frequent and as systematic in the world of
politics as in the world of commerce, and that treaties
and alliances having regard to the political government
and industrial exploitation of countries occupied by
lower races may constitute a rude sort of effective
internationalism in the early future.

Now, such political arrangements fall short in two
important respects of that genuine trust for civilisation
which alone could give moral validity to a "civilised"
control of lower peoples.   In the first place, its assignment of a sphere of interest or a protectorate to England,
to Germany, or Russia, is chiefly determined by some
particular separate interest of that country by reason
of contiguity or other private convenience, and not by
any impartial consideration of its special competence
for the work of civilisation.   If, for example, European
Powers were really animated by the desire to extend
Western civilisation to China for her own good and
that of the world, they might more favourably essay

this task by promoting the influence of Japan than by inserting their own alien occidentalism. But no one proposes to delegate to Japan this " trust "; every nation thinks of its own present commercial interests and political prestige.

Secondly, the civilisation of the lower races, even according to accepted Western lights, is nowhere adopted as the real aim of government. Even where good political order is established and maintained, as in Egypt or India, its primary avowed end, and its universally accepted standard of success, are the immediate economic benefits attributed thereto. The political government of the country is primarily directed everywhere to the rapid, secure, effective development of the national resources, and their profitable exploitation by native labour under white management. It is maintained and believed that this course is beneficial to the natives, as well as to the commerce of the controlling Power and of the world at large. That Indians or Egyptians are better off to-day than they were before our autocratic sway, not merely in economic resources but in substantial justice, may be quite true; it may even be accredited to us that many of our governors and officials have displayed some disinterested concern for the immediate well-being of the races committed (by ourselves) to our trust. But it can nowhere be sincerely contended that either we or any other Christian nation are governing these lower races upon the same enlightened principles which we profess and sometimes practise in governing ourselves. I allude here not to method of government but to ends. In the more enlightened European States and their genuine colonies, though present economic considerations bulk largely enough, they do not absorb the present and the future of public policy; provision is made for some play of non-economic forces, for the genuine culture of human life and character, for progress alike in individual growth and in the social growth which comes by free processes of self-government. These are regarded as essential conditions of the healthy growth of a nation. They are not less essential in the case of lower nations, and their exercise demands more thought and more experiment. The chief indictment of Imperialism in relation to the lower races consists in this, that it does not even pretend to apply to them the principles of education and of progress it applies at home.

IV

If we or any other nation really undertook the care and education of a "lower race" as a trust, how should we set about the execution of the trust? By studying the religions, political and other social institutions and habits of the people, and by endeavouring to penetrate into their present mind and capacities of adaptation, by learning their language and their history, we should seek to place them in the natural history of man; by similar close attention to the country in which they live, and not to its agricultural and mining resources alone, we should get a real grip upon their environment. Then, carefully approaching them so as to gain what confidence we could for friendly motives, and openly discouraging any premature private attempts of exploiting companies to work mines, or secure concessions, or otherwise to impair our disinterested conduct, we should endeavour to assume the position of advisers. Even if it were necessary to enforce some degree of authority, we should keep such force in the background as a last resort, and make it our first aim to understand and to promote the healthy free operations of all internal forces for progress which we might discover.

Natural growth in self-government and industry along tropical lines would be the end to which the enlightened policy of civilised assistance would address itself.

Now, what are the facts? Nowhere has any serious organised attempt been made, even by Great Britain, by far the largest of the trustees, to bring this scientific disinterested spirit of inquiry to bear upon the races whose destiny she dominates.[1] The publications of the Aborigines Protection Society, and the recent report of the Native Races Committee, dealing with South Africa, indicate the vast range of unexplored knowledge, and the feeble fumblings which have hitherto taken the place of ordered investigations.[2] It is natural that this should be so. White pioneers in these countries are seldom qualified to do the work required; the bias of the trader, the soldier, or the professional traveller, is fatal to sober, disinterested study of human life, while the missionary who has contributed more than the rest, has seldom been endowed with a requisite amount of the scientific spirit or the scientific training.

Even the knowledge which we do possess is seldom utilised for light and leading in our actual government of native races. There are indeed signs of an awakening intelligence in certain spots of our Empire; administrators like Sir George Grey, Lord Ripon, and Sir Marshall Clarke have brought sympathy and knowledge to the establishment of careful experiments in self-government. The forms of protectorate exercised over Basutoland and

[1] The recent formation of an African Society, in memory of Miss Mary Kingsley, for the study of the races of that continent, is a move in the right direction.

[2] No slight is here intended upon the excellent work of the Society and the Committee here named. They have handled well and accurately their material. It is the work of original research that is so lacking.

Khama's Country in South Africa, the restoration of the province of Mysore to native government, and the more careful abstention from interference with the internal policy of feudatory States in India, are favourable signs of a more enlightened policy.

In particular, the trend of liberal sentiment regarding government of lower races is undergoing a marked change. The notion that there exists one sound, just, rational system of government, suitable for all sorts and conditions of men, embodied in the elective representative institutions of Great Britain, and that our duty was to impose this system as soon as possible, and with the least possible modifications, upon lower races, without any regard to their past history and their present capabilities and sentiments, is tending to disappear in this country, though the new headstrong Imperialism of America is still exposed to the taunt that "Americans think the United States has a mission to carry 'canned' civilisation to the heathen." The recognition that there may be many paths to civilisation, that strong racial and environmental differences preclude a hasty grafting of alien institutions, regardless of continuity and selection of existing agencies and forms—these genuinely scientific and humane considerations are beginning to take shape in a demand that native races within our Empire shall have larger liberty of self-development assured to them, and that the imperial Government shall confine its interference to protection against enemies from without, and preservation of the elements of good order within.

The true "imperial" policy is best illustrated in the case of Basutoland, which was rescued in 1884 from the aggressive designs of Cape Colony, stimulated by industrial exploiters.

Here British imperial government is exercised by a

Commissioner, with several British magistrates to deal with grave offences against order, and a small body of native police under British officers. For the rest, the old political and economic institutions are preserved—government by chiefs, under a paramount chief, subject to the informal control or influence of public opinion in a national assembly; ordinary administration, chiefly consisting in allotment of land, and ordinary jurisdiction are left to the chiefs.

" As far back as 1855 Moshesh forbade the ' smelling-out' of witches, and now the British authorities have suppressed the more noxious or offensive kinds of cere-monies practised by the Kaffirs. Otherwise, they interfere as little as possible with native ways, trusting to time, peace, and the missionaries to secure the gradual civilisa-tion of the people." " No Europeans are allowed to hold land, and a licence is needed even for the keeping of a store. Neither are any mines worked. European prospectors are not permitted to come in and search for minerals, for the policy of the authorities has been to keep the country for the natives, and nothing alarms the chiefs so much as the occasional appearance of these speculative gentry, who, if admitted, would soon dis-possess them." [1]

These sentences serve to point the path by which most of our Imperialism has diverged from the ideal of a " trust for civilisation."

The widest and ultimately the most important of the struggles in South Africa is that between the policy of Basutoland and that of Johannesburg and Rhodesia; for there, if anywhere, we lay our finger on the difference between a " sane " Imperialism, devoted to the protection, education, and self-development of a " lower race," and

[1] Mr. Bryce, "Impressions of South Africa," p. 422.

an "insane" Imperialism, which hands over these races
to the economic exploitation of white colonists who will
use them as "live tools" and their lands as repositories
of mining or other profitable treasure.

V

It is impossible to ignore the fact that this "saner"
Imperialism has been vitiated in its historic origins in
almost every quarter of the globe.   Early Imperialism
had two main motives, the lust of "treasure" and the
slave trade.

Gold and silver, diamonds, rubies, pearls, and other
jewels, the most condensed forms of portable and durable
wealth by which men in a single hazardous adventure,
by fortune, fraud, or force, might suddenly enrich themselves—these from the ancient days of Tyre and Carthage
have directed the main current alike of private and
national exploration, and have laid the foundation of
white dominion over the coloured races.   From Ophir,
Golconda, and the Orinoco to Ashanti, Kimberley, Klon-
dike, the Transvaal and Mashonaland it is the same story:
to the more precious metals, tin and copper were early
added as motives of nearer and less hazardous trading
ventures, and the machine economy of recent generations
has lifted coal and iron deposits to the rank of treasures
worth capture and exploitation by civilised nations.   But
gold still holds its own as the dramatic centre of gravitation for Imperialism.

But along with these motives, and of even wider operation, has been the desire to obtain supplies of slave or serf
labour.   The earliest, the most widely prevalent, and the
most profitable trade in the history of the world has been
the slave trade.   Early forms of imperial expansion were

directed less to any permanent occupation and government of foreign countries than to the capture of large supplies of slave labour to be transmitted to the conquering country. The early Imperialism of the Greek States and of Rome was largely governed by this same motive. Greeks and Romans did not often effect large permanent settlements among the barbarians they conquered, but, contenting themselves with keeping such military and magisterial control as sufficed to secure order and the payment of tribute, drafted large numbers of slaves into their countries in order to utilise their labour. The Greek cities were mostly maritime, commercial, and industrial, and the slaves they drew from Eastern trade or from the Scythian and Thracian "hinterlands" they employed upon their ships and docks, in their mines, and as artisans and labourers in their towns: Rome, the capital of an agricultural State, used her slaves on a "plantation system," ousting by this cheap forced labour the peasantry, who, driven into Rome, were subsisted chiefly upon public charity, defrayed out of the tribute of their foreign conquests.[1]

Now modern Imperialism in its bearing on the "lower races" remains essentially of the same type: it employs other methods, other and humaner motives temper the dominance of economic greed, but analysis exposes the same character at bottom. Wherever white men of "superior races" have found able-bodied savages or lower races in possession of lands containing rich mineral or agricultural resources, they have, whenever strong enough, compelled the lower race to work for their benefit, either organising their labour on their own land, or inducing them to work for an unequal barter, or else conveying

[1] *Cf.* Mr. Gilbert Murray in "Liberalism and the Empire," pp. 126–129 (Brimley Johnson).

them as slaves or servants to another country where their labour-power could be more profitably utilised. The use of imperial force to compel "lower races" to engage in trade is commonly a first stage of Imperialism : China is here the classic instance of modern times, exhibiting the sliding scale by which sporadic trade passes through "treaties," treaty ports, customs control, rights of inland trading, mining and railway concession towards annexation and general exploitation of human and natural resources.

The slave trade or forcible capture and conveyance of natives from their own to a foreign land has in its naked form nearly disappeared from the practice of Western nations (save in the case of Belgium in the Congo), as also the working of conquered people as slaves in their own country.[1]

The entire economic basis of the industrial exploitation of inferior races has shifted with modern conditions of life and industry. The change is a twofold one: the legal status of slave has given place to that of wage-labourer, and the most profitable use of the hired labour of inferior races is to employ them in developing the resources of their own lands under white control for white men's profit.

"In ancient times the employer would not, if he could, go away from his own country to employ Libyans or Scythians in their native places. If he left home, it was not so easy to come back. He was practically in

---

[1] In the British Protectorate of Zanzibar and Pemba, however, slavery still exists (notwithstanding the Sultan's decree of emancipation in 1897) and British courts of justice recognise the status. Miss Emily Hutchinson, who is associated with the Friends' Industrial Mission at Pemba, said it was five years since the legal status of slavery was abolished in Zanzibar and Pemba. Every one, including those who were most anxious that the liberation should proceed slowly, was dissatisfied with the present state of affairs. Out of an estimated population of 25,000 slaves in Pemba less than 5000 had been liberated so far under the decree (Anti-Slavery Society Annual Meeting, April 4, 1902).

exile. In the second place, he was not sufficiently master of his slaves in their own country. If they were all of one nation and all at home, they might rebel or break loose. If a strong Government prevented that, it was at any rate much easier for individual slaves to escape—a consideration always of the utmost importance. In modern times, the increasing ease of communication has enabled white men to go abroad to all parts of the earth without suffering much real exile and without losing the prospect of returning home at will. Our Governments, judged by ancient standards, are miraculously strong; our superior weapons make rebellions almost impossible. Consequently we do not attempt to import blacks, coolies, and Polynesians into Great Britain. The opposition of the working classes at home would be furious; and, even if that obstacle were overcome, the coloured men would die too fast in our climate. The whole economic conditions are in favour of working the coloured man in his own home." [1]

This conclusion, however, requires some qualification in the case of European colonies. The British colony of Queensland and the French New Caledonia are fed still with indentured labour from Polynesia; Natal has been "worked" in large measure by a similar flow of "coolie" labour, while Chinese labour, free or indentured, has found its way into the Straits Settlements, Burma, Borneo, New Guinea, North and East Australia, and many parts of America, Oceania, and Africa, until checked or prohibited by legislation. Still, it is true that the general modern tendency is to work the coloured man in his own home, or in some neighbouring country to whose climatic and other natural characters he can easily adapt himself.

[1] Murray, "Liberalism and the Empire," p. 141.

The chief economic condition which favours this course is not, however, the greater willingness of modern white men to sojourn for a while abroad, but the ever-growing demand for tropical goods, and the abundant overflow of capital from modern industrial States, seeking an investment everywhere in the world where cheap labour can be employed upon rich natural resources.

The ancients carried off the lower races to their own country, because they could use their labour but had little use for their land; we moderns wish the lower races to exploit their own lands for our benefit. The tastes for tropical agricultural products, such as rice, tea, sugar, coffee, rubber, &c., first aroused by trade, have grown so fast and strong that we require larger and more reliable supplies than trade with ill-disciplined races can afford us; we must needs organise the industry by Western science and Western capital, and develop new supplies. So likewise with the vast mineral resources of lands belonging to lower races; Western capital and Western exploiting energy demand the right to prospect and develop them. The real history of Imperialism as distinguished from Colonialism clearly illustrates this tendency. Our first organised contact with the lower races was by means of trading companies, to which some powers of settlement and rights of government were accorded by charter as incidental to the main purpose, viz. that of conducting trade with native inhabitants. Such small settlement as took place at first was for trade and not for political expansion or genuine colonisation of a new country. This was the case even in America with the London and Plymouth Companies, the Massachusetts Bay Company, and the Hudson's Bay Company, though other colonising motives soon emerged; our first entrance into the West Indies was by a trading settlement of the London Company in Barbados; the foundation of our great Eastern Empire was laid in the trading operations of the East India Company, while the Gold Coast was first touched by the Royal Africa Company in 1692. Holland and France were moved by the same purpose, and the tropical or sub-tropical settlements which later passed from their hands into ours were mostly dominated by commercialism and a government based avowedly on commercial exploitation.[1]

As we approach more recent times, investment of capital and organisation of native labour on the land, the plantation system, play a more prominent part in the policy of new companies, and the British North Borneo Company, the Sierra Leone Company, the Royal Niger Company, the East Africa Company, the British South Africa Company, are no longer chiefly trading bodies, but are devoted more and more to the control and development of agricultural and mining resources by native labour under white management to supply Western markets. In most parts of the world a purely or distinctively commercial motive and conduct have furnished the nucleus out of which Imperialism has grown, the early trading settlement becoming an industrial settlement, with land and mineral concessions growing round it, an industrial settlement involving force, for protection, for securing further concessions, and for checking or punishing infringements of agreement or breaches of order; other interests, political and religious, enter in more largely, the original commercial settlement assumes a stronger political and military character, the reins of government are commonly taken over by the State from the company, and a vaguely defined protectorate passes gradually into the form of a colony.

[1] Cf. Morris, "The History of Colonisation," vol. ii. p. 60, &c.

Sierra Leone, Uganda, and, at no distant date, Rhodesia, will serve for recent instances of this evolution.

VI

The actual history of Western relations with lower races occupying lands on which we have settled throws, then, a curious light upon the theory of a "trust for civilisation." When the settlement approaches the condition of genuine colonisation, it has commonly implied the extermination of the lower races, either by war or by private slaughter, as in the case of Australian Bushmen, African Bushmen and Hottentots, Red Indians, and Maoris, or by forcing upon them the habits of a civilisation equally destructive to them.[1] This is what is meant by saying that "lower races" in contact with "superior races" naturally tend to disappear. How much of "nature" or "necessity" belongs to the process is seen from the fact that only those "lower races" tend to disappear who are incapable of profitable exploitation by the superior white settlers, either because they are too "savage" for effective industrialism or because the demand for labour does not require their presence.

Whenever superior races settle on lands where lower races can be profitably used for manual labour in agriculture, mining, and domestic work, the latter do not tend to die out, but to form a servile class. This is the case, not only in tropical countries where white men cannot form real colonies, working and rearing families

---

[1] Mr. Bryce (Romanes Lecture, 1902, p. 32) says: "I was told in Hawaii that the reduction of the native population, from about 300,000 in Captain Cook's time to about 30,000 in 1883, was largely due to the substitution of wooden houses for the old wigwams, whose sides, woven of long grass, had secured natural ventilation, and to the use of clothes, which the natives, accustomed to nothing more than a loin cloth, did not think of changing or drying when drenched with rain."

with safety and efficiency, and where hard manual work, if done at all, must be done by " coloured men," but even in countries where white men can settle, as in parts of South Africa and of the southern portion of the United States.

As we entered these countries for trade, so we stay there for industrial exploitation, directing to our own profitable purposes the compulsory labour of the lower races. This is the root fact of Imperialism so far as it relates to the control of inferior races; when the latter are not killed out they are subjected by force to the ends of their white superiors.

With the abolition of the legal form of slavery the economic substance has not disappeared. It is no general question of how far the character of slavery adheres in all wage labour that I am pressing, but a statement that Imperialism rests upon and exists for the sake of "forced labour," *i.e.* labour which natives would not undertake save under direct or indirect personal compulsion issuing from white masters.

There are many methods of "forcing" labour.

Wherever the question of industrial development of tropical or sub-tropical lands for agricultural or mining purposes comes up, the same difficulty confronts the white masters. The Report of the Select Committee of the House of Commons in 1842 on the state of the West Indies, subsequent to the emancipation of slaves, states the problem most succinctly : " The labourers are enabled to live in comfort and to acquire wealth without, for the most part, labouring on the estates of the planters for more than three or four days in a week, and from five to seven hours in a day, so that they have no sufficient stimulus to perform an adequate amount of work." The reason of this inadequate amount of work (how many

white men in the West Indies put in a five to seven hours'
working-day ?) is that they can get high wages, and this
is attributed "to the easy terms upon which the use of
land has been obtainable by negroes." In a word, the
Committee considered "that the cheapness of land has
been the main cause of the difficulties which have been
experienced, and that this cheapness is the natural result
of the excess of fertile land beyond the wants of the
existing population."

The negro would only put in a five to seven hours'
day at high pay because he had the option of earning
his livelihood on fertile land of his own. The same
trouble confronts the white master everywhere where the
lower races are in possession of agricultural land sufficient
for their low and unprogressive standard of comfort; they
either will not work at all for wages, or will not work
long enough or for low enough pay.

"The question, in a few words," writes Professor
Ireland, "is this—What possible means are there of
inducing the inhabitants of the tropics to undertake
steady and continuous work if the local conditions are
such that from the mere bounty of nature all the ambitions of the people can be gratified without any considerable amount of labour ?"[1]

There are only two genuinely economic forces which
will bring such labour more largely into the labour
market; the growth of population with increased difficulty
in getting a full easy subsistence from the soil is one, the
pressure of new needs and a rising standard of consumption is the other.

These may be regarded as the natural and legitimate
inducements to wage labour, and even in most tropical
countries they exercise some influence, especially where

[1] "Tropical Colonisation," p. 155 (The Macmillan Co.).

white settlements have taken up much of the best land. In the lowest races, where the increase of population is kept down by high mortality, aggravated by war and infanticide, and where new wants are slowly evolved, these inducements are feeble; but in more progressive peoples they have a fair amount of efficacy. Unfortunately, these natural forces are somewhat slow, and cannot be greatly hastened; white industrialists are in a hurry to develop the country, and to retire with large, quick profits. The case of South Africa is typical. There many of the Bantu races are fairly educable in new needs, and are willing to undertake wage labour for their satisfaction; many of them, notably the Basutos, are becoming overcrowded on their reserved lands, and are willing to go far for good wages. But the demands of a vast mining industry, growing within a few years to gigantic proportions, cannot await the working of these natural stimuli; the mine-owners want an unnatural accession to the labour market. The result is frantic efforts to scour the continents of Africa and Asia, and bring in masses of Zanzibari, Arabs, Indian coolies, or Chinese, or else to substitute for natural economic pressure various veiled modes of political or private compulsion.

The simplest form of this compulsion is that of employing armed force upon individual natives to " compel them to come in," as illustrated by the methods of the South Africa Chartered Company before 1897,[1] which,

[1] Sir Richard Martin in his report states his conviction " that the Native Commissioners, in the first instance, endeavoured to obtain labour through the Indunas, but failing that they procured it by force."

Howard Hensman, defending the administration of the Company in his " History of Rhodesia " (Blackwood & Sons), admits the practice, thus describing it: " In Rhodesia a native who declined to work " (i.e. for wages) " was taken before the Native Commissioners and sent off to some mine or public work close at hand, paid at what, to him, were very high rates, fed and housed, and then at the end of three months he was allowed to return to his kraal, where he was permitted to remain for the rest of the year " (p. 257).

when the chiefs failed to provide labour, sent out native
police to "collect the labour." Save its illegal character,
there is nothing to distinguish this from the *corvée* or
legalised forced labour imposed on natives in Natal, or
the Compulsory Labour Ordinance passed by the Gold
Coast Legislature in December 1895, reviving the lapsed
custom under which it was "obligatory on persons of the
labouring class to give labour for public purposes on being
called out by their chiefs or other native superiors," and
authorising the Government to compel native chiefs to
furnish as many carriers as were needed for the projected
expedition to Kumasi.[1]

Military service, borrowing a semblance of "civilised"
usage from the European system of conscription, is
utilised, not merely for emergencies, as in the Kumasi
expedition, and in our South African campaign, where
native labour has everywhere been "pressed," when
ordinary economic motives failed, but for regular industrial labour. The classical instance is that of the
Congo Free State, where a "militia" levy is made upon
the population, nominally for defence, but really for the
State and Chartered Company service in the "rubber"
and other industries.

In face of unrepealed decrees according "une protection spéciale aux noirs," and prescribing that "l'escla-
vage, même domestique, ne saurait être reconnu officiale-
ment," a system of "voluntary" and "militia" levies has
been instituted to be used "in the establishment of
plantations and the construction of works of public
utility." The accuracy of Mr. Fox Bourne's commentary
is attested by numerous witnesses. "The 'force publique'
with its 'agriculteurs soldats' and others subordinate to
it, when not employed on military expeditions, are used

[1] *Cf.* "Whites and Blacks in South Africa," by H. R. Fox Bourne, p. 63.

as overseers of what are virtually slave-gangs or as collectors of 'tribute' from the luckless aborigines, whose right to live in their own country, without paying heavily for the privilege, is denied." [1]

So far as "forced labour" is designed merely as a mode of revenue to the State, a system of "taxation in kind," it cannot be condemned as essentially unjust or oppressive, however liable it may be to abuses in practice. All taxation is "forced labour," whether the tax be levied in money, in goods, or in service. When such "forced labour" is confined to the needs of a well-ordered government, and is fairly and considerately administered, it involves no particular oppression. Such "servitude" as it involves is concealed under every form of government.

The case is quite different where governmental regulations and taxation are prostituted to purposes of commercial profit; where laws are passed, taxes levied, and the machinery of public administration utilised in order to secure a large, cheap, regular, efficient, and submissive supply of labourers for companies or private persons engaged in mining, agricultural, or other industries for their personal gain.

Where white settlers find "lower races" in occupation of lands rich in agricultural, mineral, or other resources, they are subject to a double temptation. They want possession of the land and control of a cheap native supply of labour to work it under their control and for their gain. If the "natives" are of too low an order or too untamable to be trained for effective labour they must be expelled or exterminated, as in the case of the "lower nomads" the Bushmen of Australia and South Africa, the Negritos, Bororos,

---

[1] "Slavery and its Substitutes in Africa," p. 11.

Veddahs, &c., and even the Indians of North America. War, murder, strong drink, syphilis and other civilised diseases are chief instruments of a destruction commonly couched under the euphemism "contact with a superior civilisation." The land thus cleared of natives passes into white possession, and white men must work it themselves, or introduce other lower industrial peoples to work it for them, as in the case of slave labour introduced into the United States and West Indies, or indentured labour into Natal, British Guiana, &c.

But where the "lower races" are capable of being set to profitable labour on their own land, as agriculturists, miners, or domestics, self-interest impels the whites to work a "forced-labour" system for their private ends. In most tropical or sub-tropical countries the natives can by their own labour and that of their families get a tolerably easy subsistence from the land. If they are to be induced to undertake wage labour for white masters, this must be put a stop to. So we have pressure brought upon government to render it impossible for the natives to live as formerly upon the land. Their land and, when they are a pastoral people, their cattle are objects of attack.

The Torrens Act, by which in 1852 the doctrine of "eminent domain" was applied to South Australia in such wise as to make all the country virtually Crown land, though not ill-meant, has furnished a baneful precedent, not only for encroachment of British settlers, but for the still more flagrant abuses of Belgian adventurers on the Congo. White settlers or explorers, sometimes using legal instruments, sometimes private force or fraud, constantly encroach upon the fertile or mineralised lands of natives, driving them into less fertile lands, crowding them into reserves, checking their nomadic habits, and otherwise making it more difficult for them to obtain a livelihood by the only methods known to them.

A chief object and a common result of this policy is to induce or compel natives to substitute wage labour, altogether or in part, for the ancient tribal life upon the land. Those ignorant of the actual conditions involved often suppose that the alienation of lands or mineral rights, or the contracts for labour, are negotiated in accordance with ordinary methods of free bargain.

The modern history of Africa, however, is rich in instances to the contrary.

The history of competitive knavery and crime, by which Lobengula was inveigled into signing away " rights " which he neither owned nor understood to the Chartered Company, cannot yet be written completely, but its outlines are plain and profitable reading.

A " free contract," implying voluntary action, full knowledge and approximate equality of gain to both parties, is almost unknown in the dealings of superior with inferior races. How political treaties and industrial concessions are actually obtained may be described for us by Major Thruston,[1] who was sent to negotiate treaties in 1893 in Uganda.

" I had been instructed by Colonel Colvile to make a treaty with Kavalli, by which he should place himself under British protection ; in fact, I had a bundle of printed treaties which I was to make as many people sign as possible. This signing is an amiable farce, which is supposed to impose on foreign Governments, and to be the equivalent of an occupation. The *modus operandi* is somewhat as follows : A ragged, untidy European, who in any civilised country would be in danger of being

---

[1] " Personal Experiences in Egypt and Unyoro " (Murray).

taken up by the police as a vagrant, lands at a native village; the people run away, he shouts after them to come back, holding out before them a shilling's worth of beads. Some one, braver than the rest, at last comes up; he is given a string of beads, and is told that if the chief comes he will get a great many more. Cupidity is, in the end, stronger than fear; the chief comes and receives his presents; the so-called interpreter pretends to explain the treaty to the chief. The chief does not understand a word of it, but he looks pleased as he receives another present of beads; a mark is made on a printed treaty by the chief, and another by the interpreter; the vagrant, who professes to be the representative of a great Empire, signs his name. The chief takes the paper, but with some hesitation, as he regards the whole performance as a new and therefore dangerous piece of witchcraft. The boat sails away, and the new ally and protégé of England or France immediately throws the treaty into the fire."

This cynical bit of realistic humour expresses with tolerable accuracy the formal process of "imperial expansion" as it operates in the case of lower races. If these are the methods of political agents, it may well be understood that the methods of private "concession-mongers" are not more scrupulous. Indeed "political protectorate" and "land concession" are inextricably blended in most instances where some adventurer, with a military or other semi-official commission, pushes across the frontier into a savage country, relying upon his Government to endorse any profitable deal he may accomplish.

But since, in the case of England at any rate, political expansion is commonly subordinate to industrial exploitation, a treaty or concession, giving rights over land or minerals, is of little value without control of labour.

Enclosure of lands, while it facilitates a supply of native labour by restricting free land for native agriculture or pasture, does not commonly suffice. Various devices are adopted for bringing pressure to bear upon individual labourers to "contract" for wage labour. The simplest, apart from direct compulsion, is to bribe chieftains to use their "influence" with members of their tribe. Such was the system devised by the philanthropic Earl Grey to procure labour for the mines in Rhodesia.[1]

Such bargaining, either with "headmen" or with individual natives, is usually conducted by professional labour touts, who practise every form of craft and falsehood so as to induce ignorant natives to enter a labour contract. In the case of the Transvaal mines this abuse had become so monstrous as to "spoil the labour market," obliging the mine-owners to go ever farther afield for their labour, and eventually compelling them to petition the Government for assistance in putting down the system of private labour touts, and substituting authorised responsible officials. Alike in the Boer Republics and in Cape Colony, the seizures of land and labour have been chief motives of the border warfare constantly recurring in the history of South Africa. The encroachments of Boers or British colonists upon native territory or reserves, or the seizure of cattle on border land by one party or the other, have led to punitive expeditions, the result of which has been further confiscation of land and capture of prisoners, who, formerly held as slaves, have in more recent times been kept to labour as "apprentices" or indentured labourers.

[1] "We propose to give to the big chiefs, when they have proved themselves worthy of trust, a salary of £5 a month and a house. . . . The indunas will then be responsible to the Government for the conduct of their people." This, Earl Grey supposes, "is the best way to secure a considerable revenue in the future in the shape of hut-tax, and to obtain a fair supply of labour for the mines" (*Times*, 28th November 1896).

The case of Bechuanaland in 1897 affords a serviceable illustration. A small local riot got up by a drunken
native sub-chief on a trifling grievance, and involving
armed resistance on the part of a few hundred Kaffirs,
easily put down by a small body of armed volunteers, was
exaggerated into a " rebellion," and was made a pretext
for driving some 8000 natives from the lands "inalien-
ably" secured to them by the Bechuanaland Annexation
Act of 1895, and for confiscating these lands for British
occupation, while the rest of the population, some
30,000, were to be gradually removed from their settlements, and given " equivalent land " in some other
district.   In the speech introducing the confiscation
measure in the Cape Parliament, Sir Gordon Sprigg
explained that this was " very valuable land, and probably would be cut up into very small farms, so that
there might be a considerable European population
established in that part of the country."   There was no
pretence that most of those who were deprived of their
lands or deported were proved to have taken part in the
" rebellion."   The sequel of this clearing is most significant.   What was to become of the people taken from
their land ?   They were offered a choice between prose-
cution " on a charge of sedition" and " service in the
colony upon such conditions and with such rates of wages
as the Government might arrange for a term of five
years."   The Government, in thus proposing to compound a felony, was well aware of the extreme difficulty
of proving " sedition " in a court of justice, and, in point
of fact, in two cases which were put on trial the Public
Prosecutor declined to bring the case before a jury.   The
object of the threat of trial was to coerce into the acceptance of " indentured labour," and in fact 584 men, with
three times as many women and children, were handed

over to serve under colonial farmers, wages being fixed at
10s. a month for able-bodied men and 7s. 6d. for women.

Thus did covetous colonials kill two birds with one
stone, obtaining the land and the labour of the Bechuana
"rebels." [1] It is not necessary to suppose that such incidents are deliberately planned : where empire is asserted over lower races in the form of protectorate,
the real government remaining in native hands, offences
must from time to time arise, local disturbances which
can by rash or brutal treatment be fanned into "rebellion" and form the pretext for confiscation and a forcing
of the landless rebels into "labour."

Among African tribes the most vulnerable point is the
cattle, which form their most important, often their only,
property. To encroach upon this is a sure way of provoking hostility. The Bechuana riot seems to have
arisen from an injudicious handling of precautions needed
to deal with the rinderpest. The second Matabele war,
with its murders of white settlers and the wholesale
slaughter in reprisal, was directly instigated by the seizure
of cattle belonging to the tribesmen, on the unproven

---

[1] The details of this business, recorded in Blue-book C. 8797, relating
to native disturbances, are most instructive to the student of Imperialism.

The Inspector of Native Locations in his report of the affair distinctly
asserts : "That it was not a general rising of the Mashowing people is certain, because there were not more than 100 natives engaged in the Kobogo
fight." Yet the whole of the Mashowing territory was confiscated and all
the population treated as rebels.

While only some 450 men were taken with arms, 3793 men, women, and
children were arrested and deported, 1871 being afterwards "indentured"
in the colony. Seven-eighths of the prisoners were women, children, or
unarmed men. Even of the men who were taken in arms at the Langeberg Sir A. Milner wrote (January 5, 1898) : "I am inclined to think that in
many other cases, if the prisoners had chosen to stand their ground, the
same difficulty (as in two cases taken to trial) would have been found in
establishing legal evidence of treason. It is probable that, of the men who
surrendered at the Langeberg, some had never fought against the Government at all, while many others had done so reluctantly. To bring home
treasonable intent to any large number of them would, I conceive, have
been a difficult matter " (p. 48).

theory that all cattle belonged to the king and thus came
into the possession of the Chartered Company. As a
sequel of the first Matabele war large quantities of cattle
had been stolen by white settlers to stock the farms
which had just been pegged out for them in the land
they had taken, and the further threat of a wholesale
confiscation of cattle, though not carried into full effect,
lay at the root of the subsequent rebellion.[1]

Everywhere these attacks upon the land and cattle
of lower races, provoking reprisals, followed by further
confiscation and a breaking-up of the old tribal life upon
the soil, have as a related secondary object the provision
of a supply of cheap labour for the new white masters,
to be employed in farming, on mines, or for military
service.

Such labour commonly preserves a semblance of
free contract, engagements "voluntarily" entered into for
a fixed period at agreed wages. The amount of real freedom depends partly upon the amount of personal pressure
brought to bear by the chief through whom bargains are
commonly struck, still more on the amount of option
which remains to get a living from the land.

[1] Here is the account of a Rhodesian writer, defending the British
policy:—

"Seeing that Lobengula only allowed his followers to own cattle on
sufferance as it were, all the herds in the country might be said to be the
property of the late king, and that was the view which the British South
Africa Company took. The number of cattle in the country at this time
was estimated at not less than a quarter of a million head, and the indunas were ordered at once to drive in the cattle from the districts over
which they had control to Buluwayo. Some of the indunas duly com-
plied with this demand, in which they saw nothing more than what was
to be expected as the outcome of the war; but others, and those chiefly
who had not taken any part in the fighting, declined to do so, and hid
the cattle away out of reach of the Native Commissioners. As the cattle
did not come in in such numbers as they ought to have done, the Government ordered the Native Commissioners to collect and send in each
month a certain number of cattle. . . . This step proved a highly unpopular one among the natives" ("History of Rhodesia," by H. Hensman,
p. 165).

This last is the vital matter in an understanding of "forced labour." In one sense all labour is "forced" or "unfree," where it is not open to the "proletariat" to get a living by cultivation of the soil: this is the normal condition of the vast majority of the people in Great Britain and in some other white man's countries. What is peculiar to the system of "forced labour," as here used, is the adoption by a white ruling race of legal measures designed expressly to compel the individual natives to whom they apply to quit land, which they occupy and by which they can live, in order to work in white service for the private gain of the white man. When lands formerly occupied by natives are confiscated, or otherwise annexed for white owners, the creation of a labour supply out of the dispossessed natives is usually a secondary object. But this "forcing" becomes a system when measures are devised by Government for the express purpose of "compelling" labour.

VII

The simplest method, that of "slavery," is generally abolished by European nations. *Corvée*, the Congo and former Rhodesian methods are seldom openly advocated or defended; but the adoption of various forms of public compulsion in order to drive natives into private service is generally approved by "colonials," and is sanctioned by imperialist statesmen. A chief instrument of this indirect compulsion is taxation. There is nothing essentially unreasonable in imposing a hut or a pole-tax upon natives to assist in defraying the expenses of government, provided that care is taken in the modes of assessment and collection, and due allowance made for the fluctuating economic circumstances of agricultural populations with narrow markets and small use of money. But these taxes are not infrequently applied so as to dispossess natives of their land, force them to work for wages, and even to drive them into insurrections which are followed by wholesale measures of confiscation.

The case of the risings in Sierra Leone during 1898 attests the nature of this impolicy, and the following passage from the report of the Special Commissioner, Sir David Chalmers, deserves attention. His conclusions as to the causes of the insurrection are thus summarised:—

"The hut-tax, together with the measures used for its enforcement, were the moving causes of the insurrection. The tax was obnoxious to the customs and feelings of the people. A peremptory and regularly recurring impost is unknown in their own practices and traditions. The English Government has not as yet conferred any such benefits as to lead to a burden of a strange and portentous species being accepted willingly. There was a widespread belief that it was a means of taking away their rights in their country and in their property."[1] "The amount of the tax is higher than the people, taken together, can pay, and the arrangements by which liability is primarily placed on the chiefs to make good definite amounts on demand are unworkable." "The mode of enforcing payment provided by the law would probably prove abortive, whether used to meet inability or unwillingness to pay." "Repugnance to the tax was

[1] Miss Mary Kingsley regards this "widespread belief" as justified.

"It has been said that the Sierra Leone hut-tax war is a 'little Indian Mutiny'; those who have said it do not seem to have known how true the statement is, for these attacks on property in the form of direct taxation are, to the African, treachery on the part of England, who, from the first, has kept on assuring the African that she does not mean to take his country from him, and then, as soon as she is strong enough, in his eyes, deliberately starts doing so" ("West African Studies," p. 372; Macmillan & Co.).

much aggravated by the sudden, uncompromising and harsh methods by which it was endeavoured to be brought into operation, not merely by the acts of native policemen, but in the whole scheme adopted by the colonial authorities."

Here Sir D. Chalmers condenses all the familiar grievances of monetary taxes imposed by strong expensive white Governments upon poor "native" races. White government, if good, is expensive, hence taxation tends to be heavy in amount; fixed in amount, it must be paid out of very fluctuating industries; levied in money, it forces self-subsisting families or tribes to find markets for their goods or labours; collected, as it must be, by native authorities, it breeds extortion, corruption, and cruelty. But Sir D. Chalmers lays his finger on the central vice when he names " a widespread belief that it was a means of taking away their rights in their country and in their property."[1]

Where there exists a large growing demand for native labour this method of compelling natives to pay money taxes is seen to have a new importance. They can only earn money by undertaking labour contracts. Hence a system of direct taxation imposed by hut, poll, or labour-taxes is devised. Everywhere, as we have seen, under free popular government, the tendency is to subordinate direct to indirect taxation. "Imperialism" alone favours direct taxation of the working classes. It does not, however, propose a general system of direct taxation applicable alike to whites and blacks. The direct taxes with

---

[1] Compare the pathetic plaint of the natives in Rhodesia, as voiced by Sir Richard Martin in his official report. "The natives practically said : ' Our country is gone and our cattle; we have nothing to live for. Our women are deserting us; the white man does as he likes with them. We are the slaves of the white man; we are nobody, and have no rights or laws of any kind ' " (Cd. 8547).

which we are here concerned are applied exclusively to the "subject" races.

In South Africa their chief avowed aim is, not to provide revenue, but to compel labour.   The hut and labour taxation is not strongly developed in Cape Colony or in Natal, because the break-up of old tribal life, and the substitution of individual economic family life favouring wage labour, has hitherto furnished a sufficient supply of labour to countries, mainly agricultural, thinly peopled by white settlers, and only in one district, that of Kimberley, developing a considerable centralised demand for native labour.   The hut-tax in these colonies has, therefore, not proved an oppressive burden.   Only when the diamond fields found difficulties in obtaining a ready supply of native labour, and wages rose, did Mr. Rhodes, a chief proprietor, use his public position as Cape Premier to procure an Act designed to assist De Beers in obtaining cheap labour. By this statute, the Glen Grey Act, it was enacted that every male native, in districts where the Act was adopted, should pay a "labour-tax" of 10s. per annum, unless he could prove that during three months of each year "he has been in service or employment beyond the borders of the district."   No secret was made of the fact that this measure was designed, not to provide revenue, but to compel to labour.   "If they could make these people work they would reduce the rate of labour in the country," said Mr. Rhodes; and in another speech in Parliament: "It was wrong that there should be a million natives in that country, and yet that they should be paying a sum equal to about £1 a week for their labour, while that labour was absolutely essential for the proper development of the country."

The "labour-tax" has not, however, operated oppressively in Cape Colony; for the diamond industry, being limited in output, has not demanded more native labour than could be easily supplied by ordinary economic inducements.

It is in the Transvaal and Rhodesia that taxation of natives ripens into a plan of forcing labour. The mine-owners of the Transvaal are agreed as to their right and their need to compel the natives to undergo the dignity of labour, and they regard taxation as one important instrument. The testimony of witnesses before the Industrial Commission in 1897 was unanimous in favouring such compulsion, and Mr. Rudd, of the Consolidated Goldfields, stated the demand very plainly at the annual meeting of his company.[1] "If we could only call upon one-half of the natives to give up three months of the year to work, that would be enough. We should try some cogent form of inducement, or practically compel the native, through taxation or in some other way, to contribute his quota to the good of the community, and to a certain extent he should then have to work." The general feeling of the "Outlanders" in the Transvaal has favoured the oppressive hut-tax of £2, imposed by the Republic in 1895, and has only complained of its inadequate enforcement.

Similarly, in Rhodesia, where mines require a larger supply of labour than can be obtained from natives by ordinary economic motives, an increase of the hut-tax and a labour-tax are an integral part of the public policy. Earl Grey, recent administrator and present director of the Chartered Company, thus states the case: "Means have to be found to induce the natives to seek, spontaneously (sic!), employment at the mines, and to work willingly for long terms of more or less

[1] November 19, 1899.

continuous employment. An incentive to labour must be provided, and it can only be provided by the imposition of taxation. I look forward to the imposition of a hut-tax of £1 per hut in conformity with the practice which exists in Basutoland, and I also hope that we may, with the permission of the imperial authorities, be able to establish a labour-tax, which those able-bodied natives should be required to pay who are unable to show a certificate of four months' work."

It remains to add that one "imperial authority" of some importance has expressly endorsed this policy of using public finance for private profit-making purposes. In a speech in the House of Commons dealing with the Chartered Company,[1] Mr. Chamberlain said: "When you say to a savage people who have hitherto found their chief occupation in war, 'You shall no longer go to war; tribal war is forbidden,' you have to bring about some means by which they may earn their living in place of it, and you have to induce them to adopt the ordinary means of earning a livelihood by the sweat of their brow. But with a race of this kind I doubt very much whether you can do it merely by preaching. I think that something in the nature of an inducement, stimulus, or pressure is absolutely necessary if you are to secure a result which is desirable in the interests of humanity and civilisation."

A far more thorough and logical application of the policy of taking natives from their life upon the land in order to perform wage labour is devised by the Transvaal mine-owners. The native labour problem there differs widely from the case of Kimberley, where only some 12,000 natives under strict control are required

[1] May 7, 1898.

for the diamond industry. The intention of working out, with the utmost rapidity, the gold of the Rand can only be accomplished by securing a vast and a growing supply of native labour on the spot. In 1899, with great difficulty and at heavy expense, less than 100,000 natives were secured for work upon the mines. If twice or thrice this number is to be procured and at lower prices, this can only be accomplished by using taxation, coercion, and persuasion to induce large numbers of Kaffirs to come and settle down with their families upon locations in the mining districts, where the amount of land provided does not enable them to get a living from agriculture, and where they will consequently be dependent on wage labour at the mines, and will breed a permanent supply of young labour on the spot. The wages paid will be determined, not by competition, but by the Chamber of Mines; the houses they will occupy will be the property of the mines, as also the shops where they will be compelled to deal. This is the policy advocated by the chief mining experts.

Break up the tribal system which gives solidarity and some political and economic strength to native life; set the Kaffir on an individual footing as an economic bargainer, to which he is wholly unaccustomed, take him by taxation or other "stimulus" from his locality, put him down under circumstances where he has no option but to labour at the mines—this is the plan which mine-owners propose and missionaries approve.[1]

[1] This has been the policy of the Glen Grey Act, and the following passage from the official report of a resident magistrate in a district of Cape Colony (Mr. W. T. Brownlie of Butterworth) makes its main economic motive transparent: "I have long held and still hold that the labour question and the land question are indissolubly bound together. In my opinion it is of little use framing enactments to compel unwilling persons to go out to work. It is like the old saw about leading a horse to the

This system of "native locations," fortified by hut and labour-taxes, and by pass laws which interfere with freedom of travel and practically form a class of *ascripti glebæ*, is the only alternative to an expensive system of indentured labour from India, China, or distant parts of Africa. It will be adopted as the cheapest mode of getting a large, reliable, submissive supply; it will be defended as a means of bringing large masses of the natives under influences of civilisation, education, and Christianity.

The tendency will be for many who suspect the means adopted to condone the methods as necessary and as serviceable to the cause of progress. Sir Harry Johnston, in his "History of the Colonisation of Africa by Alien Races," expresses a view which easily recommends itself to those who are convinced that there is but one sort of civilisation.

"In this world natural law ordains that all mankind must work to a reasonable extent, must wrest from its environment sustenance for body and mind, and a bit over to start the children from a higher level than the parents. The races that will not work persistently and doggedly are trampled on, and in time displaced, by

water; you can take him there, but you cannot make him drink. In the same way you may impose your labour-tax, but you cannot make your unwilling persons work. Create a healthy thirst in your horse and he will drink fast enough. Similarly create the necessity for the native to work and he will work and none better.

"Hitherto, under our commercial-tenure system, there has been little absolute necessity for our young natives to leave their homes to work. The land supplies them with food, and a few shillings will buy a blanket, and as soon as the young man marries he is entitled to receive his lot of arable land; but once this is stopped—and it will be stopped by the survey and individual tenure—a young man before he marries a wife will have to be in a position to support a wife, and to obtain this he must work, and once having married her he must still work to maintain her and himself, and once the necessity of work is created there will be no lack of men ready and willing to work" ("Blue-book on Native Affairs," C. 31, p. 75). For the Transvaal mine-owners' extension and systematisation of the policy, see Appendix at the close of this chapter.

those who do. Let the negro take this to heart; let him devote his fine muscular development, in the first place, to the getting of his own rank, untidy continent in order. If he will not work of his own free will, now that freedom of action is temporarily restored to him; if he will not till, and manure, and drain, and irrigate the soil of his country in a steady, laborious way as do the Oriental and the European; if he will not apply himself zealously under European tuition to the development of the vast resources of tropical Africa, where hitherto he has led the wasteful, unproductive life of a baboon; then force of circumstances, the pressure of eager, hungry, impatient outside humanity, the converging energies of Europe and Asia will once more relegate the negro to a servitude which will be the alternative—in the coming struggle for existence—to extinction."

This widely accepted theory, accompanied by the illustrations of practice given above, makes it quite evident that Imperialism in its bearing on lower races implies the use of public force to compel natives to labour for the gain of white masters, and incidentally, it is claimed, for their own education and progress. The term "servitude" is rightly used by Sir H. Johnston. It is indeed feigned that the contracts by which natives hire themselves out to their white masters are "free," in the sense in which an English mechanic is free to dispose of his labour. But investigation of the circumstances attending such contracts shows the absence of the two essential characters of a "free contract," equitable purchase and voluntary service. In almost all cases, political domination by a white race, empire, is abused in order to apply compulsion to labour which would not be possible under conditions of popular self-government.

VIII

It is, of course, not true that all labour in the tropics is subject to these abuses. It is right to consider the best as well as the worst work of Imperialism on its economic side. There can be no question but that the best administered system of tropical labour under British rule is the indentured labour system as practised under imperial protection in certain West Indian islands and in Natal. British Guiana, Mauritius, and Trinidad are the West Indian possessions where the system of importing Indian coolie labour has been most practised, and where the system is best tested.

The present law governing indentured labour in British Guiana provides against most of the abuses which beset the economic relations of white employers towards "lower races," and appears to be well administered. Here the Imperial Government in India approves all contracts with immigrants, and these contracts not only contain a full statement of time, wages, and other conditions of labour and of living for the immigrant and his family, but provide for his return, if necessary at the public expense, at the end of his time. During the term of his indenture in British Guiana he is under the protection of authorities appointed and controlled by the governor alone. An immigration agent-general, with a staff of agents, who visit all plantations where indentured labourers are employed, hear privately all complaints, and bring them, if necessary, into the courts, retaining counsel and acting in all cases as the principals. Employers of indentured labour are obliged to keep and produce full and accurate books of accounts under heavy penalties, and are forbidden to pay wages below a certain sum or to overwork their labourers. No punishment of any kind can be imposed by employers without recourse to the courts. It is contended by Professor Ireland, who has had long experience as an overseer, that this system operates with remarkable success both economically and socially [1] in British Guiana and in other West Indian islands; and in Natal, though "coolies" are regarded with anything but favour by large sections of the population, substantially the same protective legislation is in force, and there is every reason to suppose that indentured labourers are well protected as regards wages and other economic conditions.

But the very encomia passed upon this well-administered system of indenture show how defective is the grasp of the magnitude and the real nature of the issues involved in the control of tropical labour.

It seems a light and natural thing that large bodies of men, with or without their families, should be driven by economic pressure to quit their native soil in our Indian Empire and absent themselves for ten years at a time in some unknown and remote colony. Migration to, and colonisation of, sparsely peopled lands by inhabitants of thickly peopled lands is a natural and wholly beneficial movement, but the break-up of settled life, implied by long periods of alienation, is fraught with grave injuries to both countries alike. A country which relies for its economic development on continual influxes of foreign labourers who will not settle is impaired in its natural process of industrial and political self-development by this mass of unassimilated sojourners, while the country which they have abandoned suffers a corresponding injury.

[1] "Tropical Colonisation," chap. v., by Professor Ireland, gives a full and detailed account of the theory and practice of indentured labour in British Guiana.

T

Why is it necessary or desirable that large bodies of our Indian fellow-subjects should desert their native land, removing for long periods their industrial services in order to develop another country which is not theirs? If India is over-populated, permanent colonisation is surely the remedy; if it is not, this practice of "indentured labour" seems to testify to misgovernment and bad husbandry of our Indian resources. To break up considerable areas of Indian society, and remove its able-bodied males for ten years at a time, in order that these men may bring back some "savings" at the end of their term, seems at best a wanton sacrifice of the stability and normal progress of Indian society to a narrow consideration of purely monetary gain. History teaches, in fact, that a peasant people living on soil which they own will not consent thus to alienate themselves for purposes of slight economic gain, unless they are compelled by excessive taxation on the part of Government, or by extortions of money-lenders, which deprive them in large measure of the enjoyment of the fruits of their labour on their land. Certain very thickly peopled districts of China form the only instance in the modern world where the mere stress of growing population seems to be the prime motive to such alienation.

However well administered this system of indentured labour may be, it seems vitiated in origin by its artificial character and its interference with normal processes of self-development. It involves a subordination of wider social considerations to purposes of present industrial exploitation. What is true of the system, as applied in the West Indies and elsewhere for agricultural work, is still more true of industrial labour in mining processes. Whether we regard the huge barrack-prison life of the Kimberley "compounds," or the laxer, more licentious conditions of Rand or Rhodesian locations, we are confronted by convincing evidence of the damage done to native life and character by these periodic removals from normal tribal life. When "civilised" Kaffirs choose to quit their individual farms in the Transkei, or elsewhere, in order to earn extra money by three months' service in the mines, no particular harm may offset their monetary gain; but when labour agents are employed to break up tribal life and tempt "raw" Kaffirs away from their kraals and the restraints of their habitual life into the utterly strange and artificial life upon the mines, the character of the Kaffir goes to pieces; he becomes a victim to drink if he can get it, and often succumbs to the vices of the crowded, laborious, unhealthy life to which he has sold himself, while the arbitrary restrictions under which he works and lives, however justified, degrade and damage his personality. According to the evidence of most experienced and competent investigators, he returns home a "damaged" man, and often by his example a damage to his neighbours.[1] The least reflection will expose the dangers which must arise from suddenly transferring men from a semi-savage, tribal, agricultural life to a great modern, elaborate, industrial business like that of diamond and gold mining.

It may well be doubted whether there is a net gain to the civilisation of the world by increasing the supply of gold and diamonds at such a price.

IX

It may be said: "Whatever the motives of employers may be, it is surely a good thing to take natives, by persuasion or even by force, from a life of idleness and

[1] *Cf.* "Cape Colony Blue-books on Native Affairs," G. 31, 1899, pp. 5, 9, 72, 75, 91, &c.; G. 42, 1898, pp. 13, 14, 58, 82.

habituate them to labour, which educates their faculties, brings them under civilising influences, and puts money into their pockets."

Now while the statement that such Kaffirs, West Africans, and other tropical or semi-tropical men, left to themselves, lead an idle life, is commonly a gross exaggeration, due largely to the fact that their work is more irregular and capricious than that of their women, it must be admitted that the repression of internecine warfare and the restriction of hunting do set free a large quantity of male energy which it is really desirable should be utilised for industrial purposes.   But for whose industrial purposes? Surely it is far better that the "contact with civilisation" should lead these men to new kinds of industry on their own land, and in their own societies, instead of dragging them off to gang-labour on the lands or mining properties of strangers   It can do this in two ways: by acquainting them with new wholesome wants it can apply a legitimate stimulus, and by acquainting them with new industrial methods applicable to work in their own industries it can educate them to self-help.   Where native peoples are protected from the aggressive designs of white profit-mongers, this salutary evolution operates. In large districts of Basutoland and in certain reserves of Zululand the substitution of the plough for the primitive hoe or pick has led to the introduction of male labour into the fields;[1] every encouragement in stock-raising, dairy-farming, or other occupations connected with animals enhances male employment among natives; the gradual introduction of new manufacturing industries into village life leads to men's taking a larger share in those in-

[1] Cf. "Report of South African Native Races Commission," p. 52, &c.; also "The Labour Question in South Africa, " by Miss A. Werner (The Reformer, December 1901).

dustries in or near the kraal which were formerly a monopoly of women.

So far as Imperialism seeks to justify itself by sane civilisation of lower races, it will endeavour to raise their industrial and moral status on their own lands, preserving as far as possible the continuity of the old tribal life and institutions, protecting them against the force and deceit of prospectors, labour touts, and other persons who seek to take their land and entice away their labour. If under the gradual teaching of industrial arts and the general educational influences of a white protectorate many of the old political, social, and religious institutions decay, that decay will be a natural wholesome process, and will be attended by the growth of new forms, not forced upon them, but growing out of the old forms and conforming to laws of natural growth in order to adapt native life to a changed environment.

But so long as the private, short-sighted, business interests of white farmers or white mine-owners are permitted, either by action taken on their own account or through pressure on a Colonial or Imperial Government, to invade the lands of "lower peoples," and transfer to their private profitable purposes the land or labour, the first law of "sane" Imperialism is violated, and the phrases about teaching "the dignity of labour" and raising races of "children" to manhood, whether used by directors of mining companies or by statesmen in the House of Commons, are little better than wanton exhibitions of hypocrisy. They are based on a falsification of the facts, and a perversion of the motives which actually direct the policy.

X

In setting forth the theory which sought to justify Imperialism as the exercise of forcible control over lower races, by regarding this control as a trust for the civilisation of the world, we pointed out three conditions essential to the validity of such a trust: first, the control must be directed to the general good, and not to the special good of the "imperialist" nation; secondly, it must confer some net advantage to the nation so controlled; lastly, there must exist some organisation representative of international interests, which shall sanction the undertaking of a trust by the nation exercising such control.

The third condition, which is fundamental to the validity of the other two, we saw to be unfulfilled, inasmuch as each nation claiming to fulfil the trust of governing lower races assumed this control upon its own authority alone.

The practice of Imperialism, as illustrated in a great variety of cases, exhibits the very defects which correspond with the unsound theory. The exclusive interest of an expanding nation, interpreted by its rulers at some given moment, and not the good of the whole world, is seen to be the dominant motive in each new assumption of control over the tropics and lower peoples; that national interest itself commonly signifies the direct material self-interest of some small class of traders, mine-owners, farmers, or investors who wish to dispose of the land and labour of the lower peoples for their private gain. Other more disinterested motives woven in may serve to give an attractive colouring to each business in hand, but it is impossible to examine the historic details in any important modern instance without recognising the supremacy of economic forces. At best it is impossible to claim more than this, that some consideration is taken of justice and humanity in the exercise of the authority assumed, and that incidentally the welfare of the lower race is subserved by the play of economic and political forces not primarily designed to secure that end.

Everywhere, in the white administration of these lower races, considerations of present order are paramount, and industrial exploitation of the land and labour under private management for private immediate gain is the chief operative force in the community, unchecked, or inadequately checked, by imperial or other governmental control. The future progress of the lower race, its gradual education in the arts of industrial and political self-government, in most instances do not at all engage the activity of imperial government, and nowhere are such considerations of the welfare of the governed really paramount.

The stamp of " parasitism " is upon every white settlement among these lower races, that is to say, nowhere are the relations between whites and coloured people such as to preserve a wholesome balance of mutual services. The best services which white civilisation might be capable of rendering, by examples of normal, healthy, white communities practising the best arts of Western life, are precluded by climatic and other physical conditions in almost every case : the presence of a scattering of white officials, missionaries, traders, mining or plantation overseers, a dominant male caste with little knowledge of or sympathy for the institutions of the people, is ill-calculated to give to these lower races even such gains as Western civilisation might be capable of giving.

The condition of the white rulers of these lower races is distinctively parasitic ; they live upon these natives,

their chief work being that of organising native labour
for their support.   The normal state of such a country
is one in which the most fertile lands and the mineral
resources are owned by white aliens and worked by
natives under their direction, primarily for their gain :
they do not identify themselves with the interests of the
nation or its people, but remain an alien body of sojourners, a "parasite" upon the carcass of its "host,"
destined to extract wealth from the country and retire
to consume it at home.   All the hard manual or other
severe routine work is done by natives; most of the real
labour of administration, or even of aggression, is done
by native overseers, police and soldiery.   This holds of
all white government in the tropics or wherever a large
lower population is found.   Even where whites can live
healthily and breed and work, the quantity of actual
work, physical or mental, which they do is very small,
where a large supply of natives can be made to work for
them.   Even in the parts of South Africa where whites
thrive best, the life they lead, when clearly analysed, is
seen to be parasitic.   The white farmer, Dutch or British,
does little work, manual or mental, and tends everywhere
to become lazy and "unprogressive"; the trading, professional or official classes of the towns show clear signs
of the same laxity and torpor, the brief spasmodic flares
of energy evoked by dazzling prospects among small
classes of speculators and business men in mushroom
cities like Johannesburg serving but to dazzle our eyes
and hide the deep essential character of the life.

If this is true of South Africa, much more is it
true of countries where climate inhibits white settlement and white energy, the general condition of those
countries which represent the expansion of modern
Imperialism.

Nowhere under such conditions is the theory of white government as a trust for civilisation made valid; nowhere is there any provision to secure the predominance of the interests, either of the world at large or of the governed people, over those of the encroaching nation, or more commonly a section of that nation. The relations subsisting between the superior and the inferior nations, commonly established by pure force, and resting on that basis, are such as preclude the genuine sympathy essential to the operation of the best civilising influences, and usually resolve themselves into the maintenance of external good order so as to forward the profitable development of certain natural resources of the land, under "forced" native labour, primarily for the benefit of white traders and investors, and secondarily for the benefit of the world of white Western consumers.

This failure to justify by results the forcible rule over alien peoples is attributable to no special defect of the British or other modern European nations. It is inherent in the nature of such domination. "The government of a people by itself has a meaning and a reality, but such a thing as government of one people by another does not and cannot exist. One people may keep another as a warren or preserve for its own use, a place to make money in, a human cattle-farm, to be worked for the profits of its own inhabitants; but if the good of the governed is the proper business of a government, it is utterly impossible that a people should directly attend to it." [1]

---

[1] J. S. Mill, "Representative Government," p. 326.

APPENDIX

THE LABOUR POLICY OF TRANSVAAL MINE-OWNERS

This policy is most succinctly stated in the language of the President of the Chamber of Mines, at Johannesburg, in his annual address for 1898:—

"I consider that one of our chief aims should be to get a class of labour that stays, and in that direction I should consider it a distinct advantage if we had been allowed to establish at a short distance from here some huge location where the natives could live with their families, but having no other means of earning their livelihood except by working in the mines, they would have secured a supply of skilled labour constantly available" (Cd. 9345, p. 31).

Here is the mining policy in a nut-shell. Natives are to be induced to come from a distance "with their families." At present they leave these families behind, and when they have earned enough money go away with it, and resume their tribal life of agriculture. But if they can be got to bring their families, they will have broken their tribal ties, and however much they may afterwards regret their action and desire to return, they will have given hostages to fortune; they cannot carry off their families, trek many hundreds of miles, and resume the old tribal life. In their new location they are not to be allowed land to cultivate, but are to be kept in an economic condition, which allows them no option but continuous work at the mines. These "location" natives will no longer work three or six months, and go away with their wages as heretofore; the conditions named above, supported by a rigorous enforcement of the pass law, will oblige them to stay all their working life in the service of the mines. Here is one great advantage of the location over the compound. Another advantage hardly less important is that by this location system the mines will " breed" their labour on the spot, young Kaffirs ripening in reliable crops every year to meet the growing demands of the labour market, with no option of turning to any other market or of making a living off the soil.

No wonder the location policy is popular among mine owners and managers. This is the scheme which is approved by all the witnesses before the Industrial Commission. Mr. Albu " would not recommend the compound system," because " it would hurt the industrial community" (p. 25); but says, " I think if the natives had their locations here, and had their wives and families, they would make this place their home " (p. 24).

Mr. Way, mine manager, when asked, " Can you suggest any plan by which a permanent supply could be relied upon for the Rand, skilled principally?" replied : "The only way is to give natives facilities for family life. We do it to a certain extent on the George Goch, and we get into considerable trouble for doing it. We have a location upon our lower claims, and I have boys who have their wives and families, who have been working at the mine for the last eight years. If locations could be established somewhere in the neighbourhood of the mines—within walking distance—so that the natives could bring down their wives and families, I think you would have a far greater supply than you require " (p. 43).

Mr. S. J. Jennings (p. 46), Mr. Brakhan (p. 184), Mr. Denny (p. 376), Mr. W. Hall (p. 429), the other mining witnesses examined on this subject, all endorsed the

location policy, the last named giving his opinion as
follows :—

"As to the Kaffir, he cannot be made to become a
progressive and reliable employee under the unnatural
condition in which he is now held. That he should
have at least a temporary home, within no great distance
from the mine centre, to which he could inexpensively
retire after his engagements on mine service are over,
and with the end of returning to mine work, seems to
me to be absolutely essential to the end in view; or else
he must be carried by rail, at a merely nominal rate,
practically to and from the country of his birth"
(p. 429).

This last passage indicates a new "economy" of the
location system. The demand for labour on the mines
has been, and will continue to be, irregular, and subject
to swift and sudden fluctuation. It is therefore important for the mine-owners to have upon the spot "a far
greater supply than you require," in Mr. Way's words,
so that you may get your increase quick and cheap
when you want it, and may force it "inexpensively"
to retire into unemployment when it is no longer
wanted.

One other economy is subserved by the location.
The miner will be forced to spend all his earnings, not
merely in the country, but on the spot, in shops owned,
rented, financed, or otherwise controlled by the mining
companies, or by the members of those companies in
some other business capacity.

The advocacy of the location system is, however,
not confined to the mine-owner. The clergy and missionaries, who profess the deepest concern for the "elevation"
of the natives, are divided between advocacy of the
compounds and advocacy of the location. While the

Rev. J. S. Moffat is persuaded of the beneficial moral influences of imprisonment in the Kimberley compound, the Rev. J. M. Bovill, rector of the Cathedral Church, Lorenzo Marques, champions the location. In his instructive book, " Natives under the Transvaal Flag," he states the case as follows :—

" Let native reserves or locations be established on the separated mines, or groups of mines, where the natives can have their huts built, *and live more or less under the same conditions as they do in their native kraals.* If a native found that he could live on the Rand under similar conditions to those he has been accustomed to, he will soon be anxious to save enough money to bring his wife and children there, and remain in the labour district for a much longer period than at present is the case. It would be a distinct gain to the mining industry as well as to the native " (p. 59).

This may be taken as a characteristic utterance of the sham philanthropy of the professional harmoniser of God and Mammon. For Mr. Bovill, who displays throughout his book an intimate acquaintance with the mining industry, must be well aware of the falsehood which is contained in the words we have italicised. These natives are not intended to live " more or less under the same conditions as they do in their native kraals," where their life is entirely agricultural and pastoral. On the contrary, it is, as we said, clearly recognised that they must not be allowed to work on the land, but must work in the mines for wages. In the location Mr. Bovill would not even leave them property in their own huts.

" Huts could be erected on a mine, or group of mines, at a very small cost, and I am sure that the natives would be quite willing to pay a monthly rent if they

were properly housed. Their huts, of course, would be
the property of the mines, built on ground belonging to
the mines, and under the supervision of the mines, much
as our miners' houses are in some of our colliery districts " (p. 61).

In order to complete the picture of economic servitude,
it is right to understand the wage system under which
these Kaffirs will work. Mr. Bovill does not trouble to
explain this, but the admission of mining witnesses before
the Industrial Commission and subsequent events supply
the lack. When Kaffirs with their families are "induced"
to settle in these locations, and to live in huts supplied
by mining companies, not only must they work for wages
in the mines, spending those wages in rent for their huts
and for goods purchased from the mining companies, but
they must work for whatever wages their employers
choose to pay. They will have no voice whatever in
determining their wages; no power of bargain will be
left to them. Their wages will be fixed, not by competition, but by the dictation of a complete monopoly.
For years past the policy of the various mining companies
upon the Rand has been to adopt a fixed tariff of wages;
this has been from the first a chief object of the Chamber
of Mines. The 30 per cent. reduction of wages in 1897
was successfully carried out by joint action, and Mr.
Albu, when asked, "Is there competition among the mines
with regard to the wages?" replied, "I don't think so at
the present moment." To the further question, "Is it
in the power of the mining industry to regulate the
wages of Kaffirs?" he answered, "To a great extent it
is, provided that the Government assists us in bringing
labour to this market" (p. 14).

Since 1897 the amalgamation of mining interests
has proceeded apace, and the virtual supremacy of the

Eckstein group greatly facilitates joint action. Before the war great progress had been made in common action as regards both Kaffir and white wages, and there is a plain recognition of the necessity of dealing with the native labour question by united co-operation with the Government. How clearly this need was recognised four years ago appears in the evidence of Mr. Wm. Hall, who put the matter thus :—

"In short, the mine managements must work together in this matter. For that purpose they must be organised as one institution, and every mine management must be in it. This could only be effected under a law of the Republic. The details of the law should be presented by the representative Chamber of Mines. The operation of it should be wholly in the hands of the organisation created by it, under general supervision—not absolute dictation—of the Government. By some such means only can I see the way at all clear to handle the Kaffir labour problem of the future of the Rand" (p. 428).

Before the war the fact that so much labour must be brought from a distance at great expense, and the difficulty of getting and keeping enough Kaffirs, made it difficult to prevent mine managers from contravening secretly the regulations of the Chamber, and trying to entice away the labour from other mines, a selfish policy, facilitated by the loose administration of the pass law. With large native locations, a fixed population of native families, and a rigorous pass law, the wages schedule will be strictly adhered to, and natives will have to work for the mines adjoining their location at wages dictated by the Chamber of Mines. The special laws under which they will live would render strikes or other organised labour action impossible, while their utter dependence on the mines for a livelihood and their inability to leave the neighbourhood will make all effective resistance to reduction of wages ineffectual. The natives upon their locations will be *ascripti glebæ*, living in complete serfdom, with no vote or other political means of venting their grievances, and with no economic leverage for progress.

CHAPTER V

IMPERIALISM IN ASIA

I

THE great test of Western Imperialism is Asia, where vast peoples live, the inheritors of civilisations as complex as our own, more ancient and more firmly rooted by enduring custom in the general life. The races of Africa it has been possible to regard as savages or children, "backward" in their progress along the same general road of civilisation in which Anglo-Saxondom represents the vanguard, and requiring the help of more forward races. It is not so easy to make a specious case for Western control over India, China, and other Asiatic peoples upon the same ground. Save in the more recent developments of the physical sciences and their application to industrial arts, it cannot be contended that these peoples are "backward," and though we sometimes describe their civilisations as "arrested" or "unprogressive," that judgment either may imply our ignorance of the pace at which civilisations so much older than our own must continue moving, or it may even afford unconscious testimony to a social progress which has won its goal in securing a well-nigh complete adjustment between human life and its stable environment.

The claim of the West to civilise the East by means of political and military supremacy must rest ultimately upon the assumption that civilisations, however various in their surface growths, are at root one and the same,

U

that they have a common nature and a common soil.
Stripped of metaphor, this means that certain moral and
intellectual qualities, finding embodiment in general forms
of religion, law, customs, and arts of industry, are essential
to all local varieties of civilisation, irrespective of race,
colour, climate, and other conditions; that Western
nations, or some of them, possess these qualities and
forms of civilisation in a pre-eminent degree, and are
able to impart them to Eastern nations by government
and its accompanying political, religious, and industrial
education. It certainly seems as if "humanity" implies
such common factors. The ethics of the Decalogue appears
to admit of a wide common application; certain rights of
the individual, certain elements of social justice, embodied
in law and custom, appear capable of universal appeal;
certain sorts of knowledge and the arts of applying them
appear useful to all sorts and conditions of men. If
Western civilisation is richer in these essentials, it seems
reasonable to suppose that the West can benefit the East
by imparting them, and that her government may be
justified as a means of doing so.

The British Empire in India may be taken as the
most serviceable test. We did not, indeed, go there in
the first instance for the good of the Indians, nor have
our various extensions of political power been motived
primarily by this consideration; but it is contended that
our government of India has in point of fact conferred
upon the people the benefits arising from our civilisation,
and that the conferring of these benefits has of later
years played a larger and a larger part in our conscious
policy. The experiment has been a long and varied one,
and our success in India is commonly adduced as the
most convincing argument in favour of the benefits
accruing to subject races from Imperialism.

The real questions we have to answer are these: "Are we civilising India?" and "In what does that civilisation consist?" To assist in answering there exists a tolerably large body of indisputable facts. We have established a wider and more permanent internal peace than India had ever known from the days of Alexander the Great. We have raised the standard of justice by fair and equal administration of laws; we have regulated and probably reduced the burden of taxation, checking the corruption and tyranny of native princes and their publicans. For the instruction of the people we have introduced a public system of schools and colleges, as well as a great quasi-public missionary establishment, teaching not only the Christian religion but many industrial arts. Roads, railways, and a network of canals have facilitated communication and transport, and an extensive system of scientific irrigation has improved the productiveness of the soil; the mining of coal, gold, and other minerals has been greatly developed; in Bombay and elsewhere cotton mills with modern machinery have been set up, and the organisation of other machine industries is helping to find employment for the population of large cities. Tea, coffee, indigo, jute, tobacco, and other important crops have been introduced into Indian agriculture. We are gradually breaking down many of the religious and social superstitions which sin against humanity and retard progress, and even the deeply rooted caste system is modified wherever British influence is felt. There can be no question that much of this work of England in India is well done. No such intelligent, well-educated, and honourable body of men has ever been employed by any State in the working of imperial government as is contained in the Civil Service of India. Nowhere else in our Empire has so much really disinterested and thoughtful energy been applied in the work of government. The same may be said of the line of great statesmen sent out from England to preside over our government in India. Our work there is the best record British Imperialism can show. What does it tell us about the capacity of the West to confer the benefits of her civilisation on the East ?

·Take first the test of economic prosperity. Are the masses of the people under our rule wealthier than they were before, and are they growing wealthier under that rule ? There are some who maintain that British government is draining the economic life-blood of India and dragging her population into lower and more hopeless poverty. They point to the fact that one of the poorest countries in the world is made to bear the cost of a government which, however honestly administered, is very expensive ; that one-third of the money raised by taxation flows out of the country without return ; that India is made to support an army admittedly excessive for purposes of self-defence, and even to bear the cost of wars in other parts of the Empire, while nearly the whole of the interest on capital invested in India is spent out of the country. The statistical basis of this argument is too insecure for much reliance to be placed on it : it is probably untrue that the net cost of British government is greater than the burden of native princes which it has largely[1] superseded, though it is certainly true that the extortionate taxation under native rule was expended in the·country on productive work or unproductive native services. Whether the increasing drain of wheat and other food–stuffs from India exceeds the gain from improved irrigation, and whether the real

[1] About three-eighths of the country is still under native government, with British supervision.

income of the "ryot" or other worker is increasing or
diminishing, cannot be established, so far as the whole
country is concerned, by any accurate measure. But
it is generally admitted, even by British officials strongly
favourable to our rule, that we have not succeeded in
giving any considerable economic prosperity to India. I
quote from a recent source strongly favourable to our rule:

"The test of a people's prosperity is not the extension of exports, the multiplication of manufactures or
other industries, the construction of cities. No. A
prosperous country is one in which the great mass of
the inhabitants are able to procure, with moderate toil,
what is necessary for living *human* lives, lives of frugal
and assured comfort. Judged by this criterion, can
India be called prosperous?

"Comfort, of course, is a relative term. . . . In a
tropical country, like India, the standard is very low.
Little clothing is required there. Simple diet suffices.
Artificial wants are very few, and, for the most part, are
not costly. The Indian Empire is a peasant Empire.
Ninety per cent. of the people live upon the land. . . .
An unfailing well of water, a plot of land, and a bit of
orchard—that will satisfy his heart's desire, if indeed
you add the cattle needful to him, 'the ryot's children,'
as they are called in many parts. Such is the ryot's
ideal. Very few realise it. An acre may stand for the
modus agri, the necessary plot of ground. A man to an
acre, or 640 men to the square mile, is the utmost
density of population which India can comfortably support, except near towns or in irrigated districts. But
millions of peasants in India are struggling to live on
half an acre. Their existence is a constant struggle
with starvation, ending too often in defeat. Their difficulty is not to live *human* lives—lives up to the level

of their poor standard of comfort—but to live at all and not die. . . . We may truly say that in India, except in the irrigated tracts, famine is chronic—endemic."[1]

A century of British rule, then, conducted with sound ability and goodwill, has not materially assisted to ward off the chronic enemy, starvation, from the mass of the people. Nor can it be maintained that the new industrialism of machinery and factories, which we have introduced, is civilising India, or even adding much to her material prosperity. In fact, all who value the life and character of the East deplore the visible decadence of the arts of architecture, weaving, metal work and pottery, in which India had been famed from time immemorial. "Architecture, engineering, literary skill are all perishing out, so perishing that Anglo-Indians doubt whether Indians have the capacity to be architects, though they built Benares; or engineers, though they dug the artificial lakes of Tanjore; or poets, though the people sit for hours or days listening to the rhapsodists as they recite poems, which move them as Tennyson certainly does not move our common people."[2] The decay or forcible supersession of the native industrial arts is still more deplorable, for these always constitute the poetry of common life, the free play of the imaginative faculty of a nation in the ordinary work of life.

Sir George Birdwood, in his great work on "The Industrial Arts of India," written more than twenty years ago, gives a significant judgment upon the real meaning of a movement which has ever since been advancing at an accelerating pace: "If, owing to the operation of certain economic causes, machinery was to be gradually introduced into India for the

[1] "India and its Problems," by W. S. Lilly, pp. 284, 285 (Sands & Co.).
[2] "Asia and Europe," by Meredith Townsend, p. 102 (Constable & Co.).

manufacture of its great traditional handicrafts, there would ensue an industrial revolution which, if not directed by an intelligent and instructed public opinion and the general prevalence of refined taste, would inevitably throw the traditional arts of the country into the same confusion of principles, and of their practical application to the objects of daily necessity, which has for three generations been the destruction of decorative art and of middle-class taste in England and North-Western Europe and the United States of America. The social and moral evils of the introduction of machinery into India are likely to be greater." Then follows a detailed account of the free picturesque handicrafts of the ordinary Indian village, and the author proceeds: " But of late these handicraftsmen, for the sake of whose works the whole world has been ceaselessly pouring its bullion into India, and who, for all the marvellous tissue they have wrought, have polluted no rivers, deformed no pleasing prospects, nor poisoned any air; whose skill and individuality the training of countless generations has developed to the highest perfection—these hereditary handicraftsmen are being everywhere gathered from their democratic village communities in hundreds and thousands into the colossal mills of Bombay, to drudge in gangs for tempting wages, at manufacturing piece goods, in competition with Manchester, in the production of which they are no more intellectually and morally concerned than the grinder of a barrel organ in the tunes turned out from it."

Even from the low standpoint of the world-market this hasty destruction of the native arts for the sake of employing masses of cheap labour in mills is probably bad policy; for, as the world becomes more fully opened up and distant countries are set in closer communication with one another, a land whose industries had so unique and interesting a character as those of India would probably have found a more profitable market than by attempting to undersell Lancashire and New England in stock goods.

But far more important are the reactions of these changes on the character of the people. The industrial revolution in England and elsewhere has partaken more largely of the nature of a natural growth, proceeding from inner forces, than in India, and has been largely coincident with a liberation of great popular forces finding expression in scientific education and in political democracy: it has been an important phase of the great movement of popular liberty and self-government. In India, and elsewhere in the East, there is no such compensation.

An industrial system, far more strongly set and more closely interwoven in the religious and social system of the country than even were the crafts and arts in Europe, has been subjected to forces operating from outside, and unchecked in their pace and direction by the will of the people whose life they so vitally affected. Industrial revolution is one thing when it is the natural movement of internal forces, making along the line of the self-interests of a nation, and proceeding *pari passu* with advancing popular self-government; another thing when it is imposed by foreign conquerors looking primarily to present gains for themselves, and neglectful of the deeper interests of the people of the country. The story of the destruction of native weaving industry[1] for the benefit of mills started by the Company will illustrate the selfish, short-sighted economic policy of the late eighteenth and

[1] *Cf.* the careful summary of official evidence in Mr. Romesh Dutt's "Economic History of British India," chap. xv. (Kegan Paul).

early nineteenth centuries. " Under the pretence of Free Trade, England has compelled the Hindus to receive the products of the steam-looms of Lancashire, Yorkshire, Glasgow, &c., at mere nominal duties; while the hand-wrought manufactures of Bengal and Behar, beautiful in fabric and durable in wear, have had heavy and almost prohibitive duties imposed on their importation to England." [1] The effect of this policy, rigorously maintained during the earlier decades of the nineteenth century, was the irreparable ruin of many of the most valuable and characteristic arts of Indian industry. " In India the manufacturing power of the people was stamped out by Protection against her industries, and then Free Trade was forced on her so as to prevent a revival." [2]

When we turn from manufacture to the great industry of agriculture, which even now occupies nine-tenths of the population, the difficulty of alien administration, with whatever good intention, is amply illustrated. Not a few of our greatest Indian statesmen, such as Munro, Elphinstone, and Metcalfe, have recognised in the village community the true embodiment of the spirit of Eastern civilisation.

" The village communities," wrote Sir C. Metcalfe,[3] " are little republics, having nearly everything that they can want within themselves, and almost independent of any foreign relations. They seem to last where nothing else lasts. Dynasty after dynasty tumbles down; revolution succeeds to revolution; Hindu, Pathan, Moghul, Mahratta, Sikh, English, are masters in turn; but the village communities remain the same." " The union

---

[1] " Eastern India," by Montgomery Martin (London, 1838), vol. iii. Introd. (quoted Romesh Dutt, p. 290).

[2] Romesh Dutt, p. 302.

[3] Letter to the Board of Revenue, April 1838 (quoted Romesh Dutt, p. 386).

of the village communities, each one forming a separate little State in itself, has, I conceive, contributed more than any other cause to the preservation of the people of India through all revolutions and changes which they have suffered, and it is in a high degree conducive to their happiness and to the enjoyment of a great portion of freedom and independence. I wish, therefore, that the village constitutions may never be disturbed, and I dread everything which has a tendency to break them up."

Yet the whole efforts of British administration have been directed to the destruction of this village self-government in industry and politics. The substitution of the individual ryot for the community as the unit of revenue throughout Bombay and Madras struck a fatal blow at the economic life of the village, while the withdrawal of all real judicial and executive powers from the zemindars or headmen, and their concentration in British civil courts and executive officers, virtually completed the destruction of the strongest and most general institution of India—the self-governing village.

Both these important steps were taken in furtherance of the new Western idea of individual responsibility as the only sound economic basis, and centralised government as the most efficacious mode of political machinery. The fact that it should be considered safe and profitable suddenly to subvert the most ancient institutions of India, in order thus to adapt the people to English modes of life, will be taken by sociologists as one of the most amazing lessons of incompetence in the art of civilisation afforded by modern history. Indeed the superior prosperity of a large part of Bengal, attributable in part at any rate to the maintenance of a local landlord class, who served as middlemen between the State and the individual cultivators, and mitigated the mechanical rack-rent of the land-tax, is a sufficiently remarkable testimony to the injury inflicted upon other parts of India by sudden ill-advised application of Western economic and political methods.[1]

II

When we turn from industry to the administration of justice and the general work of government in which the ability and character of British officialism finds expression, we are led to further questioning. Is Great Britain able to Anglicise the government of India, is she doing so, and is she thereby implanting Western civilisation in India? How much a few thousand British officials, endowed with the best ability and energy, can achieve in stamping British integrity and efficiency upon the practical government of three hundred million people of alien race and character it is difficult to judge. Numbers are not everything, and it is probable that these diffused units of British authority exercise directly and indirectly a considerable influence upon the larger affairs of government, and that this influence may sometimes permeate far down among native official circles. But it must be kept in mind that those few British officials are rarely born in India, have seldom any perfect understanding of the languages of the people, form a close "caste," never mingling in free social intercourse with those whom they govern, and that the laws and regulations they administer are largely foreign to the traditionary institutions of the

[1] The prosperity of districts under the Bengal settlement, as compared with other parts of British India, must however be imputed largely to the fact that this settlement enables Bengal to evade its full proportion of contribution to the revenue of India, and throws therefore a disproportionate burden upon other parts.

Indian peoples. When we remember how large a share of real government is the personal administration of detail, the enforcement of law or regulation upon the individual citizen, and that in the overwhelming majority of cases this work must always be left to native officials, it is evident that the formal virtues of British law and justice must admit much elasticity and much perversion in the actual processes of administration.

"No one can deny that this system of civil and criminal administration is vastly superior to anything which India ever possessed under former rulers. Its defects arise chiefly from causes extraneous to it. The unblemished integrity and unswerving devotion to duty of the officials, whether English or Indian, who occupy the higher posts, no one will call in question. The character of the subordinate officials is not always so entirely above suspicion, and the course of justice is too often perverted by a lamentable characteristic of the Oriental mind. 'Great is the rectitude of the English, greater is the power of a lie' is a proverbial saying throughout India. Perhaps the least satisfactory of the government departments is the police. A recent writer says, 'It is difficult to imagine how a department can be more corrupt.' This, too, may be an over-statement. But, taken on the whole, the rank and file of the Indian police are probably not of higher integrity and character than those of New York."[1] Now one sentence of this statement deserves special attention. "Its defects arise chiefly from causes extraneous to it." This is surely incorrect. It is an essential part of our system that the details of administration shall be in native hands: no one can contemplate any considerable displacement of lower native officials by English; the latter could not do the work and would not

[1] "India and its Problems," p. 182.

if they could, nor could the finances, always precarious, possibly admit of so huge an increase of expenditure as would be involved by making the government of India really British in its working. The tendency, in fact, is all the other way, and makes for the more numerous employment of natives in all but the highest grades of the public service. If it is true that corruption and mendacity are deeply rooted in all Eastern systems of government, and that the main moral justification of our rule consists in their correction by British character and administration, it is pretty clear that we cannot be performing this valuable work, and must in the nature of the case be disabled from even understanding where and how far we fall short of doing so. The comment made by Mr. Lilly upon Indian police is chiefly significant because this is the one department of detailed practical government where special scandals are most likely to reveal the failure of our excellent intentions as embodied in criminal codes and judicial procedure. One would wish to know whether the actual native officer who collects the land-tax or other dues from the individual ryot practises the integrity of his British superior official or reverts to the time-honoured and universal practice of the East.

How much can a handful of foreign officials do in the way of effectual check and supervision of the details of government in a country which teems with populations of various races, languages, creeds, and customs? Probably not very much, and *ex hypothesi* they, and so we, cannot know their failures.

The one real and indisputable success of our rule in India, as indeed generally through our Empire, is the maintenance of order upon a large scale, the prevention of internecine war, riot, or organised violence. This, of course, is much, but it is not everything; it is not enough in itself to justify us in regarding our imperial rule as a success. Is British justice, so far as it prevails, and British order good for India? will seem to the average Briton a curious question to ask. But Englishmen who have lived in India, and who, on the whole, favour the maintenance of our authority, sometimes ask it. It must, in the first place, be remembered that some of the formal virtues of our laws and methods which seem to us most excellent may work out quite otherwise in practice. The rigorous justice in the exaction of the land-tax and in the enforcement of the legal claims of usurers is a striking instance of misapplied notions of equity. Corrupt as the practice of Eastern tax-gatherers has ever been, tyrannical as has been the power of the usurer, public opinion, expediency, and some personal consideration 'have always qualified their tyranny: the mechanical rigour of British law is one of the greatest sources of unpopularity of our government in India, and is probably a grave source of actual injury.

There is even some reason to suspect that Indians resent less the illegal and irregular extortion of recognised native autocrats, whose visible authority is familiarly impressed on their imaginations, than the actually lighter exactions of an inhuman, irresistible and immitigable machine, such as the British power presents itself to them.

It is pretty clear that, so far as the consent of the governed in any active sense is a condition of success in government, the British Empire in India has not succeeded. We are deceived by Eastern acquiescence, and our deception may even be attended by grave catastrophe unless we understand the truth. Mr. Townsend, who has brought close thought to bear upon the conditions of our hold of India, writes thus :—

" Personal liberty, religious liberty, equal justice, perfect security—these things the Empire gives; but then are these so valued as to overcome the inherent and incurable dull distaste felt by the brown men to the white men who give them ?   I doubt it greatly."[1]

The reasons he gives for his doubt are weighty.   The agricultural populace, whom we have, he holds, materially benefited, is an inert mass: the active classes endowed with initiative, political ambition, patriotism, education are silently but strongly hostile to our rule.   It is natural this should be so.   We have spoiled the free career open to these classes under native government; the very order we have imposed offends their instincts and often thwarts their interests.   The caste system, which it is the boast of our more liberal laws and institutions to moderate or disregard, is everywhere consciously antagonistic to us in its self-defence, and deeply resents any portion of our educative influences which impairs its hold upon the minds of the people.   This force is well illustrated by the almost complete failure of our energetic Christian missions to make converts out of any members of the higher castes.   The testimony of one of the most devoted of Roman Catholic missionaries after thirty years of missionary labours deserves attention :—

"During the long period I have lived in India in the capacity of a missionary, I have made, with the assistance of a native missionary, in all between two and three hundred converts of both sexes.   Of this number two-thirds were Pariahs or beggars, and the rest were composed of Sudras, vagrants and outcasts of several tribes, who, being without resources, turned Christians in order to form connections, chiefly for the purpose of marriage, or with some other interested views."[2]

[1] " Asia and Europe," p. 101.
[2] Quoted Lilly, " India and its Problems," p. 163.

This view is borne out in the general treatment of Christian missions in Mr. Barrie's report on the census in 1891. "The greatest development (of Christianity) is found where the Brahmanic caste system is in force in its fullest vigour, in the south and west of the Peninsula, and among the hill tribes of Bengal. In such localities it is naturally attractive to a class of the population whose position is hereditarily and permanently degraded by their own religion."

If British Christianity and British rule were welcomed by large bodies of the ryots and the low-caste and Pariah populations, the opposition of the native "classes" might seem a strong testimony to the beneficence of our rule, as an instrument for the elevation of the poorer working people who always form the great majority. Unfortunately no such result can seriously be pretended. There is no reason to suppose that we hold the allegiance of any large section of the people of India by any other bond than that of fear and respect for our external power. Mr. Townsend puts the matter in a nut-shell when he affirms: "There is no corner in Asia where the life of a white man, if unprotected by force, either actual or potential, is safe for an hour; nor is there an Asiatic State which, if it were prudent, would not expel him at once and for ever."[1] There are, according to this view, no psychical roots to the civilisation we are imposing upon India: it is a superficial structure maintained by force, and not grafted on to the true life of the nation so as to modify and educate the soul of the people. Mr. Townsend is driven with evidently deep reluctance to the conclusion that "the Empire hangs in air, supported by nothing but the minute white garrison and the unproved assumption that the people of India desire it

[1] "Asia and Europe," p. 98.

to continue to exist." [1]   It was indeed pointed out by
Professor Seeley, and is generally admitted, that our
Empire in India has only been rendered possible by the
wide cleavages of race, language, religion and interests
among the Indian populations, first and foremost the
division of Mohammedan and Hindu.

But it may be fairly contended that the forcible
foundation of our rule and the slowness and reluctance of
the natives to appreciate its benefits are no proof that it
is not beneficial or that in process of time we may not infuse
the best principles of Western civilisation into their life.

Are we doing this ?   Is the nature of our occupation
such as to enable us to do it ?   Apart from the army,
which is the aspect of the Empire most in evidence, there
is a British population of some 135,000, less than 1 to
every 2000 of the natives, living neither the normal life
of their own country nor that of the foreign country
which they occupy, in no sense representative units of
British civilisation, but exotics compelled to live a highly
artificial life and unable to rear British families or to
create British society of such a sort as to embody and
illustrate the most valuable contents of our civilisation.

It is certain that the machinery of government,
however excellent, can of itself do little to convey the
benefits of civilisation to an alien people.   The real forces
of civilisation can only be conveyed by contact of individual with individual.   Now the conditions of free,
close, personal contact between British and Indians are
virtually non-existent.   There is no real, familiar, social
intercourse on equal terms, still less is there intermarriage, the only effective mode of amalgamating two
civilisations, the only safeguard against race hatred and
race domination.   " When intermarriage is out of the

[1] " Asia and Europe," p. 89.

question," writes Dr. Goldwin Smith, "social equality cannot exist; without social equality political equality is impossible, and a republic in the true sense can hardly be."[1]

The vast majority of whites admittedly live their own life, using natives for domestic and industrial service, but never attempting to get any fuller understanding of their lives and character than is required to exact these services from them or to render official services in return.   The few who have made some serious attempt to penetrate into the Indian mind admit their failure to grasp with any adequacy even the rudiments of a human nature which differs, in its fundamental valuations and its methods of conduct, so radically from our own as to present for its chief interest a series of baffling psychological puzzles. It is indeed precisely from these students that we come to understand the impossibility of that close, persistent, interactive contact of mind with mind which is the only method by which that "mission of civilisation" which we profess is capable of fulfilment.   Even those English writers who seem to convey most forcibly what is called the spirit of the East as it shows forth in the drama of modern life, writers such as Mr. Kipling and Mrs. Steel, hardly do more than present a quaint alluring atmosphere of unintelligibility; while study of the great Indian literature and art which may be taken as the best expression of the soul of the people exhibits the hitherto unbridgeable divergence of the British conception of life from the Indian.   The complete aloofness of the small white garrison is indeed in no small measure due to an instinctive recognition of this psychical chasm and of their inability to enter into really vital sympathy with these members of an "inferior" race.   They are not to blame,

---

[1] "Commonwealth or Empire" (Macmillan & Co.).

but rather the conditions which have brought them there and imposed on them a task essentially impossible, that of implanting genuine white civilisation on Asiatic soil. It must clearly be understood that it is not a question of the slowness of a process of adaptation: the really vital process of change is not taking place.   We are incapable of implanting our civilisation in India by present methods of approach: we are only capable of superficially disturbing their civilisation.   Even the external life of the vast bulk of the population we hardly touch; the inner life we do not touch at all.   If we are deceived by the magnitude of the area of our political control and the real activity of the machinery of government into supposing that we are converting the Indian peoples to British Christianity, British views of justice, morality, and to the supreme value of regular intense industry in order to improve the standard of material comfort, the sooner we face the facts the better.   For that we are doing none of these things in an appreciable degree is plain to most British officials.   Of the nearest approaches to such success they are openly contemptuous, condemning outright the Eurasian and ridiculing the " stucco civilisation of the baboo."   The idea that we are civilising India in the sense of assisting them to industrial, political, and moral progress along the lines either of our own or their civilisation is a complete delusion, based upon a false estimate of the influence of superficial changes wrought by government and the activity of a minute group of aliens.   The delusion is only sustained by the sophistry of Imperialism, which weaves these fallacies to cover its nakedness and the advantages which certain interests suck out of empire.

    This judgment is not new, nor does it imply the spirit of a "little Englander."   If there is one writer who, more than another, is justly accredited with the stimulation of large ideas of the destiny of England, it is the late Professor Seeley. Yet this is his summary of the value of the "imperial" work which we have undertaken in India :—

"At best we think of it as a good specimen of a bad political system. We are not disposed to be proud of the succession of the Grand Mogul. We doubt whether, with all the merits of our administration, the subjects of it are happy. We may even doubt whether our rule is preparing them for a happier condition, whether it may not be sinking them lower in misery; and we have our misgivings that perhaps a genuine Asiatic Government, and still more a national Government springing up out of the Hindu population itself, might, in the long run, be more beneficial, because more congenial, though perhaps less civilised, than such a foreign, unsympathetic Government as our own." [1]

III

While India presents the largest and most instructive lesson in distinctively British Imperialism, it is in China that the spirit and methods of Western Imperialism in general are likely to find their most crucial test. The new Imperialism differs from the older, first, in substituting for the ambition of a single growing empire the theory and the practice of competing empires, each motived by similar lusts of political aggrandisement and commercial gain; secondly, in the dominance of financial or investing over mercantile interests.

The methods and motives of the European Powers are not open to serious dispute. The single aim of

[1] "The Expansion of England," pp. 273, 274.

Chinese policy from time immemorial had been to avoid all dealings with foreigners which might lead to the establishment of inter-governmental relations with them. This did not imply, at any rate until recently, hostility to individual foreigners or a reluctance to admit the goods or the ideas which they sought to introduce. Arabs and other Asiatic races of the West had traded with China from very early times. Roman records point to intercourse with China as early as Marcus Aurelius. Nor were their relations with the outside world confined to trade. Christianity was introduced some fifteen hundred years ago by the Nestorians, who propagated their religious views widely in the Central Kingdom; Buddhist foreign missionaries were well received, and their teaching found wide acceptance. Indeed few nations have displayed so much power of assimilating foreign religious notions as the Chinese. Roman Catholic missionaries entered China during the Mongol dynasty, and later in the Ming dynasty.[1] Jesuits not only propagated Christianity, but introduced Western science into Pekin, attaining the climax of their influence during the latter part of the seventeenth century. Not until the arrival of the Dominicans introduced an element of religious faction, attended by political intrigue, did Christianity come into disrepute or evoke any sort of persecution. With the introduction of Protestant missions during the nineteenth century, the trouble has grown apace. Though the Chinese as a nation have never displayed religious intolerance, they have naturally mistrusted the motives of Westerns who, calling themselves Christians, quarrelled amongst themselves, and by their tactless zeal often caused local rioting which led to diplomatic or armed interference for their protection. Almost all

[1] A.D. 1368 to 1644.

lay European authorities in China bear out the following judgment of Mr. A. J. Little :—

"The riots and consequent massacres resulting from mission work throughout Indo-China may be justified by the end; but it is certain our relations with the Chinese would be far more cordial than they are, were we not suspected of an insidious design to wean them from such habits of filial piety and loyalty as they possess, to our advantage." [1]

The main outlines of Chinese policy are quite intelligible. Though not averse from incidental contact with Europeans or with other Asiatics, traders, travellers, or missionaries, they have steadily resisted all attempts to disturb their political and economic system by organised pressure of foreign Powers. Possessing in their enormous area of territory, with its various climatic and other natural conditions, its teeming industrial population, and its ancient, well-developed civilisation, a full material basis of self-sufficiency, the Chinese, following a sound instinct of self-defence, have striven to confine their external relations to a casual intercourse. The successful practice of this policy for countless centuries has enabled them to escape the militarism of other nations; and though it has subjected them to a few forcible dynastic changes, it has never affected the peaceful customary life of the great mass of little self-sufficing industrial villages of which the nation is composed. The sort of politics of which Western history is mainly composed has meant virtually nothing to the Chinese. It is the organised attempt of Western nations to break through this barrier of passive resistance, and to force themselves, their wares, their political and industrial control, on China that gives importance to Impe-

[1] "Through the Yang-Tse Gorges," edition 1888, p. 334.

rialism in the Far East. It is not possible here to trace, even in bare outlines, the history of this pressure, how quarrels with traders and missionaries have been utilised to force trade with the interior, to establish treaty ports, to secure special political and commercial rights for British or other European subjects, to fasten a regular system of foreign political relations upon the central government, and at the conclusion of the nineteenth century to drive China into wars, first with Japan, next with a confederacy of European Powers, which threaten to break up the political and industrial isolation of forty centuries, and to plunge China into the great world-competition.

The conduct of European Powers towards China will rank as the clearest revelation of the nature of Imperialism. Until late years Great Britain, with France as a poor second, had made the pace in pursuit of trade, covering this trading policy with a veneer of missionary work, the real relative importance of the two being put to a crucial test by the opium war. The entrance of Germany and America upon a manufacturing career, and the occidentation of Japan, enhanced the mercantile competition, and the struggle for the Far Eastern markets became a more definite object of national industrial policy. The next stage was the series of forceful moves by which France, Russia, Germany, Great Britain, and Japan have fastened their political and economic fangs into some special portion of the body of China by annexation, sphere of influence, or special treaty rights, their policy at this stage culminating in the ferocious reprisals of the recent war, and the establishment of a permanent menace in the shape of international political and financial conditions extorted from a reluctant and almost impotent central government by threats of further violence.

It is now hardly possible for any one who has carefully followed recent events to speak of Europe undertaking "a mission of civilisation" in China without his tongue in his cheek.[1] Imperialism in the Far East is stripped nearly bare of all motives and methods save those of distinctively commercial origin. The schemes of territorial acquisition and direct political control which Russia, Germany, and France have developed, the "sphere of influence" which has oscillated with "an open door" in our less coherent policy, are all manifestly motived by commerce and finance.

China seems to offer a unique opportunity to the Western business man. A population of some four hundred millions endowed with an extraordinary capacity of steady labour, with great intelligence and ingenuity, inured to a low standard of material comfort, in occupation of a country rich in unworked minerals and destitute of modern machinery of manufacture or of transport, opens up a dazzling prospect of profitable exploitation.

In our dealings with backward races capable of instruction in Western industrial methods there are three stages. First comes ordinary commerce, the exchange of the normal surplus produce of the two countries. Next, after Great Britain or some other Western Power has acquired territory or invested capital

---

[1] The *Times* correspondent, in describing the forcible entrance of the allied troops into Pekin, affords this glimpse into Christianity *à la mode* in China. "The raising of the siege was signalised by the slaughter of a large number of Chinese who had been rounded up into a *cul-de-sac* and who were killed to a man, the Chinese Christian converts joining with the French soldiers of the relieving force, who lent them bayonets, and abandoned themselves to the spirit of revenge. Witnesses describe the scene as a sickening sight, but in judging such acts it is necessary to remember the provocation, and these people had been sorely tried" (The *Times*, October 16, 1900).

in the foreign country with the aim of developing the resources, she enjoys a period of large export trade in rails, machinery, and other forms of capital, not necessarily balanced by the import trade since it really covers the process of investment. This stage may continue long, when capital and business capacity cannot be obtained within the newly developed country. But a third stage remains, one which in China at any rate may be reached at no distant period, when capital and organising energy may be developed within the country, either by Europeans planted there or by natives. Thus fully equipped for future internal development in all the necessary productive powers, such a nation may turn upon her civiliser, untrammelled by need of further industrial aid, undersell him in his own market, take away his other foreign markets and secure for herself what further developing work remains to be done in other undeveloped parts of the earth. The shallow platitudes by which the less instructed Free Trader sometimes attempts to shirk this vital issue have already been exposed. It is here enough to repeat that Free Trade can nowise guarantee the maintenance of industry or of an industrial population upon any particular country, and there is no consideration, theoretic or practical, to prevent British capital from transferring itself to China, provided it can find there a cheaper or more efficient supply of labour, or even to prevent Chinese capital with Chinese labour from ousting British produce in neutral markets of the world. What applies to Great Britain applies equally to the other industrial nations which have driven their economic suckers into China. It is at least conceivable that China might so turn the tables upon the Western industrial nations, and, either by adopting their capital

and organisers or, as is more probable, by substituting
her own, might flood their markets with her cheaper
manufactures, and refusing their imports in exchange
might take her payment in liens upon their capital,
reversing the earlier process of investment until she
gradually obtained financial control over her quondam
patrons and civilisers. This is no idle speculation. If
China in very truth possesses those industrial and business capacities with which she is commonly accredited,
and the Western Powers are able to have their will in
developing her upon Western lines, it seems extremely
likely that this reaction will result.

IV

The inner significance of the joint attack of Western
Powers in China lies here. It is the great speculative
coup of international capitalism not fully ripened for
international co-operation, but still hampered by the
necessity under which the groups of capitalists lie, of
using national feelings and policies to push their special
interests. So long as it is necessary to use diplomatic
pressure and armed force in order to secure some special
field of investment in railroads, mining rights, or other
development, the peace of Europe is endangered by
national intrigues and bickering. Though certain areas
may be considered as more or less definitely allocated,
Manchuria to Russia, the southern provinces of Tonking,
with Hainan to France, Shan-tung to Germany, Formosa
and Fokien to Japan, for industrial exploitation and
for political control, there are large areas where the
industrial and future political control, as spheres of influence, is likely to cause grave discord. Yunnan and
Quan-tung on the southern boundary are disputed

territory between England and France, the Chinese Government having given to each of these Powers a similar assurance that these provinces should not be alienated to any other Power. Great Britain's claim to the vast indefinite area known as the Yang-Tse basin as her separate sphere of influence for industrial concessions and political dominance is now exposed to the serious avowed encroachments of Germany, while Corea remains an open sore between Russia and Japan. The United States, whose interest in China for investment and for trade is developing faster than that of any European Power, will certainly insist upon an open door, and will soon be in a position to back her claim by strong naval force. The present epoch, therefore, is one of separate national policies and special alliances, in which groups of financiers and capitalists urge their Governments to obtain leases, concessions, or other preferences over particular areas. It is quite possible that the conflicts of national Imperialism thus provoked, skilfully used for self-defence by the Chinese Government, may retard for a long time any effective opening up of China by Western enterprise, and that China may defend herself by setting her enemies to fight among themselves.

But it is idle to suppose that the industrial attack on China can be ultimately evaded. Unless China can be roused quickly from the sleep of countless centuries of peace and can transform herself into a powerful military nation, she cannot escape the pressure of the external powers. To suppose that she can do this, because her individual citizens show a capacity for drill and discipline, is to mistake the issue. The whole genius of the Chinese peoples, so far as it is understood, is opposed to militant patriotism and to the strongly cen-

tralised government required to give effect to such a
policy.   The notion of China organising an army of six
millions under some great general, and driving "the
foreign devil" out of the country, or even entering
herself upon a career of invasion and conquest, ignores
the chief psychological and social factors of Chinese
life.   At any rate this is the least likely of all early
issues in the Far East.

Far more reasonable is it to suppose that capitalism,
having failed to gain its way by national separatist
policies issuing in strife of Western peoples, may learn
the art of combination, and that the power of international capitalism, which has been growing apace,
may make its great crucial experiment in the exploitation of China.   The driving force of the competing
Imperialism of Western nations has been traced to the
interests of certain small financial and industrial groups
within each nation, usurping the power of the nation
and employing the public force and money for their
private business ends.   In the earlier stage of development, where the grouping of these forces is still
distinctively national, this policy makes for wars in
pursuit of "national" markets for investments and
trade.   But the modern science of militarism renders
wars between "civilised" Powers too costly, and the
rapid growth of effective internationalism in the financial and great industrial magnates, who seem destined
more and more to control national politics, may in
the future render such wars impossible.   Militarism
may long survive, for that, as has been shown, is
serviceable in many ways to the maintenance of a
plutocracy.   Its expenditure furnishes a profitable
support to certain strong vested interests, it is a decorative element in social life, and above all it is

necessary to keep down the pressure of the forces of internal reform. Everywhere the power of capital in its more concentrated forms is better organised than the power of labour, and has reached a further stage in its development; while labour has talked of international co-operation, capital has been achieving it. So far, therefore, as the greatest financial and commercial interests are concerned, it seems quite probable that the coming generation may witness so powerful an international union as to render wars between the Western nations almost impossible. Notwithstanding the selfish jealousies and the dog-in-the-manger policies which at present weaken European action in the Far East, the real drama will begin when the forces of international capitalism, claiming to represent the civilisation of united Christendom, are brought to bear on the peaceful opening up of China. It is then that the real "yellow peril" will begin. If it is unreasonable to expect that China can develop a national patriotism which will enable her to expel the Western exploiters, she must then be subjected to a process of disintegration, which is more aptly described as "the break-up" of China than by the term "development."

Not until then shall we realise the full risks and folly of the most stupendous revolutionary enterprise history has known. The Western nations may then awaken to the fact that they have permitted certain little cliques of private profit-mongers to engage them in a piece of Imperialism in which every cost and peril of that hazardous policy is multiplied a hundred-fold, and from which there appears no possibility of safe withdrawal. The light-hearted, casual mood in which the nations have been drawn on to the opening up of a country with a population almost as large as that of Europe, nineteen-twentieths of whom are perfectly unknown to us, is the crowning instance of irrational government. In large measure such an enterprise must rank as a plunge in the dark. Few Europeans even profess to know the Chinese, or to know how far the Chinese they do know are representative of the nation as a whole. The only important fact upon which there is universal agreement is that the Chinese are of all the "lower races" most adaptable to purposes of industrial exploitation, yielding the largest surplus product of labour in proportion to their cost of keep. In a word, the investors and business managers of the West appear to have struck in China a mine of labour power richer by far than any of the gold and other mineral deposits which have directed imperial enterprise in Africa and elsewhere; it seems so enormous and so expansible as to open up the possibility of raising whole white populations of the West to the position of "independent gentlemen," living, as do the small white settlements in India or South Africa, upon the manual toil of these laborious inferiors. For a parasitic exploit so gigantic the competing groups of business men who are driving on their respective Governments might even abate their competition and co-operate in the forceful steps required in starting their project. Once encompass China with a network of railroads and steamer services, the size of the labour market to be tapped is so stupendous that it might well absorb in its development all the spare capital and business energy the advanced European countries and the United States can supply for generations. Such an experiment may revolutionise the methods of Imperialism; the pressure of working-class movements in politics and industry in the West can be met by a flood of China goods, so as to keep down wages and compel industry, or, where the power of the imperialist oligarchy is well set, by menaces of yellow workmen or of yellow mercenary troops, while collaboration in this huge Eastern development may involve an understanding between the groups of business politicians in the Western States close enough and strong enough to secure international peace in Europe and some relaxation of militarism.

This would drive the logic of Imperialism far towards realisation; its inherent necessary tendencies towards unchecked oligarchy in politics, and parasitism in industry, would be plainly exhibited in the condition of the "imperialist" nations. The greater part of Western Europe might then assume the appearance and character already exhibited by tracts of country in the South of England, in the Riviera, and in the tourist-ridden or residential parts of Italy and Switzerland, little clusters of wealthy aristocrats drawing dividends and pensions from the Far East, with a somewhat larger group of professional retainers and tradesmen and a large body of personal servants and workers in the transport trade and in the final stages of production of the more perishable goods: all the main arterial industries would have disappeared, the staple foods and manufactures flowing in as tribute from Asia and Africa.[1] It is of course idle to suppose that the industrialisation of China by Western methods can be achieved without effective political control, and just in proportion as Western Europe became dependent economically upon China would the maintenance of that joint imperial control react upon Western

[1] Mr. Bryce, in his Romanes Lecture, p. 9, seems to hint at the probability of such a development. "It is hardly too much to say that for economic purposes all mankind is fast becoming one people, in which the hitherto backward nations are taking a place analogous to that which the unskilled workers have held in each one of the civilised nations. Such an event opens a new stage in world history."

politics, subordinating all movements of domestic reform to the need of maintaining the Empires, and checkmating the forces of democracy by a skilful use of a highly centralised bureaucracy and army.

It is true that things may work out otherwise in the Far East. It is conceivable, though hardly probable, that China herself under the pressure of events may become a centralised military Empire, and, either alone, or with the aid of the neighbour whose interests are most closely bound with hers, Japan, may beat back the power of Western civilisation from her shores. Again, China, passing more quickly than other "lower races" through the period of dependence on Western science and Western capital, and quickly assimilating what they have to give, may re-establish her own economic independence, finding out of her own resources the capital and organising skill required for the machine industries, and, cutting short the second stage described above, may quickly launch herself upon the world-market as the biggest and most effective competitor, taking to herself first the trade of Asia and the Pacific, and then swamping the free markets of the West and driving the closed markets of the West to an ever more rigorous Protection with its corollary of diminished production. Lastly, it is conceivable that the powerful industrial and financial classes of the West, in order better to keep the economic and political mastery at home, may combine to reverse the policy which has hitherto been gaining ground in the United States and in our white colonies, and may insist upon the free importation of yellow labour for domestic and industrial service in the West. This is a weapon which they hold in reserve, should they need to use it in order to keep the populace in safe subjection.

Those who regard with complacency the rapid development of China, because of a general conviction that the liberation of these great productive forces must by ordinary processes of commercial intercourse be beneficial to the Western nations, entirely miss the issue. The peaceful, equitable distribution over the industrial world of the increase of world-wealth rising from the development of China implies a successful movement of industrial democracy in the Western nations, yielding not merely increased productivity of their national resources, but a continual rise in standard of consumption of the peoples. Such a condition might, by securing ordinary processes of world-exchange, enrich the nations with a legitimate share of the prosperity of China. But the economic *raison d'être* of Imperialism in the opening up of China is, as we see, quite other than the maintenance of ordinary commerce: it consists in establishing a vast new market for Western investors, the profits of which will represent the gains of an investing class and not the gains of whole peoples. The normal healthy processes of assimilation of increased world-wealth by nations are inhibited by the nature of this Imperialism, whose essence consists in developing markets for investment, not for trade, and in using the superior economies of cheap foreign production to supersede the industries of their own nation, and to maintain the political and economic domination of a class.

IV

So far the influence of the "opening" or "break-up" of China upon the Western world has been the subject of inquiry. Let us now ask what this "break-up" means for China. Certain plain features stand out in the structure of Chinese society. China has never been a great Empire, or had any strong national existence in the

Y

European sense. The central government has always
been very slight, virtually confined to a taxing power
exercised through the provincial government, and to a
small power of appointment of high officials. Even the
provincial government has, in ordinary times, touched the
actual life of the mass of the people lightly and at few
points. China may be described properly as a huge nest
of little free village communes, self-governing, and animated by a genuine spirit of equality. Mr. Colquhoun
names the faculty of local self-government as "a main
source of national vitality." "Groups of families constitute villages, which are self-governing, and the official
who ventures to trench on their immemorial rights to the
point of resistance is, according to an official code not
confined to China, disavowed by his superiors, and
generally finds a change of scene imperative." "The
family system, with its extension to village and town
groups, is the cheapest form of government extant, for
it dispenses with police, while disposing effectually of
offenders against the peace or respectability of the community." [1] Similarly the great German explorer Richt-
hofen: "No people in the world are more exempt from
official interference."

"The great fact," says Colquhoun, "to be noted as
between the Chinese and the Government is the almost
unexampled liberty which the people enjoy, and the
infinitesimally small part which Government plays in the
scheme of national life." [2]

The family is the political, economic, and moral unit
of society, the village commune being either a direct
enlargement of a single family or a group of closely
related families. Sometimes communal ownership is

[1] "Transformation in China," by A. R. Colquhoun, p. 176.
[2] Op. cit., p. 296.

maintained, but usually a division takes place with each growth of family, and the operative principle in general vogue is an occupying ownership of small proprietors, paying a low land-tax to the State, the sole landlord, in return for a lease in perpetuity. The land-tax is based on profitable use, and unoccupied lands revert to the community. Patrimonial institutions prevent accumulation of large properties. Numerous provisions of law and custom provide against land-grabbing and monopoly. " Nowhere in China would it be possible for a rich man to take possession of a spring and convey its water to his pond by subterranean drains, leaving dry the fields under which it passed. Water is as indispensable to life as air and land. No individual has the right to say ' It is mine, it belongs to me.' This feeling is very strongly rooted in China." [1]

A family council, partly elective, partly hereditary, settles most important issues, punishing crimes, collecting the taxes, and settling divisions of property; recourse to legal processes is rare, the moral authority of the family commonly sufficing to preserve order.

This moral factor is, indeed, the one great vital principle in Chinese life. It not only governs economic relations, and presents a substitute for wider politics, but it figures prominently in the education and the religious or ethical system of the people. " Life seems so little worth living to a man outlawed from family and home that even capital sentences are executed by consent "; [2] and where growth of population drives male members to seek employment in the towns, the closest family associations are retained. The reverence for family history and for the moral obligations it entails constitutes the kernel

[1] Colquhoun.
[2] Simcox, "Primitive Civilisations," vol. ii.

of national culture and the great stimulus to individual education and ambition in life.

Upon this basis is built one of the most extraordinary civilisations the world has known, differing in certain very vital matters from the civilisation of the West.

Two points merit particular attention, because they drive down into the roots of Chinese civilisation. The first is the general recognition of that "dignity of labour" which in the West has degenerated into a cant phrase so far as the common forms of work are concerned. Manual labour is not only a necessary means of livelihood, but a genuinely absorbing personal interest for the entire body of the nation; with simple tools, and scarcely any use of machinery, minute personal skill is applied to agriculture and the manufactures; most workers have some considerable variety of occupation, and see and enjoy the useful results of their toil. The whole economic system stands on a broad basis of "bread labour," applied in intensive cultivation of the land; destitute of Western science or Western machinery, the detailed empirical study of agriculture has been carried farther than in any other country, and this "gardening" life is the most prominent factor in the external civilisation of the country.

The second point is the wide diffusion of some sort of literary education and a genuine reverence for "things of the mind." The high respect in which a narrow conservative and pedantic literary system is held, the extraordinary importance attached to verbal memory and trivialities of ritual in their culture, have not unnaturally aroused much astonishment and some contempt among educated Westerns. But the general prevalence of schools and libraries, the democratisation of the machinery of education, the opening of the highest

offices of State to a free competition of the people, conducted on an intellectual test, are indicative of a standard
of valuation which entitles China to rank high among the
civilisations of the world. In no Western nation do the
man of learning and the gardener rank higher in the
common regard of the people than the soldier. These ·
valuations, economic and intellectual, lie firmly rooted in
the Chinese mind, and have helped through countless
generations to mould the social institutions of the people.
The civilisation, sprung up under these conditions, manifests some serious defects, compared with the best
standards of the West. Life and conduct seem unduly
cramped by detailed conventions; outside officialism
there seems little scope for individual distinction;
beyond the range of family, emotional life appears atten-
uated; the fine arts have never flourished, literature is
conventional, morals are closely practical; the rigorous
economy of material life seems attended by a less sensitive,
nervous organisation than that of any Western nation, and
individual life seems to run upon a somewhat lower level
of consciousness, and to be valued proportionately less.

But it should be recognised that the merits of this
civilisation are better attested than the defects, for the
fruits of Chinese industry, honesty, orderly behaviour,
and high regard for learning, are easily discernible by
foreigners, while the more serious defects might vanish
or be deeply modified by a more intimate understanding
of Chinese psychology than any foreigner is likely to
possess. The "barbarities" which have commonly won
for China an ill-fame in Western lands, the savage punish-
ments inflicted on criminals, the exposure of female
infants, the brutal assaults on foreigners, are no normal
part of the conduct of the nation, but rather sporadic
survivals of brute habits and instincts, not more to be

regarded as final tests of the civilisation of China than negro-lynching of that of America or wife-kicking of that of England.

If this brief conspectus of the essential features of Chinese civilisation is substantially correct, it is evident that "the break-up" brought about by the forces of Western nations will destroy the very foundations of the national order.

Its first fruits have been to impair security of life, peaceful industry and property over large areas of territory, to arouse a disorderly spirit of guerilla, to erect large public debts and so to enhance the burden of central government upon the body of the people, diminishing their communal independence. As the Western economic forces make further way, they must, partly by increased taxation needed for an expensive central government with armies, elaborate civil services and military debts, partly by the temptation of labour agents, draw large numbers of the workers from the position of independent little farmers into that of town wage-earners. This drain of population into industrial cities and mining districts, and the specialisation of agriculture for large markets, will break up the communal land system with its fixed hereditary order and will sap the roots of family solidarity, introducing those factors of fluidity, minute sub-division, and concentration of labour which are the distinctive characteristic of Western industry. The economic and social equality which belongs to ordinary Chinese life will disappear before a new system of industrial caste which capitalism will entail. The decay of morals, which is so noticeable in the *declassés* Chinese, will spread with the decay of the family power, and an elaborate judicial and punitory machinery will replace the rule of the self-governing family. This collapse of local status will react upon the habit of commercial integrity attested throughout China by the inviolability of business pledges; the new credit system of elaborate Western commerce will involve a network of commercial law and an education in that habit of litigiousness which exercises so dangerous a fascination over some other Asiatic peoples. The increase of wealth which this new industrialism would bring would either flow in economic tribute to the West, or would go to the endowment of a new powerful capitalist caste in China itself, who, following the Western lines, would ally themselves with imperialist politics in order to protect their vested interests. Capitalism, centralised government, militarism, protection, and a whole chain of public regulations to preserve the new order against the rising of old conservative traditional forces—such would be the inevitable outcome. The changes of external environment which have come with dangerous rapidity on Europe during the nineteenth century, forced still more rapidly on China by foreign profit-seekers, would produce reactions of incalculable peril upon the national life and character.

It would seem to imply no less than the destruction of the existing civilisation of China and the substitution in its place of what? There has been no serious pretence that European nations can impose or inculcate the essentials of their civilisation on China. The psychology of the Chinese is a *terra incognita*: the most experienced European residents are those who are the frankest in declaring their inability to grapple with the mysteries of Chinese character and Chinese morality; where less discreet writers venture on generalisations, their pages are riddled with the wildest contradictions and inconsistencies. What is, however, pretty clear is this: the Chinaman who detaches himself from the family bond and its moral associations and adopts European manners is distrusted alike by his fellow-countrymen and by his new patrons; Christianity makes no way among "respectable" Chinese, the educated classes presenting no ground of appeal for any form of supernaturalism; though Western science may hope in time to make a legitimate impression upon the intellectual life of China, the process will be one of slow absorption from within and cannot be imposed by alien instruction from without.

That the squabbles of European potentates for territorial expansion, the lusts of merchants or financiers, the ludicrously false expectations of missionaries, the catch-words of political parties in European elections, should be driving European nations to destroy the civilisation of a quarter of the human race without possessing the ability or even recognising the need to provide a substitute, ought surely to give pause to those Imperialists who claim to base their policy on reason and the common good.

No thinking man can seriously question the immense importance of free intercourse between the West and the East, or doubt the gain that would accrue to the civilisation of the world by a wise communication to the Eastern mind of those arts which peculiarly represent Western civilisation, the laborious, successful study of the physical sciences and their application to the arts of industry, the systematic development of certain definite principles and practices of law and government, and the thought and literature which are the conscious flowering of this growth of practical achievement.

That Europe could in this way render an invaluable service to Asia is certain.

"Some strange fiat of arrest, probably due to mental exhaustion, has condemned the brown men and the yellow men to eternal reproduction of old ideas."[1] To revivify the mind of Asia, to set it working again along new lines of rich productivity, this might be the boon of Europe. And for this service she too might take a rich reward. The brooding mind of Asia gave to sluggish Europe in past ages the great moments in religion and philosophy and in the mathematics; even in its sleep, or what appears to us the sleep of many centuries, it may have had its noble and illuminative dreams. The reason of the West may yet need the insight of the East. An union so profitable in the past may not be barren for the future. It is the right condition of this wholesome intercourse which is of supreme importance to the cause of civilisation. Now one thing at least is certain. Force and the pushful hand of material greed inhibit the free interaction of mind and mind essential to this intercourse. The ancient civilisations of India and China, whose duration bears testimony to inherent qualities of worth, have not been directed chiefly to the attainment of progress in the arts of material wealth, though the simpler industries have in parts of China and India attained a high perfection, but rather to the maintenance of certain small types of orderly social life, with a strong hierarchy of social and industrial ranks in India, with a fundamentally democratic character in China.

The energy spared from political and industrial struggles, and in China from military practices, has gone, partly to the cultivation of certain simple qualities of domestic life and personal conduct, partly to the wide diffusion of a certain real life of the soul, animated by profound religious and philosophic speculations and

[1] "Asia and Europe," p. 9.

contemplations in India, or by the elaboration of a more
practical, utilitarian wisdom in China. These Eastern
civilisations alone have stood the test of time; the
qualities which have enabled them to survive ought surely
to be matter of deep concern for the mushroom civilisations
of the West. It may even be true that the maintenance
of these younger and more unstable civilisations depends
upon unlocking the treasure-house of the wisdom of the
East. Whether this be so or not, the violent breaking
down of the characteristic institutions of Asia to satisfy
some hasty lust of commerce, or some greed of power,
is quite the most fatally blind misreading of the true
process of world-civilisation that it is possible to conceive.
For Europe to rule Asia by force for purposes of gain,.
and to justify that rule by the pretence that she is civilising Asia and raising her to a higher level of spiritual
life, will be adjudged by history, perhaps, to be the
crowning wrong and folly of Imperialism. What Asia
has to give, her priceless stores of wisdom garnered from
her experience of ages, we refuse to take; the much or
little which we could give we spoil by the brutal manner
of our giving. This is what Imperialism has done, and
is doing, for Asia.

CHAPTER VI

IMPERIAL FEDERATION

I

THE imperial policy of Great Britain since 1870, and more particularly since 1885, has been almost entirely absorbed in promoting the subjugation and annexation of tracts of territory where no genuine white settlement of any magnitude is contemplated. This policy, as we have seen, differs essentially from colonisation; and from the standpoint of government it implies a progressive diminution of freedom in the British Empire by constantly increasing the proportion of its subjects who are destitute of real power of self-government.

It is important to consider how this new Imperialism reacts, and is likely in the future to react, upon the relations between Great Britain and her self-governing colonies. Will it stimulate these colonies to an assertion of growing independence and final formal severance from the mother country, or will it lead them to form a closer political union with her upon a basis, no longer of Empire, but of a Federation of equal States? This is a vital issue, for it is quite certain that the present relations will not be maintained.

Hitherto the tendency has been towards a steady consistent increase of self-government, and a growing relaxation of Empire in the shape of control exercised by the home Government. In Australasia, North America, and South Africa seventeen self-governing colonies have been established, endowed with reduced types of the British constitution. In the case of Australia and of Canada the growth of self-government has been formally and actually advanced by acts of federation, which have, in fact, especially in Australia, compensated the restriction of the power of the federated States by a more than equivalent increase of governing power vested in the federal Government.

Great Britain has in the main learned well the lesson of the American Revolution; she has not only permitted but favoured this growing independence of her Australian and American colonies. During the very period when she has been occupied in the conscious policy of extending her Empire over lands which she cannot colonise and must hold by force, she has been loosening her "imperial" hold over her white colonies. While 1873 removed the last bond of economic control which marked the old "plantation" policy, by repealing the Act of 1850 which had forbidden Australian colonies from imposing differential duties as between the colonies and foreign countries, and permitting them in future to tax one another's goods, the Australian Commonwealth Act of 1900 has, by the powers accorded to its Federal Judicature, reduced to the narrowest limits yet attained the constitutional control of the Privy Council, and has by the powers enabling the Federal Government to raise a central armed force for defence obtained a new substantial basis for a possible national independence in the future. Though it is unlikely for some time to come that the federal Government which is contemplated for British South Africa will be accorded powers equivalent to those of the Australian or even the Canadian Federations, the same tendency to increased self-government has in the past steadily prevailed in Cape Colony and

Natal, and it is tolerably certain that, if the racial animosities between the two white races are abated, a South African Commonwealth would soon be found in possession of a far larger measure of real self-government than the British colonies which enter it have hitherto possessed.

But while the trend of British colonialism has uniformly been towards increased self-government or practical independence, and has been appreciably strengthened by the process of federating colonial States, it is evident that the imperial statesmen who have favoured most this federation policy have had in view some larger recasting of the political relations with the mother country, which should bind parent and children in closer family bonds, not merely of affection or of trading intercourse, but of political association. Though imperial federation for British purposes is no modern invention, Lord Carnarvon was the first Colonial Secretary to set it before him as a distinct object of attainment, favouring federation in the various groups of colonies as the first step in a process which should federate the Empire. The successful completion in 1873 of the process of federation which formed the Dominion of Canada doubtless stimulated Lord Carnarvon, entering office the next year, to further experiments along similar lines. Unfortunately he laid hands upon South Africa for his forcing process, and suffered a disastrous failure. Twenty years later Mr. Chamberlain resumed the task, and, confronted by the same essential difficulties, the forcible annexation of the two Dutch Republics, and the coercion of Cape Colony, has brought his federation policy in South Africa towards completion, while the federation of Australian States marks another and a safer triumph of the federation principle.

The process of federation, as bearing on the relations of the federating colonies, is of course a triumph for the centripetal forces; but, by securing a larger measure of theoretical and practical independence for the federal Governments, it has been centrifugal from the standpoint of the Imperial Government. The work of securing an effective political imperial federation implies, therefore, a reversal of hitherto dominant tendencies.

It is quite evident that a strong and increasing desire for imperial federation has been growing among a large number of British politicians. So far as Mr. Chamberlain and some of his friends are concerned, it dates back to the beginning of the struggle over Mr. Gladstone's Home Rule for Ireland policy. Speaking on Mr. Gladstone's Home Rule Bill in 1886, Mr. Chamberlain said: " I should look for the solution in the direction of the principle of federation. My right honourable friend has looked for his model to the relations between this country and her self-governing and practically independent colonies. I think that is of doubtful expediency. The present connection between our colonies and ourselves is no doubt very strong, owing to the affection which exists between members of the same nation. But it is a sentimental tie, and a sentimental tie only. . . . It appears to me that the advantage of a system of federation is that Ireland might under it really remain an integral part of the Empire. The action of such a scheme is centripetal and not centrifugal, and it is in the direction of federation that the democratic movement has made most advances in the present century."

Now, it is quite true that the democratic movement, both now and in the future, seems closely linked with the formation of federal States, and the federation of the parts of the British Empire appears to suggest, as a next step and logical outcome, the federation of the whole.

Holding, as we must, that any reasonable security for good order and civilisation in the world implies the growing application of the federation principle in international politics, it will appear only natural that the earlier steps in such a process should take the form of unions of States most closely related by ties of common blood, language, and institutions, and that a phase of federated Britain or Anglo-Saxondom, Pan-Teutonism, Pan-Slavism, and Pan-Latinism might supervene upon the phase already reached. There is perhaps a suspicion of excessive logic in such an order of events, but a broad general view of history renders it plausible and desirable enough. Christendom thus laid out in a few great federal Empires, each with a retinue of uncivilised dependencies, seems to many the most legitimate development of present tendencies, and one which would offer the best hope of permanent peace on an assured basis of inter-Imperialism. Dismissing from our mind the largest aspect of this issue, as too distant for present profitable argument, and confining our attention to British imperial federation, we may easily agree that a voluntary federation of free British States, working peacefully for the common safety and prosperity, is in itself eminently desirable, and might indeed form a step towards a wider federation of civilised States in the future.

The real issue for discussion is the feasibility of such a policy, and, rightly stated, the question runs thus: "What forces of present or prospective self-interest are operative to induce Great Britain and her colonial groups to reverse the centrifugal process which has hitherto been dominant?" Now, there are many reasons for

Great Britain to desire political federation with her self-governing colonies, even upon terms which would give them a voice proportionate to their population in a Parliament or other council charged with the control of imperial affairs, provided the grave difficulties involved in the establishment of such a representative, responsible governing body could be overcome.   The preponderance of British over colonial population would enable the mother country to enforce her will where any conflict of interest or judgment arose in which there was a sharp line of division between Great Britain and the colonies: the distribution of imperial burdens and the allocation of imperial assistance would be determined by Great Britain.   If the Crown colonies and other non-self-governing parts of the Empire were represented in the imperial council, the actual supremacy of the mother country would be greater still, for these representatives, either nominated by the Crown (the course most consonant with Crown colony government), or elected on a narrow franchise of a small white oligarchy, would have little in common with the representatives of self-governing colonies, and would inevitably be more amenable to pressure from the home Government. A chief avowed object of imperial federation is to secure from the colonies a fair share of men, ships, and money for imperial defence, and for those expansive exploits which in their initiation almost always rank as measures of defence. The present financial basis of imperial defence is one which, on the face of it, seems most unfair; Great Britain is called upon to support virtually the whole cost of the imperial navy, and, with India, almost the whole cost of the imperial army, though both these arms are at the service of any of our self-governing colonies that is threatened by external enemies or internal disorders.

In 1899, while the population of these colonies was
close upon one-third of that of the United Kingdom,
their revenue nearly one-half, and the value of their
sea-borne commerce one-fifth of the entire commerce
of the Empire, the contribution they were making to
the cost of the naval defence of the Empire was less
than one-hundredth part.[1]   These colonies raise no regular or irregular military force available for the general
defence of the Empire, though they have supported small
contingents of imperial troops quartered upon them by
the Imperial Government, and have maintained considerable militia and volunteer forces for home defence.
The colonial contingents taking part in the South African
war, though forming a considerable volunteer force, fell
far short of an imperial levy based upon proportion of
population, and their expenses were almost entirely
borne by the United Kingdom.   From the standpoint
of the unity of the British Empire, in which the colonies
are presumed to have an interest equivalent to that of
the United Kingdom, it seems reasonable that the latter
should be called upon to bear their fair share of the
burden of imperial defence; and an imperial federation
which was a political reality would certainly imply a
provision for such equal contribution.   Whatever were
the form such federation took, that of an Imperial
Parliament, endowed with full responsibility for imperial
affairs under the Crown, or of an Imperial Council, on
which colonial representatives must sit to consult with

[1] 1899.	Population.	Revenue.	Trade.	Naval Contribution.
United King- dom . .	39,000,000	£104,000,000	£766,000,000	£24,734,000
Self-governing Colonies .	12,000,000	46,000,000	222,000,000	177,000

Z

and advise the British ministry, who still retained the
formal determination of imperial policy, it would certainly imply a compulsory or quasi-compulsory contribution on the part of the colonies proportionate to that
of the United Kingdom.

Now it is quite evident that the self-governing
colonies will not enter such an association, involving
them in large new expenses, out of sentimental regard for
the British Empire.   The genuineness and the warmness
of the attachment to the British Empire and to the
mother country are indisputable, and though they were
not called upon to make any considerable self-sacrifice in
the South African campaign, it is quite evident that their
present sentiments are such as would lead them voluntarily to expend both blood and money where they
thought the existence, the safety, or even the honour of
the Empire was at stake.   But it would be a grave error
to suppose that the blaze of enthusiastic loyalty, evinced
at such a period of emergency, can be utilised in order to
reverse the general tendency towards independence, and
to "rush" the self-governing colonies into a closer formal
union with Great Britain, involving a regular continuous
sacrifice.   If the colonies are to be induced to enter
any such association, they must be convinced that it is
essential to their individual security and prosperity.   At
present they get the protection of the Empire without
paying for it; as long as they think they can get adequate protection on such terms, it is impossible to suppose
they would enter an arrangement which required them
to pay, and which involved an entire recasting of their
system of revenue.   The temper of recent discussions in
the Australian and Canadian Parliaments, amid all the
enthusiasm of the South African war, makes it quite clear
that no colonial ministry could in time of peace persuade

the colonists to enter such a federation as is here out-
lined, unless they had been educated to the conviction
that their individual colonial welfare was to be subserved.
Either Australia and Canada must be convinced that imperial defence of Australia or Canada upon the present
basis is becoming more inadequate, and that such defence
is essential to them, or else they must be compensated
for the additional expense which federation would involve by new commercial relations with the United
Kingdom which will give them a more profitable market
than they possess at present.

Now the refusal of the self-governing colonies hitherto
to consider any other contribution to imperial defence
than a small voluntary one has been based upon a conviction that the virtual independence they hold under
Great Britain is not likely to be threatened by any great
Power, and that, even were it threatened, though their
commerce might suffer on the sea, they would be competent to prevent or repel invasion by their own internal powers of self-defence. The one exception to this
calculation may be said to prove the rule. If Canada
were embroiled in war with her great republican neighbour, she is well aware that though the British navy
might damage the trade and the coast towns of the
United States, she could not prevent Canada from being
over-run by American troops, and ultimately from being
subjugated.

But, it may at least be urged, the importance of
maintaining a British navy adequate to protect their
trade will at least be recognised; the colonies will perceive that in face of the rising wealth and naval preparations of rival Empires, in particular Germany, France,
and the United States, the United Kingdom cannot
bear the financial strain of the necessary increase of

ships without substantial colonial assistance. This is doubtless the line of strongest pressure for imperial federation. How far is it likely to prove effective? It is certain to educate colonial politicians to a closer consideration of the future of their colony; it will force them to canvass most carefully the net advantages or disadvantages of the imperial connection. Such consideration seems at least as likely to lead them towards that definite future severance from Great Britain which, during the last half-century, none of them has seriously contemplated, as it is to bring them into a federation. This consummation, if it ultimately comes about, will arise from no abatement of natural good feeling and affection towards the United Kingdom, but simply from a conflict of interests.

If the movement towards imperial federation fails, and the recent drift towards independence on the part of the self-governing colonies is replaced by a more conscious movement in the same direction, the cause will be Imperialism. A discreet colonial statesman, when invited to bring his colony closer to Great Britain, and to pay for their joint support while leaving to Great Britain the virtual determination of their joint destiny, is likely to put the following pertinent questions: Why is Great Britain obliged to increase her expenditure in armaments faster than the growth of trade or income, so that she is forced to call upon us to assist? Is it because she fears the jealousy and the hostility of other Powers? Why does she arouse these ill feelings? To these questions he can hardly fail to find an answer. "It is the new Imperialism that is wholly responsible for the new perils of the Empire, and for the new costs of armaments." He is then likely to base upon this answer further questions. Do we self-governing colonies benefit by this new Imperialism ? If we decide that we do not, can we stop it by entering a federation in which our voices will be the voices of a small minority ? May it not be a safer policy for us to seek severance from a Power which so visibly antagonises other Powers, and may involve us in conflict with them on matters in which we have no vital interest and no determinant voice, and either to live an independent political life, incurring only those risks which belong to us, or (in the case of Canada) to seek admission within the powerful republic of the United States ?

However colonial history may answer these questions, it is inevitable that they will be put. Imperialism is evidently the most serious obstacle to " imperial federation," so far as the self-governing colonies are concerned. Were it not for the presence of these unfree British possessions and for the expansive policy which continually increases them, a federation of free British States throughout the world would seem a reasonable and a most desirable step in the interests of world-civilisation. But how can the white democracies of Australasia and North America desire to enter such a hodge-podge of contradictory systems as would be presented by an imperial federation, which might, according to a recent authority,[1] be compiled in the following fashion : first a union of Great Britain, Ireland, Canada, West Indies, Australia, Tasmania, New Zealand, Newfoundland, Mauritius, South Africa, Malta, to be followed later by the admission of Cyprus, Ceylon, India, Hong-Kong, and Malaysia, with an accompaniment of semi-independent States such as Egypt, Afghanistan, Natal, Bhutan, Jehore, and perhaps the kingdoms of Uganda and of Barotse, each with some sort of representation on an Imperial Council and some voice in the determination of the imperial destiny ?

[1] Sir H. H. Johnston, *Nineteenth Century*, May 1902.

Is it likely that the great rising Australian Commonwealth or the Dominion of Canada will care to place her
peaceful development and her financial resources at the
mercy of some Soudanese forward movement or a pushful policy in West Africa?

An imperial federation comprising all sorts and
conditions of British States, colonies, protectorates, veiled
protectorates, and nondescripts, would be too unwieldy,
and too prolific of frontier questions and of other hazards,
to please our more isolated and self-centred free colonies;
while, if these former were left without formal representation as special protégés of the United Kingdom, their
existence and their growth would none the less hang like
a mill-stone round the neck of the federal Government,
constantly compelling the United Kingdom to strain the
allegiance of her confederates by using her technical
superiority of voting power in what she held to be their
special interest and hers.

The notion that the absence of any real strong
identity of interest between the self-governing colonies
and the more remote and more hazardous fringes of the
Empire can be compensated by some general spirit of
loyalty towards and pride in "the Empire" is a delusion
which will speedily be dispelled. The detached colonies
of Australasia may not unreasonably argue that the very
anxiety of British statesmen to draw them into federation
is a confession of the weakening of that very protection
which constitutes for them the chief value of the present
connection. "The United Kingdom," they may say,
" asks us to supply men and ships and money in a binding engagement in order to support her in carrying
farther the very imperialist policy which arouses the
animosity of rival Powers and which disables her for
future reliance on her own resources to sustain the

Empire. For our increased contribution to the imperial resources we shall therefore receive in return an increase of peril. Is it not something like asking us, out of pure chivalry, to throw in our lot with a sinking vessel ? " It will doubtless be replied that a firmly federated Empire will prove such a tower of strength as will enable her to defy the increased jealousy of rival Powers. But this tempting proposition will be submitted to cool calculation in our colonies, which will certainly refuse to be " rushed " into a change of policy implying a reversal of the general tendency of half a century. Admitting the obvious political and military gain of co-operative action in the face of an enemy, the colonists will ask whether this gain is not offset by an increased likelihood of having to face enemies, and when they reflect that they are really invited to federate, not merely with the England whom they love and admire, but with an ever-growing medley of savage States, the balance of judgment seems likely to turn against federation, unless other special inducements can be applied.

II

There are two special inducements which might bring the self-governing colonies, or some of them, to favour a closer political union with Great Britain. The first is a revision of the commercial and financial policy of the mother country, so as to secure for the colonies an increased market for their produce in Great Britain and in other parts of the British Empire. In discussion of this issue it is customary to begin by distinguishing the proposal to establish an Imperial Zollverein, or Customs Union, from the proposal for a preferential tariff. But very little reflection suffices to perceive the futility of the former without the latter as an appeal to the self-interest

of the colonies. Will these colonies assimilate their
financial policy to that of Great Britain, abolishing their
protective tariffs and entering a full Free Trade career?
The most sanguine Free Trader suggests no such possibility, nor indeed would such a course afford any real
guarantee of increasing the commercial inter-dependence
of the Empire. It would simply force the colonies upon
processes of direct taxation repugnant to their feelings.
Is Free Trade within the Empire, with a maintenance of
the *status quo* as regards foreign countries, really more
feasible? It would simply mean that the colonies gave
up the income they obtained from taxing the goods of
one another and of Great Britain, each getting in return
a remission of tariffs from the other colonies with which
its trade is small and no remission from Great Britain,
which would continue to receive its goods free as before.
Though this same policy would ultimately be beneficial
to their commerce, it would only encourage the existing
tendency to trade less with the Empire and more with
foreign nations, while it would involve a revolution of
their fiscal method. No; Free Trade within the Empire is
only conceivable upon the basis of Great Britain agreeing
to abandon Free Trade with countries outside the Empire.
Even were Great Britain prepared to adopt such a course,
it would remain most unlikely that the colonies would
make the sacrifice of customs income involved by admitting goods from all the Empire free; for this course
would entail a sacrifice much greater than at first sight
appears, inasmuch as such discrimination would virtually enable the goods admitted free to displace the taxed
goods, reducing to quite insignificant dimensions the
income still derived from customs.

Engaged as we are now in finding special inducements to draw the colonies into closer political union

with Great Britain, we need not discuss the probability of an extension of the policy which Canada initiated by her preferential tariff, according to Great Britain a preferential tariff by a surrender of duties upon British imports amounting to 33 per cent. It is needless to discuss the motives which may have animated this advance. If we look to its result we find that it has been quite inoperative, regarded as a stimulus to British trade. "In spite of the preferential tariff, the percentage of American goods entering Canada has continued to increase and the percentage of British goods to decline."[1] This is attributed to the "sham" character of the concession, as illustrated by the fact that "before giving a preference to British goods the Laurier ministry was careful to raise the duties on cotton goods largely coming from Great Britain, while lowering or abolishing the duties on raw materials coming from the United States."

Thus the much-boasted British preference is to a large extent a delusion. In spite of the preference, British goods still pay a higher average tax on entering Canada than American goods. Here are the figures:—

CANADIAN IMPORT DUTIES.

Year ending June 30.	Average Duty on British Goods.	Average Duty on American Goods.
1897	21.1 per cent.	14.3 per cent.
1901	18.3 per cent.	12.4 per cent.

Even if it is claimed that the act was a pure offering of goodwill, it is not contended that the colonies will generally follow the example, making concessions and receiving no preference in return. The only Zollverein

[1] Harold Cox, "The Canadian Preferential Tariff," from which the accompanying figures are also taken.

proposal which claims serious discussion is one based upon the general adoption of preferential treatment within the Empire, involving on the part of Great Britain herself an abandonment of Free Trade with foreign countries. Here, at least, the colonies would have some *quid pro quo*, a guaranteed monopoly of the imperial market for their exports, in compensation for their loss of customs revenue from admitting imperial imports free, or at a lower rate of duties. Assuming that the colonies would enter such an arrangement, Great Britain would have to pay a heavy price for the political and military support which such a commercial policy was designed to purchase. Apart from the immediate dislocation of her industries, which would follow this partial abandonment of Free Trade on her part, and which would be more serious than a carefully imposed tariff applied equally to all imports, it would tax all classes of consumers and producers in this country by raising the prices of ordinary necessaries and conveniences of life, and of materials imported from abroad to be employed in home industry. Grain and flour, cattle and meat, wool, timber, and iron would form the chief commodities which, in the supposed interests of our colonies, would be taxed first. Unless it did raise these prices it could have no effect in enabling colonial producers to displace foreign producers: the tariff, to be operative at all, must remove all profit from some portion of foreign goods previously imported, and, by preventing such goods from entering our markets in the future, reduce the total supply: this reduction of supply acts of necessity in raising the price for the whole market. This well-recognised automatic operation of the law of supply and demand makes it certain that English consumers would pay in enhanced prices a new tax, part of which would be handed over to colonists in payment for their new " loyalty," part would go to the British exchequer, and part to defray expenses of collection.

Nor is this all, or perhaps the worst. By this very method of binding our colonies closer to us we take the surest way of increasing the resentment of those very nations whose political and military rivalry impels us to abandon Free Trade. The vast and increasing trade we have with France, Germany, Russia, and the United States is the most potent guarantee of peace which we possess. Reduce the volume and the value of our commerce with these nations, by means of the re-establishment of a tariff avowedly erected for the purpose, and we should convert the substantial good-will of the powerful financial, mercantile, and manufacturing interests in these countries into active and dangerous hostility. It would be far worse for us that we had never been a Free Trade country than that we relapsed into a protective system motived by the desire to weaken our commercial bonds with the political and commercial Powers whose rivalry we have most to fear. By the statistics of an earlier chapter[1] it has been shown that not merely is our trade with these foreign nations far greater than the trade with the self-governing colonies, but that it is growing at a faster rate. To offend and antagonise our better customers in order to conciliate our worse is bad economy and much worse politics.

The shrewder politicians in our colonies might surely be expected to look such a gift-horse in the mouth. For the very bribe which is designed to win them for federation is one which enhances for them enormously and quite incalculably the perils of a new connection by

[1] *Cf*. Part I., chap. ii.

which they throw in their lot irrevocably with that of Great Britain. A monopoly of the imperial market for their exports may be bought too dear, if it removes the strongest pledge for peace which England possesses, at a time when that pledge is needed most. Nor would these colonies share only the new peril of England; their own discriminative tariffs would breed direct ill-feeling against them on the part of foreigners, and would drag them into the vortex of European politics. Finally, by distorting the more natural process of commercial selection, which, under tariffs equally imposed, has in the past been increasing the proportion of the trade done by these colonies with foreign countries, and reducing the proportion done with Great Britain, we shall be forcing them to substitute a worse for a better trade, a course by which they will be heavy losers in the long run.

It cannot be too clearly understood that not merely is the natural tendency of development in our self-governing colonies towards a decreasing commercial dependence upon Great Britain, but the same commercial separatist tendency operates among the colonies in their relations to one another. The colonies do not find their interests to lie in increasing the proportion of their trading intercourse with one another. Professor Flux in his close investigation of the statistics comes to the following conclusion:—

"As for the trade between the colonies, the Australian inter-colonial trade, which we have stated at £22,500,000 for 1892-96, was only between £7,000,000 and £8,000,000 at the earlier date here considered. Other inter-colonial trade has hardly grown in value. It was recorded at about £20,000,000 on the import side and £25,000,000 on the export side during the years 1867-71. Thus nearly 76 per cent. of colonial imports were derived from the Empire, and about 73 per cent. of the exports went to the Empire, or about 74 per cent. of the total trade was carried on with other parts of the Empire, as compared with the 65 per cent. at the more recent date, as recorded above." [1] Why should we persuade our self-governing colonies to reverse the natural tide of their commerce, which flows towards internationalism, and force it into the narrower channel of Imperialism?

III

In face of such facts it will be impossible for Great Britain to offer the self-governing colonies a sufficient commercial inducement to bring them into imperial federation. Is there any other possible inducement or temptation? There is, I think, one, viz. to involve them on their own account in Imperialism, by encouraging and aiding them in a policy of annexation and the government of lower races. Independently of the centralised Imperialism which issues from Great Britain, these colonies have within themselves in greater or less force all the ingredients out of which an Imperialism of their own may be formed. The same conspiracy of powerful speculators, manufacturing interests and ambitious politicians, calling to their support the philanthropy of missions and the lust for adventure which is so powerful in the new world, may plot the subversion of honest self-developing democracy, in order to establish class rule, and to employ the colonial resources in showy enterprises of expansion for their own political and commercial ends.

Such a spirit and such a purpose have been plainly operative in South Africa for many years past. That

---

[1] *Journal of the Statistical Society*, vol. lxii. p. 498.

which appears to us an achievement of British Imperialism, viz. the acquisition of the two Dutch Republics
and the great North, is and always has appeared something
quite different to a powerful group of business politicians
in South Africa. These men at the Cape, in the Transvaal and in Rhodesia, British or Dutch, have fostered
a South African Imperialism, not opposed to British
Imperialism, willing when necessary to utilise it, but
independent of it in ultimate aims and purposes. This
was the policy of "colonialism" which Mr. Rhodes
espoused so vehemently in his earlier political career,
seeking the control of Bechuanaland and the North for
Cape Colony and not directly for the Empire. This has
been right through the policy of an active section of
the Africander Bond, developing on a large scale the
original "trek" habit of the Dutch. This was the
policy to which Sir Hercules Robinson gave voice in
his famous declaration of 1889 regarding Imperialism:
" It is a diminishing quantity, there being now no longer
any permanent place in the future of South Africa for
direct imperial rule on any large scale." A distinctively
colonial or South African expansion was the policy of
the politicians, financiers, and adventurers up to the
failure of the Jameson Raid; reluctantly they sought
the co-operation of British Imperialism to aid them in
a definite work for which they were too weak, the seizure
of the Transvaal mineral estates; their absorbing aim
hereafter will be to relegate British Imperialism to what
they conceive to be its proper place, that of an *ultima
ratio* to stand in the far background while colonial
Imperialism manages the business and takes the profits.
A South African federation of self-governing States will
demand a political career of its own, and will insist
upon its own brand of empire, not that of the British

Government, in the control of the lower races in South Africa.

Such a federal State will not only develop an internal policy regarding the native territories different from, perhaps antagonistic to, that of British Imperialism, but its position as the "predominant" State of South Africa will develop an ambition and a destiny of expansion which may bring it into world politics on its own account.

Australasia similarly shows signs of an Imperialism of her own. She has recently taken over New Guinea, and some of her sons are hankering after the New Hebrides, quite willing to incite Great Britain to break away from the joint-control over these islands which she holds along with France.

If this is a substantially correct view of Australasian tendencies, it has a most important bearing upon the feasibility of imperial federation, because it indicates another force which might be utilised for a reversal of the centrifugal movement hitherto dominant in colonial policy. If Great Britain is prepared to guarantee to Australasia and to South Africa a special imperial career of their own, placing the entire federal resources of the Empire at the disposal of the colonial federal States, to assist them in fulfilling an ambition or a destiny which is directed and determined by their particular interests and will, such a decentralisation of Imperialism might win the colonies to a closer federal union with the mother country. For Great Britain herself it would involve great and obvious dangers, and some considerable sacrifice of central imperial power; but it might win the favour and support of ambitious colonial politicians and capitalists desirous to run a profitable Imperialism of their own and to divert the democratic forces from domestic agitation into foreign enterprises.

If Australasia can get from Great Britain the services
of an adequate naval power to enforce her growing
" Monroe doctrine" in the Pacific without paying for it,
as British South Africa has obtained the services of our
land forces, she will not be likely to enter closer formal
bonds which will bind her to any large financial contribution towards the expenses of such a policy.   But if
Great Britain were willing to organise imperial federation
upon a basis which in reality assigned larger independence
to Australia than she has at present, by giving her a call
upon their imperial resources for her own private imperial
career in excess of her contribution towards the common
purse, the business instincts of Australia might lead her
to consider favourably such a proposal.

How fraught with peril to this country such imperial federation would be it is unnecessary to prove.
Centralised Imperialism, in which the Government of
Great Britain formally reserves full control over the
external policy of each colony, and actually exercises this
control, affords some considerable security against the
danger of being dragged into quarrels with other great
Powers: the decentralised Imperialism, involved in imperial federation, would lose us this security.   The
nascent local Imperialism of Australasia and of South
Africa would be fed by the consciousness that it could
not be checked or overruled in its expansive policy as it is
now; and the somewhat blatant energy of self-expression
in colonial Governments would be likely to entangle us
continually with Germany and the United States in the
Pacific, while Canada and Newfoundland would possess a
greatly enhanced power to embroil us with France and
the United States.   If it be urged that after all no
serious steps in Australian, Canadian or South African
" Imperialism " could be taken without the direct

conscious consent of Great Britain, who would, by virtue of population and prestige, remain the predominant partner, the answer is that the very strengthening of the imperial bond would give increased efficacy to all the operative factors in Imperialism. Even as matters stand now there exists in Great Britain a powerful organised business interest which is continually inciting the Imperial Government to a pushful policy on behalf of our colonies: these colonies, the Australasian in particular, are heavily mortgaged in their land and trade to British financial companies; their mines, banks, and other important commercial assets are largely owned in Great Britain; their enormous public debts[1] are chiefly held in Great Britain. It is quite evident that the classes in this country owning these colonial properties have a stake in colonial politics, different from and in some cases antagonistic to that of the British nation as a whole: it is equally evident that they can exercise an organised pressure upon the British Government in favour of their private interests that will be endowed with enhanced efficacy under the more equal conditions of an imperial federation.

Whether the bribe of a preferential tariff, or of a delegated Imperialism, or both, would suffice to bring the self-governing colonies into a closer formal political

---

[1] In 1900 the public debts of the Australasian colonial Governments amounted to £194,812,289 for a population of 3,756,894, while the New Zealand debt was £46,930,077 for a population of 756,510 (Statesman's "Year-book," 1901).

New South Wales	.	.	.	.	£65,332,993
Victoria	.	.	.	.	48,774,885
Queensland	.	.	.	.	34,338,414
South Australia	.	.	.	.	26,156,180
West Australia	.	.	.	.	11,804,178
Tasmania	.	.	.	.	8,395,639

£194,812,289

2 A

federation with Great Britain may, however, well be doubted. Still more doubtful would be their permanent continuance in such a federation. It is at least conceivable that the colonial democracies may be strong and sane enough to resist temptation to colonial Imperialism, when they perceive the dangerous reactions of such a course. Even were they induced to avail themselves of the ample resources of the Empire to forward their local imperial policy, they would, in Australia as in South Africa, be disposed to break away from such a federation when they had got out of it what advantages it could be made to yield, and they felt strong enough for an independent Empire of their own.

It is no cynical insistence upon the dominance of selfish interests which leads us to the conviction that the historic drift towards independence will not be reversed by any sentiments of attachment towards Great Britain. "My hold of the colonies," wrote Burke, "is the close affection which grows from common names, from kindred blood, from similar privileges, and equal protection. These are ties which, though light as air, are as strong as links of iron."[1] But in these ties, save the last only, there is nothing to demand or to ensure political union. The moral bonds of community of language, history and institutions, maintained and strengthened by free social and commercial intercourse, this true union of hearts, have not been weakened by the progress towards political freedom which has been taking place in the past, and will not be weakened if this progress should continue until absolute political independence from Great Britain is achieved.

It is quite certain that the issue must be determined in the long run by what the colonies consider to be their

[1] "Conciliation with America."

policy of net utility. That utility will be determined primarily by the more permanent geographical and economic conditions. These have tended in the past, so far as they have had free play, towards political independence: they will have a freer play in the future, and it seems, therefore, unlikely that their tendency will be reversed. Though the element of distance between the parts of an Empire is now less important than formerly as a technical difficulty in representation, the following pithy summary of American objections to schemes of imperial federation in the eighteenth century, as recorded by Pownall, still has powerful application :—

"The Americans also thought that legislative union would be unnecessary, inexpedient, and dangerous, because—

"(1) They had already sufficient legislatures of their own.

"(2) If the colonies were so united to England they would share the burden of British taxes and debt.

"(3) Representatives in England would be too far from their constituents, and the will of the colonies would, therefore, be transferred out of their power, and involved in that of a majority in which the proportion of their representatives would hold no balance."[1]

While then it is conceivable, perhaps possible, that, for a time at any rate, the self-governing colonies might be led into an imperial federation upon terms which should secure their private industrial and political ambitions as colonies, it is far more reasonable to expect that Canada would drift towards federation with her southern neighbour, and Australasia and South Africa towards independent political entities, with a possible

[1] Holland, *Imperium et Libertas*, p. 82.

future re-establishment of loose political relations in an Anglo-Saxon federation.

It is no aspersion on the genuineness and the strength of the " loyalty " and affection entertained by the colonies towards England to assert that these sentiments cannot weigh appreciably in the determination of the colonial " destiny " against the continuous pressure of political, industrial, and financial forces making towards severance. Though a few politicians, or even a party in these colonies, may coquet with the notion of close federation on an equal basis, the difficulties, when the matter is resolved, as it must be, into financial terms, will be found insuperable.   The real trend of colonial forces will operate in the same direction as before, and more persistently, when the nature of the burdens they are invited to undertake is disclosed to them.

The notion that one great result of the South African war has been to generate a large fund of colonial feeling which will materially affect the relations of the colonies with Great Britain is an amiable delusion based upon childish psychology.   While the rally of sentiment has been genuine, so has been the discovery of the perils of the mother country which have made colonial assistance so welcome and caused it to be prized so highly that imperial statesmen essay to turn the tide of colonial development by means of it.

Reflection, which follows every burst of sentiment, cannot fail to dwell upon the nature of the peril which besets an empire so vast, so heterogeneous, and so dispersed as the British Empire.   When the glamour of war has passed away, and history discloses some of the brute facts of this sanguinary business which have been so carefully kept from the peoples of Australia, New Zealand and Canada, their relish for the affair will diminish: they will be more suspicious in the future of issues whose character and magnitude have been so gravely misrepresented to them by the Imperial Government.[1] But the discovery likely to weigh most with the colonial democracies is the unsubstantial assets of the new Imperialism. It is one thing to enter a federation of free self-governing States upon an equal footing, quite another to be invited to contribute to the maintenance and acquisition of·an indefinitely large and growing number of dependencies, the property of one of the federating States. The more clearly the colonies recognise the precarious nature of the responsibilities they are asked to undertake, the more reluctant will they show themselves. Unless the democratic spirit of these colonies can be broken and they can be driven to " Imperialism " upon their own account, they will refuse to enter a federation which, whatever be the formal terms of entrance, fastens on them perils so incalculable. The new Imperialism kills a federation of free self-governing States: the colonies may look at it, but they will go their way as before.

The sentimental attractions which the idea may at first present will not be void of practical results. It may lead them to strengthen their preparation for internal defence, and to develop, each of them, a firmer national spirit of their own. The consciousness of this gain in defensive strength will not the more dispose them to closer formal union with Great Britain; it is far more likely to lead them to treat with her upon the terms of independent allies. The direction in which the more clear-sighted colonial statesmen are moving is and always

[1] Public feeling in Australia and New Zealand was of a particularly simple manufacture in the autumn of 1899. Mr. Chamberlain communicated the "facts" of the South African war to the Premiers of the colonies and they served them out to the press. This official information was not checked by any really independent news.

has been tolerably clear. It is towards a slighter bond of union with Great Britain, not a stronger. The near goal is one clearly marked out for the American colonies by Jefferson as early as 1774, and one which then might have been attained if England had exercised discretion. Jefferson thus describes his plan in the draft of instructions to delegates sent by Virginia to Congress: "I took the ground that from the beginning I had thought the only one orthodox or tenable, which was that the relation between Great Britain and those colonies was exactly the same as that of England and Scotland after the accession of James and until after the Union, and the same as the present relation with Hanover, having the same executive chief, but no other necessary political connection." [1]   This same project, that of narrowing down the imperial connection to the single tie of a common monarchy, was avowed by the "Reformers" who in Upper Canada usually made a majority of the Legislative Assembly during 1830–40, and underlies the conscious or unconscious policy of all our self-governing colonies when subject to normal influences. Brief, temporary set-backs to this movement under the stress of some popular outburst of enthusiasm or some well-engineered political design are possible, but unless the real forces of colonial democracy can be permanently crushed they will continue to drive colonial policy towards this goal. Whether they will drive still farther, to full formal severance, will depend upon the completeness with which Great Britain has learnt during the last century and a half the lesson of colonial government which the American Revolution first made manifest. At present, owing to our liberal rendering of the term "responsible self-government," there exists no powerful set of conscious

[1] Quoted *Imperium et Libertas*, p. 70.

forces making for complete independence in any of our colonies, save in South Africa, where our exceptional policy has given birth to a lasting antagonism of economic interests, which, working at present along the lines of race cleavage, must in the not distant future arouse in the people of a federated South Africa a demand for complete severance from British control as the only alternative to a control which they, British and Dutch, will regard as an intolerable interference with their legitimate rights of self-government.

This forcible interference of the Imperial Government with the natural evolution of a British South Africa, accompanied by a direct attack upon colonial liberties and a substitution of mechanical stimulation for organic growth in the process of a South African federation, will come home later to the other self-governing colonies through its reaction upon British policy. The legacy of this disastrous imperial exploit is enhanced militarism for Great Britain, and the rapacious dominance of armaments over public finance. These considerations almost inevitably goad public policy in Great Britain to make eager overtures to the colonies which will be rightly understood as an invitation to share risks and burdens in large excess of all assured advantages. The endeavours on our part to secure the closer political connection of the colonies are more likely than any other cause to bring about a final disruption; for the driving force behind these endeavours will be detected as proceeding from national rather than imperial needs. Australia, New Zealand, Canada have had no voice in determining recent expansion of British rule in Asia and Africa; such expansion serves no vital interest of theirs; invited to contribute a full share to the upkeep and furtherance of such Empire, they will persistently refuse, preferring to make full preparation for such self-defence as will enable them to dispense with that protection of the British flag which brings increasing dangers of entanglement with foreign Powers.

The new Imperialism antagonises colonial self-government, tends to make imperial federation impracticable, and furnishes a disruptive force in the relations of Great Britain with the self-governing colonies.

CHAPTER VII

THE OUTCOME

I

IF Imperialism may no longer be regarded as a blind inevitable destiny, is it certain that imperial expansion as a deliberately chosen line of public policy can be stopped?

We have seen that it is motived, not by the interests of the nation as a whole, but by those of certain classes, who impose the policy upon the nation for their own advantage. The amalgam of economic and political forces which exercises this pressure has been submitted to close analysis. But will the detection of this confederacy of vicious forces destroy or any wise abate their operative power? For this power is a natural outcome of an unsound theory in our foreign policy. Put into plain language, the theory is this, that any British subject choosing, for his own private pleasure or profit, to venture his person or his property in the territory of a foreign State can call upon this nation to protect or avenge him in case he or his property is injured either by the Government or by any inhabitant of this foreign State. Now this is a perilous doctrine. It places the entire military, political, and financial resources of this nation at the beck and call of any missionary society which considers it has a peculiar duty to attack the religious sentiments or observances of some savage people, or of some reckless explorer who chooses just those spots of earth known to be inhabited by hostile peoples ignorant of British power ; the speculative trader or the mining prospector gravitates naturally towards dangerous and unexplored countries, where the gains of a successful venture will be quick and large. All these men, missionaries, travellers, sportsmen, scientists, traders, in no proper sense the accredited representatives of this country, but actuated by private personal motives, are at liberty to call upon the British nation to spend millions of money and thousands of lives to defend them against risks which the nation has not sanctioned. It is only right to add that unscrupulous statesmen have deliberately utilised these insidious methods of encroachment, seizing upon every alleged outrage inflicted on these private adventurers or marauders as a pretext for a punitive expedition which results in the British flag waving over some new tract of territory. Thus the most reckless and irresponsible individual members of our nation are permitted to direct our foreign policy. Now that we have some four hundred million British subjects, any one of whom in theory or in practice may call upon the British arms to extricate him from the results of his private folly, the prospects of a genuine *pax Britannica* are not particularly bright.

But those sporadic risks, grave though they have sometimes proved, are insignificant when compared with the dangers associated with modern methods of international capitalism and finance. It is not long since industry was virtually restricted by political boundaries, the economic intercourse of nations being almost wholly confined to commercial exchanges of goods. The recent habit of investing capital in a foreign country has now grown to such an extent that the well-to-do and politically powerful classes in Great Britain to-day derive

a large and ever larger proportion of their incomes from
capital invested outside the British Empire. This growing stake of our wealthy classes in countries over which
they have no political control is a revolutionary force
in modern politics; it means a constantly growing tendency to use their political power as citizens of this
State to interfere with the political condition of those
States where they have an industrial stake.

The essentially illicit nature of this use of the public
resources of the nation to safeguard and improve private
investments should be clearly recognised. If I put my
savings in a home investment, I take into consideration all the chances and changes to which the business
is liable, including the possibilities of political changes
of tariff, taxation, or industrial legislation which may
affect its profits. In the case of such investment, I am
quite aware that I have no right to call upon the public
to protect me from loss or depreciation of my capital due
to any of these causes. The political conditions of my
country are taken into calculation at the time of my
investment. If I invest in consols, I fully recognise that
no right of political interference with foreign policy affecting my investment is accorded to me in virtue of my
interest as a fund-holder. But, if I invest either in the
public funds or in some private industrial venture in a
foreign country for the benefit of my private purse, getting specially favourable terms to cover risks arising from
the political insecurity of the country or the deficiencies
of its Government, I am entitled to call upon my Government to use its political and military force to secure
me against those very risks which I have already dis-
counted in the terms of my investment. Can anything
be more palpably unfair ?

It may be said that no such claim of the individual

investor upon State aid is admitted. But while the
theory may not have been openly avowed, recent history
shows a growth of consistent practice based upon its tacit
acceptance. I need not retrace the clear chain of evidence,
consisting chiefly of the admissions of the mining capitalists, by which this claim to use public resources for
their private profit has been enforced by the financiers
who seduced our Government and people into our latest
and most costly exploit. This is but the clearest and
most dramatic instance of the operation of the world-
wide forces of international finance. These forces are
commonly described as capitalistic, but the gravest danger
arises not from genuine industrial investments in foreign
lands, but from the handling of stocks and shares based
upon these investments by financiers. Those who own a
genuine stake in the natural resources or the industry
of a foreign land have at least some substantial interest
in the peace and good government of that land; but the
stock speculator has no such stake: his interest lies in
the oscillations of paper values, which require fluctuation
and insecurity of political conditions as their instrument.

As these forms of international investment and
finance are wider spread and better organised for economic
and political purposes, these demands for political and
military interference with foreign countries, on the
ground of protecting the property of British subjects,
will be more frequent and more effective; the demands
of investors will commonly be backed by personal grievances of British outlanders, and we shall be drawn into
a series of interferences with foreign Governments, which,
if we can conduct them successfully, will lead to annexation of territory as the only security for the lives and
property of our subjects.

That this policy marks a straight road to ruin there

can be no doubt. But how to stop it. What principle of safety can we lay down? Only one—an absolute repudiation of the right of British subjects to call upon their Government to protect their persons or property from injuries or dangers incurred on their private initiative. This principle is just and expedient. If we send an emissary on a public mission into a foreign country, let us support and protect him by our public purse and arms; if a private person, or a company of private persons, place their lives or property in a foreign land, seeking their own ends, let them clearly understand that they do so at their own risk, and that the State will not act for their protection.

If so complete a reversal of our consistent policy be regarded as a counsel of perfection involving a definite abandonment of domiciliary, trading, and other rights secured by existing treaties or conventions with foreign States, upon the observance of which we are entitled to insist, let us at any rate lay down two plain rules of policy. First, never to sanction any interference on the part of our foreign representatives on general grounds of foreign misgovernment outside the strict limits of our treaty rights, submitting interpretation of such treaty rights to arbitration. Secondly, if in any case armed force is applied to secure the observance of these treaty rights, to confine such force to the attainment of the specific object which justifies its use.

II

Analysis of Imperialism, with its natural supports, militarism, oligarchy, bureaucracy, protection, concentration of capital and violent trade fluctuations, has marked it out as the supreme danger of modern national States.

The power of the imperialist forces within the nation to use the national resources for their private gain, by operating the instrument of the State, can only be overthrown by the establishment of a genuine democracy, the direction of public policy by the people for the people through representatives over whom they exercise a real control. Whether this or any other nation is yet competent for such a democracy may well be matter of grave doubt, but until and unless the external policy of a nation is "broad-based upon a people's will" there appears little hope of remedy. The scare of a great recent war may for a brief time check the confidence of these conspirators against the commonwealth, and cause them to hold their hands, but the financial forces freshly generated will demand new outlets, and will utilise the same political alliances and the same social, religious, and philanthropic supports in their pressure for new enterprises. The circumstances of each new imperialist exploit differ from those of all preceding ones: whatever ingenuity is requisite for the perversion of the public intelligence, or the inflammation of the public sentiment, will be forthcoming.

Imperialism is only beginning to realise its full resources, and to develop into a fine art the management of nations: the broad bestowal of a franchise, wielded by a people whose education has reached the stage of an uncritical ability to read printed matter, favours immensely the designs of keen business politicians, who, by controlling the press, the schools, and where necessary the churches, impose Imperialism upon the masses under the attractive guise of sensational patriotism.

The chief economic source of Imperialism has been found in the inequality of industrial opportunities by which a favoured class accumulates superfluous elements

of income which, in their search for profitable investments,
press ever farther afield: the influence on State policy of
these investors and their financial managers secures a
national alliance of other vested interests which are
threatened by movements of social reform: the adoption
of Imperialism thus serves the double purpose of securing
private material benefits for favoured classes of investors
and traders at the public cost, while sustaining the
general cause of conservatism by diverting public energy
and interest from domestic agitation to external employment.

The ability of a nation to shake off this dangerous
usurpation of its power, and to employ the national resources in the national interest, depends upon the education of a national intelligence and a national will, which
shall make democracy a political and economic reality.
To term Imperialism a national policy is an impudent
falsehood: the interests of the nation are opposed to
every act of this expansive policy. Every enlargement
of Great Britain in the tropics is a distinct enfeeblement
of true British nationalism. Indeed, Imperialism is
commended in some quarters for this very reason, that
by breaking the narrow bounds of nationalities it facilitates and forwards internationalism. There are even
those who favour or condone the forcible suppression of
small nationalities by larger ones under the impulse of
Imperialism, because they imagine that this is the
natural approach to a world-federation and eternal
peace. A falser view of political evolution it is difficult
to conceive. If there is one condition precedent to
effective internationalism or to the establishment of any
reliable relations between States, it is the existence of
strong, secure, well-developed, and responsible nations.
Internationalism can never be subserved by the sup-

pression or forcible absorption of nations; for these practices react disastrously upon the springs of internationalism, on the one hand setting nations on their armed defence and stifling the amicable approaches between them, on the other debilitating the larger nations through excessive corpulence and indigestion. The hope of a coming internationalism enjoins above all else the maintenance and natural growth of independent nationalities, for without such there could be no gradual evolution of internationalism, but only a series of unsuccessful attempts at a chaotic and unstable cosmopolitanism. As individualism is essential to any sane form of national socialism, so nationalism is essential to internationalism: no organic conception of world-politics can be framed on any other supposition.

Just in proportion as the substitution of true national governments for the existing oligarchies or sham democracies becomes possible will the apparent conflicts of national interests disappear, and the fundamental co-operation upon which nineteenth-century Free Trade prematurely relied manifest itself. The present class government means the severance or antagonism of nations, because each ruling class can only keep and use its rule by forcing the antagonisms of foreign policy: intelligent democracies would perceive their identity of interest, and would ensure it by their amicable policy. The genuine forces of internationalism, thus liberated, would first display themselves as economic forces, securing more effective international co-operation for postal, telegraphic, railway, and other transport services, for monetary exchange and for common standards of measurement of various kinds, and for the improved intercommunication of persons, goods, and information. Related and subsidiary to these purposes would come a growth of machinery of courts and congresses, at first informal and private, but gradually taking shape in more definite and more public machinery : the common interests of the arts and sciences would everywhere be weaving an elaborate network of intellectual internationalism, and both economic and intellectual community of needs and interests would contribute to the natural growth of such political solidarity as was required to maintain this real community.

It is thus, and only thus, that the existing false antagonisms of nations, with their wastes and perils and their retardation of the general course of civilisation, can be resolved. To substitute for this peaceful, discovery and expression of common interests a federal policy proceeding upon directly selfish political and military interests, the idea which animates an Anglo-Saxon alliance or a Pan-Teutonic empire, is deliberately to choose a longer, more difficult, and far more hazardous road to internationalism. The economic bond is far stronger and more reliable as a basis of growing internationalism than the so-called racial bond or a political alliance constructed on some short-sighted computation of a balance of power. It is, of course, quite possible that a Pan-Slav, Pan-Teutonic, Pan-British, or Pan-Latin alliance might, if the federation were kept sufficiently voluntary and elastic, contribute to the wider course of internationalism. But the frankly military purpose commonly assigned for such alliances bodes ill for such assistance. It is far more likely that such alliances would be formed in the interests of the "imperialist" classes of the contracting nations, in order the more effectively to exploit the joint national resources.

We have foreshadowed the possibility of even a larger alliance of Western States, a European federation of great Powers which, so far from forwarding the cause of world-civilisation, might introduce the gigantic peril of a Western parasitism, a group of advanced industrial nations, whose upper classes drew vast tribute from Asia and Africa, with which they supported great tame masses of retainers, no longer engaged in the staple industries of agriculture and manufacture, but kept in the performance of personal or minor industrial services under the control of a new financial aristocracy. Let those who would scout such a theory as undeserving of consideration examine the economic and social condition of districts in Southern England to-day which are already reduced to this condition, and reflect upon the vast extension of such a system which might be rendered feasible by the subjection of China to the economic control of similar groups of financiers, investors, and political and business officials, draining the greatest potential reservoir of profit the world has ever known, in order to consume it in Europe. The situation is far too complex, the play of world-forces far too incalculable, to render this or any other single interpretation of the future very probable: but the influences which govern the Imperialism of Western Europe to-day are moving in this direction, and, unless counteracted or diverted, make towards some such consummation.

If the ruling classes of the Western nations could realise their interests in such a combination (and each year sees capitalism more obviously international), and if China were unable to develop powers of forcible resistance, the opportunity of a parasitic Imperialism which should reproduce upon a vaster scale many of the main features of the later Roman Empire visibly presents itself.

Whether we regard Imperialism upon this larger

scale or as confined to the policy of Great Britain, we find much that is closely analogous to the Imperialism of Rome.

The rise of a money-loaning aristocracy in Rome, composed of keen, unscrupulous men from many nations, who filled the high offices of State with their creatures, political " bosses " or military adventurers, who had come to the front as usurers, publicans, or chiefs of police in the provinces, was the most distinctive feature of later imperial Rome. This class was continually recruited from returned officials and colonial millionaires. The large incomes drawn in private official plunder, public tribute, usury and official incomes from the provinces had the following reactions upon Italy. Italians were no longer wanted for working the land or for manufactures, or even for military service. " The later campaigns on the Rhine and the Danube," it is pointed out, " were really slave-hunts on a gigantic scale."[1]

The Italian farmers, at first drawn from rural into military life, soon found themselves permanently ousted from agriculture by the serf labour of the *latifundia*, and they and their families were sucked into the dregs of town life, to be subsisted as a pauper population upon public charity. A mercenary colonial army came more and more to displace the home forces. The parasitic city life, with its lowered vitality and the growing infrequency of marriage, to which Gibbon draws attention,[2] rapidly impaired the physique of the native population of Italy, and Rome subsisted more and more upon immigration of raw vigour from Gaul and Germany. The necessity of maintaining powerful . mercenary armies to hold the provinces heightened continually the peril, already manifest in the last years of the Republic, arising

---

[1] Adams, "Civilisation and Decay," p. 38.　　[2] Chap. xii.

from the political ambitions of great pro-consuls conspiring with a moneyed interest at Rome against the
Commonwealth. As time went on, this moneyed oligarchy
became an hereditary aristocracy, and withdrew from military and civil service, relying more and more upon hired
foreigners: themselves sapped by luxury and idleness,
and tainting by mixed servitude and licence the Roman
populace, they so enfeebled the State as to destroy the
physical and moral vitality required to hold in check and
under government the vast repository of forces in the
exploited Empire. The direct cause of Rome's decay
and fall is expressed politically by the term "over-centralisation," which conveys in brief the real essence of Imperialism as distinguished from national growth on the
one hand and colonialism upon the other. Parasitism,
practised through taxation and usury, involved a constantly increasing centralisation of the instruments of
government, and a growing strain upon this government,
as the prey became more impoverished by the drain
and showed signs of restiveness. "The evolution
of this centralised society was as logical as every
other work of nature. When force reached the stage
where it expressed itself exclusively through money
the governing class ceased to be chosen because they
were valiant or eloquent, artistic, learned or devout, and
were selected solely because they had the faculty of
acquiring and keeping wealth. As long as the weak
retained enough vitality to produce something which
could be absorbed, this oligarchy was invariable; and, for
very many years after the native peasantry of Gaul and
Italy had perished from the land, new blood, injected
from more tenacious races, kept the dying civilisation
alive. The weakness of the moneyed class lay in this
very power, for they not only killed the producer, but in

the strength of their acquisitiveness they failed to propagate themselves." [1]

This is the largest, plainest instance history presents of the social parasitic process by which a moneyed interest within the State, usurping the reins of government, makes for imperial expansion in order to fasten economic suckers into foreign bodies so as to drain them of their wealth in order to support domestic luxury. The new Imperialism differs in no vital point from this old example. The element of political tribute is now absent or quite subsidiary, and the crudest forms of slavery have disappeared : some elements of more genuine and disinterested government serve to qualify and mask the distinctively parasitic nature of the later sort. But nature is not mocked : the laws which, operative throughout nature, doom the parasite to atrophy, decay, and final extinction, are not evaded by nations any more than by individual organisms. The greater complexity of the modern process, the endeavour to escape the parasitic reaction by rendering some real but quite unequal and inadequate services to "the host," may retard but cannot finally avert the natural consequences of living upon others. The claim that an imperial State forcibly subjugating other peoples and their lands does so for the purpose of rendering services to the conquered equal to those which she exacts is notoriously false : she neither intends equivalent services nor is capable of rendering them, and the pretence that such benefits to the governed form a leading motive or result of Imperialism implies a degree of moral or intellectual obliquity so grave as itself to form a new peril for any nation fostering so false a notion of the nature of its conduct. " Let

---

[1] Adams, "Civilisation and Decay," p. 44.

the motive be in the deed, not in the event," says a Persian proverb.

Imperialism is a depraved choice of national life, imposed by self-seeking interests which appeal to the lusts of quantitative acquisitiveness and of forceful domination surviving in a nation from early centuries of animal struggle for existence. Its adoption as a policy implies a deliberate renunciation of that cultivation of the higher inner qualities which for a nation as for an individual constitutes the ascendency of reason over brute impulse. It is the besetting sin of all successful States, and its penalty is unalterable in the order of nature.

INDEX

THE END

Printed by BALLANTYNE, HANSON & Co.
Edinburgh & London

CPSIA information can be obtained
at www.ICGtesting.com
Printed in the USA
BVHW091924150519
548354BV00008B/459/P